MW01259470

Wally

Thanks for
your help.

Gary Reiss

7/9/96

Classic

American Pottery

from the

30s, 40s, 50s AND 60s

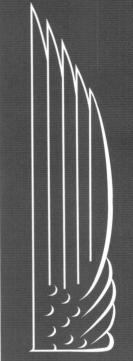

RED WING
ART POTTERY

including pottery made for

RumRill

WRITTEN AND PHOTOGRAPHED BY RAY REISS
Foreword by Marion John Nelson

Designer: Kirsten Ulve

Production Manager: Tomasz Rostowski

Marketing Director: Maureen O'Meara Follis

Thou Shalt Not Steal

COPYRIGHT 1996 Ray Reiss. All Rights Reserved.

No part of this book may be reproduced by any means including photocopying without written permission from the author, except in the case of brief quotations in critical articles.

Library of Congress Catalog Card Number: 94-067711
ISBN: 0-9642087-0-9

Reiss, Ray.
    Red Wing art pottery : including pottery made for Rum Rill /
written & photographed by Ray Reiss.
    p. cm.
    Includes bibliographical references and index.
    "Classic American pottery from the 30s, 40s, 50s and 60s."
    ISBN 0-9642087-0-9

    1. Red Wing Potteries.   2. Art Pottery--Minnesota.   I. Title.

NK4210.R4R45 1996   738.3'0977
                                             QBI95-1461

-Printed in the U.S.A-

Printed by:
MARATHON COMMUNICATIONS
Wausau, WI

Bound by:
MIDWEST EDITIONS
Minneapolis, MN

Published and distributed by:
PROPERTY
Chicago, IL

The author is always interested in historical photographs and printed information on Red Wing Potteries and George Rumrill.

Additional copies can be ordered by writing:
RED WING ART POTTERY   2144 N. LEAVITT   CHICAGO, IL   60647

Or calling:
800-355-2324

While shopping at flea markets in Wisconsin in the mid-70s, I often found beautiful vases with unusual shapes and incredible glazes. I would buy them for next to nothing, thinking all the while—what is wrong here? When I began to research, I found very little information on Red Wing Art Pottery. When I turned forty, I felt that I needed a mid-life crisis project. As a commercial photographer I began with the idea of doing a beautifully photographed coffee table book of my Red Wing collection. I then decided that perhaps I should do a few weeks of research to supplement my photographs. Two years later I felt that I had acquired enough data—from original sources—to clear up many of the mistaken notions about Red Wing Art Pottery. Thus my vision for this book expanded until I hoped to be able to publish one of the best collector books ever produced. I hope you will agree. This book could not have been created without the help of many wonderful people. Above all I wish to express my sincere appreciation to the Red Wing Art Pottery experts who have shared their knowledge and resources with me: Gary Antoline, Stan Bougie, Belle Kogan, Marie Murphy, Gary and Bonnie Tefft, Tom Trulen, and the Red Wing Collectors Society. I am most appreciative, too, for Marion Nelson's insightful essay that places Red Wing into its proper niche in the Art Pottery pantheon. I am especially grateful to the people who allowed me to photograph parts of their collection, namely Ron Linde, Mike and Dianna Rice, Cliff and Margaret Ekdahl, Dave and Ardelle Johnson, Larry and Pauline Peterson, Jan and Al of Hill Street Antiques, Delores and Morris Callstrom of Teahouse Antiques/Octagon House, Jewell Peterson, and Dana L. Mueller. Numerous institutions were very helpful in my search for original source material. I'm grateful to staff members at the Goodhue County Historical Society, Red Wing Pottery Sales, the Red Wing Public Library, the Minnesota Historical Society, The Center for Research Libraries, the Cleveland Public Library, the Old State House Museum in Little Rock, Arkansas, the Ohio Historical Society, the Library of Congress, the Smithsonian Institution, and the Chicago Public Library. Many other people helped me in this project by providing information, advice and even sometimes a kind word. I would like to express my appreciation to Bernie and Barb Banet, Ann Layfield Bates, Louise Bauer, Helen Bell, Carol Berg, Laura and Bill Blankenship, Christine Boos, Bill Burgess, Evelyn Christianson, Harvey Duke, Rolland and Evelyn Everts, John Falconer, Leo and Wendy Frese, Richard A. Gillmer, Byron Gunderson, Scott Henriquez, Ron Hoopes, Art Kuhn, Scott Lewis, Jim and Bev Mangus, John Mehrkens, Georgine R. Mickler, Jim and Phylis Miller, Marion Mincieli, Russell Nolting, Jim Norine, Jim Pfeifer, Richard Quade, Harry Rumrill, Bunnye Simone, Bill Smith, Alan and Lynn Stine, Lynn Streit, Harold "Dutch" West, Mike Zaeske, and Capt. Zoloft. A special thanks to Nicol Knappen for all his professional guidance and to my assistant Tomasz Rostowski for his enthusiasm, dedication and ability to persevere no matter how stormy the weather. For the kindness, support and patience of everyone else I encountered during this arduous creative process, my profound thanks.

—Ray Reiss

Chicago, 1995

CONTENTS

Shape #1336 is 9" tall in a glaze called *Eggshell Crackle*— *Bronze Footed and Lined*

FOREWORD

Since most Red Wing Art Pottery was made in molds, one's appraisal of it will depend in part on one's position regarding cast versus hand-thrown ceramics. From a strictly aesthetic standpoint, this should not matter. It is the product that should count, not how it was made. But the latter in the case of pottery does affect the product, the hand-thrown having qualities that cannot be replicated in a mold.

The difference lies primarily in feel. One characteristic of the hand-thrown pot is a variation in the thickness of the body, generally greatest at the base and diminishing toward the top. There is a logic in this that pleases, and it also relates to the stability of the piece. Another such pleasing characteristic is the slightly undulated surface that results from the organic nature of the human hand restricting the outward thrust of the whirling clay and giving the piece its shape. This undulation, more evident to the hand than to the eye, puts one in direct physical contact with the potter. If such are the things one seeks in ceramics, Red Wing may not be the place to turn.

But there is another side of pottery, the purely visual: color, contour, three-dimensional shape (as defined by light and shade), surface design, and surface quality (glossy, matt, textured). These can all be present in cast ware, and such elements as contour and shape can have possibilities in them that are difficult to achieve or that seem forced in handmade pottery. It is by building on these that cast ware can match hand produced ware in effectiveness, but it does so through the eye rather than touch. What it conveys is more abstract and intellectual than sensuous and human. To some people that is enough. If you are among them, Red Wing at its best can offer you much.

The shift from handmade to cast pottery does not have to be looked on solely as decline resulting from concern with faster production and greater profits. The fine arts at the time of the transition were also moving away from emphasis on the personal and sensuous to the abstract and intellectual. That is what Cubism, which came into being around 1906, was primarily about, and it has left its mark in one way or another on much that has happened in art since. Andy Warhol in the 1960s blatantly equated art with the impersonal, seeing as ideal that which could be recorded and mass-produced by a machine.

In an aesthetic atmosphere like the above, the mold makes more sense for Art Pottery than the wheel. William Gates of Chicago perceived this just before Cubism developed, and turned almost exclusively to molds for his Teco ware. Its highly esteemed buttressed shapes were totally unsuited to throwing. The choice was as much aesthetic as economic—or probably a combination of the two—which is generally what gives art its specific character at any one time. Frank Lloyd Wright in 1901 foresaw that the new arts and crafts would have to embrace both science and technology.

My lofty tone thus far is to point out that it is time to take a serious look at the mass produced material which, in the 20th century, has been replacing what we had called art. Perhaps it too is art, but in a context that makes it different. Red Wing was not unaware of the new artistic potential offered by casting. The strong, simple contours of its early art ware are capitalized on by glazing the pieces in rich pure colors: primarily blues, yellows, and mulberry. The company also offered combinations of glazes, but these were generally not of the old airbrushed type that weakened rather than emphasized the silhouette of the piece. Combinations were also less used than single colors.

Red Wing also kept the concept of the divided mold present in much of its designing, having handles or other decorative elements projecting out in two directions. These disguise unpleasant mold marks while not concealing that the piece is cast. The greatest achievement in integrating design and casting technique is Belle Kogan's *Prismatique* from the early 1960s, in which the divisions between facets in the shape correspond to those between sections of the mold. The forms in this line also blatantly break with turned prototypes and grow directly out of the technology used in production.

Such leaps in concept are not easy, although they had been taken by Weller and Muncie, not quite as successfully to be sure, about 30 years earlier. A Charles Murphy "modern" Red Wing line, on the other hand, in which cube bases—perfect shapes for the mold—are juxtaposed with thin vessels of organic form, is without prototype in commercial art pottery.

But much Red Wing cast ware was indeed directly imitative of classic turned shapes, those with which the general public still felt most comfortable and which were also excellent vehicles for displaying the beauty of glazes. Neither these more conservative pieces, however, nor those that were just cute or pretty to suit popular taste can any longer be ignored. With the increasing awareness of diversity in American culture, the common people must not be forgotten. Popular as well as fine art has a place in the total picture of art in America.

Ray Reiss is bringing balance into our concept of Art Pottery, not only by taking seriously a category that has been considered of peripheral significance, but by elevating it—through his superb photography—to the level of fine art.

—Marion John Nelson
Minneapolis, 1995

Fig. 1-1.
Commonly
referred to as the
"Lion Vase,"
shape #164S is
7⅜" tall. This glaze
is called
*Combination Tan
and Gray,* and is
very similar to the
Nokomis glaze.[1]

An
Introduction to
Red Wing Art Pottery

While artistic expression in ceramic form is ancient, the term "Art Pottery" is used today to describe the decorative clayworks inspired by the Arts and Crafts movement of the late 19th century. The Arts and Crafts movement began as a reaction to the mass production methods of the industrial age and it celebrated the individual's ability to craft beautiful, useful objects. In England particularly, proponents hoped that by renewing familiarity with traditional crafts, a return to a simpler, self-sufficient lifestyle would be possible for the working class. Initially, Art Pottery—an important component of the movement—was mostly made by hand on a piece-by-piece basis.

In America, the Arts and Crafts movement was perceived more as a style of decoration than a utopian philosophy, and mass production methods were seen by most as an economic necessity. Many American potteries manufactured enormous quantities of Art Pottery, or artware—as factory produced Art Pottery is often called—from the end of the 19th century until well into the middle of the 20th century.

Red Wing Potteries, Inc. of Red Wing, Minnesota, was in many ways a typical artware manufacturer. Although Red Wing got into the game a little later than better-known Ohio-based manufacturers like Weller and Roseville, it was not the only latecomer. Pottery companies all across the country that had enjoyed success as manufacturers

Fig. 1-2. Red Wing's #249–11" vase was offered in three glazes: *Yellow, Light Green* and *Dark Blue.*

of utilitarian stoneware products began to look for related fields to exploit as the demand for stoneware decreased. From the turn of the century on, Art Pottery, along with tile and dinnerware, became a logical product for these companies.

Red Wing made glazed Art Pottery from about 1929 until it closed in 1967. The company manufactured primarily vases, but also—in no small numbers—planters, figurines, candleholders, bowls, compotes, ashtrays, and whatnots, all of which were made from molds and offered in a staggering diversity of styles, shapes and glazes. Despite this seeming abundance, Art Pottery was always a small part of the company's product output, accounting for only about 15 percent of its total sales in later years.

At various times while Red Wing was making Art Pottery, it also was producing stoneware, dinnerware, flowerpots, and gardenware as well as many items in a category it called "kitchenware." Kitchenware included cookie jars, teapots, coffee servers, water pitchers, mugs, casseroles, bowls and serving plates. The company also had a lamp division, and it produced promotional items for other manufacturing or service companies.

Red Wing produced Art Pottery for the mass market at affordable prices. To gain a perspective on Red Wing's market, note that its top-of-the-line vase—a #249 (Fig. 1–2) Art Deco vase with nude figures as handles—wholesaled for $4 in 1931, whereas in 1930, America's premier Art Pottery manufacturer, the Rookwood Pottery Co. of Cincinnati, retailed a single piece for $100.

During the four decades of Red Wing Art Pottery production, the nation and its tastes went through many changes and Red Wing tried to keep pace. Generally, a new catalog was published twice yearly by (1) adding new product lines or modifying existing ones, (2) adding or dropping individual pieces not in any specific line, or (3) reintroducing older shapes in new glazes. In addition, some Red Wing Art Pottery

Fig. 1-3. #674-15" From the RumRill *Neo-Classic Group.* This vase in *Gypsy Orange*[2] was the tallest in that group.

pieces were produced in glazes other than those listed in Red Wing catalogs.

Over the years, the company produced at least 1,929 uniquely styled shapes of Art Pottery. That figure does not include lamp bases, kitchenware, specialty items or products manufactured by other distinctly separate company divisions such as dinnerware and stoneware. A certain number of these shapes represent different sizes of the same design.

By and large each piece of Art Pottery was assigned its own shape number, although some of the numbers were used twice. Conveniently for collectors today, that number—also commonly referred to as a mold number—is almost always found on a piece of Red Wing Art Pottery, usually on the bottom. Shape numbers also appear on some kitchenware pieces.

With the benefit of hindsight one might attempt to classify Red Wing Art Pottery according to its aesthetic characteristics. However, this text is organized according to the chronology of the company's Art Pottery production. Separate sections discuss kitchenware, dinnerware, lamps and specialty items. Additionally, the book includes identification photos and extensive coverage of manufacturing techniques as well as short biographies of the principal Red Wing designers, shape number charts, and a section on care and cleaning.

Fig. 1–4. #251–10″ in *Yellow.* **This vase was included in one of Red Wing's initial Art Pottery offerings, the 1931 price list.**

The Potter

ALBERT. H. OLSON

Fig. 2-1.
A sculpture of a potter at work made by a Red Wing potter named Albert H. Olson (later Albert Stenwick). (Courtesy of Goodhue County Historical Society, Red Wing, Minnesota)

CHAPTER 2

The History of Pottery in Red Wing

Some fifty-four miles southeast of Minneapolis/St. Paul, the picturesque city of Red Wing, Minnesota, is nestled along the Mississippi River. Surely Red Wing's first pottery was made before recorded history: Native Americans made the area a campground as they traveled through this beautiful part of the country. The Mdewakanton Dakota settled in the area, and it is one of their chiefs for whom the city of Red Wing is named.

By 1860 European settlers had built a city; there were two millinery shops, five real estate offices, five saloons, three banks and four lumber yards doing business in Red Wing.[1] The city was incorporated in 1864, just six years after Minnesota was admitted to the Union.

Fig. 2–2. By the late 19th century, with its manufacturing, grain elevators and river port, Red Wing had become an industrial giant in the upper Midwest. When clay pits were found near the town, Red Wing soon became the largest single producer of utilitarian stoneware in the nation.[2] By the middle of the 20th century, dinnerware was its major product. For four decades during this long period of mass production, a small division of the company made Art Pottery. (Photo courtesy of Minnesota Historical Society)

Fig. 2–3. A selection of the variety of stoneware and utilitarian items Red Wing made prior to entering the Art Pottery field. Crocks such as those above marked 10 and 20 (gallons) commonly were made in sizes up to 60 gallons.

Red Wing Pottery in the 19th Century

A German immigrant potter named John Paul is credited with discovering Red Wing's clay pits in 1861.[3] He sold his handmade items to neighbors. Small-scale potteries soon followed. The first was owned by W. M. Philleo; another was owned by David Hallum. The city also acquired a terra cotta company, a brickyard and sewer pipe companies.

In 1877 a group of city businessmen bought out David Hallum and hired him to help set up a new firm, incorporated as the Red Wing Stoneware Company. The company's new factory was operational by 1878, and it was successful from the beginning, selling everything it could produce.

In 1883 a new company—the Minnesota Stoneware Company—was formed by many of the original Red Wing Stoneware Company investors. Nine years later, in 1892, a third company was formed called the North Star Stoneware Company. In 1894, a downturn in the economy prompted the three companies to join in the formation of a separate sales agency in order to reduce their shipping and distribution costs. This agency was called the Union Stoneware Company.

In 1896 North Star Stoneware Company was bought by the other two companies, and in 1906 they merged, forming Red Wing Union Stoneware Company.

20th Century Red Wing

Soon after the turn of the century—with the advent of electrical refrigeration and the increased use of tin and glass containers for storage—the demand for stoneware crocks and jugs began to decline. The Volstead Act of 1920 and the subsequent thirteen years of Prohibition probably kept stoneware production alive: large, non-porous containers were required for home brewing.[4]

Like other manufacturers of utilitarian stoneware, Red Wing had to diversify. In the late 1920s the company started its first glazed Art Pottery line, although decorative flowerpots and kitchenware had been produced at the company for many years. In 1932, Red Wing began to produce Art Pottery for marketing agent George Rumrill. Red Wing made pottery for Rumrill (marked with his last name) until 1937.

In 1936 the company changed its name to Red Wing Potteries. About this time it began producing dinnerware, which eventually became the mainstay of the firm.

By the end of World War II the market for pottery had changed considerably. In 1947 the company terminated stoneware production altogether.

A company outlet store in Red Wing—which initially sold only discounted seconds—became a tourist attraction, eventually accounting for nearly 25 percent of the company's total sales.

In the 1950s, low-tariff ceramic imports from Japan, an increase in plastic products,

Fig. 2-4. One of several variations of "little boy" statues from Red Wing's early years. Gary and Bonnie Tefft in "Red Wing Potters and their Wares" theorize that these were derived from chalkware figures that were popular Victorian decorations.

Chronology of the companies that became known as the Red Wing Potteries, Inc.

1878-1906	Red Wing Stoneware Co.
1883-1906	Minnesota Stoneware Co.
1892-1896	North Star Stoneware Co.
1894-1906	Union Stoneware Co.
1906-1936	Red Wing Union Stoneware Co.
1936-1967	Red Wing Potteries, Inc.

"Judge/Yellowstone"

But for a stockholder's preoccupation with his upcoming vacation to Yellowstone Park, Red Wing Potteries might never have existed.

In August 1890, the Red Wing Stoneware Company and the Minnesota Stoneware Company nearly were absorbed by the amalgamation of several potteries throughout Minnesota, Iowa, Illinois and Missouri into a corporation that was to be named Western Stoneware. (No connection was found between that company and the one that was to form later in Monmouth, Illinois.)

A Chicagoan, Mr. Delos P. Phelps, had acquired options on all of the stock of the Red Wing companies, except for that owned by a Judge Wilder. The judge said he intended to participate, although he explained, "I am unable to give this matter any attention before I leave as every moment of my time will be taken up in making preparations for my trip."[5]

Somehow, after the judge returned from Yellowstone, what had seemed like a locked deal fell apart. A final letter regarding the stock sale states that none of the stockholders wanted to sell because they were making a 20 percent return on their investment.

and an out-of-date manufacturing facility combined to make Red Wing Potteries' profitability marginal at best. The final blow came with a 1967 strike by the plant workers. Company shareholders voted to close the factory. All the remaining products were bought by the president, Richard A. Gillmer, whose family continues to run the company outlet store. As of this writing, a few remaining pieces of dinnerware made at the Red Wing Potteries could still be bought new there.

Red Wing Approaches the 21st Century

On the edge of Red Wing stands a pottery factory called the Red Wing Stoneware Company. It was founded in 1987 by John Falconer. Although it uses glaze formulas of the defunct Red Wing firms on some of its products, it has no official connection to any of the companies that preceded it. This company manufactures reproduction crocks, jugs and other gift items, and it offers tours so that visitors can observe its traditional pottery-making techniques. Thus, the pottery industry continues to the present day in Red Wing.

In 1977 a group of interested collectors formed the Red Wing Collectors Society, an organization devoted to the study of pottery making in Red Wing. Today, with over 6,000 members from all across the country, the organization is a living monument to the talented and industrious potters of a small town in Minnesota.

Fig. 3-1.
#127-6⅜"
vases in
Bronze Tan,
Dark Green
and *Light*
Green

CHAPTER 3

BRUSHED WARE
Stoneware Evolves into Artware

What was the first piece of Art Pottery Red Wing produced? Surely the hand-crafted farm animals that were part of the company's offering in the 1800s qualify as Art Pottery. Many of the handmade, one-of-a-kind items workers made (theoretically during their lunch hour and thus called "lunch-hour pieces") also must be considered Art Pottery. These and other stoneware pieces of superior artistic merit, however, have been discussed in books about Red Wing stoneware, and so will not be discussed here. The focus here will be on Red Wing products *intended to be sold* as Art Pottery.

Even with that distinction, the origins of the company's Art Pottery production are cloudy. Although most likely experimental, at least one colorfully glazed piece has been found with a Minnesota Stoneware Co. stamp, dating its manufacture to sometime before 1906. Undoubtedly Red Wing's first official production artware (as it was initially termed) was its *Brushed Ware*. Made with a stoneware clay body, the molded *Brushed Ware* forms were colored with a stain that was quickly "brushed" off to reveal the clay color underneath. Decorated with designs of leaves, scenery, or geometric patterns, the motifs chosen lent themselves to high relief molding so that the exposed clay highlights would accentuate the design. Interiors were glazed with a solid glaze that approximated the color of the exterior stain.

The earliest documented piece that Red Wing made in the *Brushed Ware* style is the Cleveland Vase (Fig. 3–2). The original vase was made for Mrs. Grover Cleveland when she and the President came through town in October 1887. The train on which they were traveling slowed down but did not actually stop. When the President and his wife appeared on the rear platform, *"employees of the Red Wing Stoneware Co. caused an elegant present for Mrs. Cleveland to be put upon it."*[1] Decidedly not elegant—at least by today's standards—some people in Red Wing maintained that as soon as the town was out of

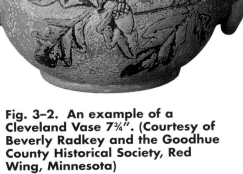

Fig. 3–2. An example of a Cleveland Vase 7¾". (Courtesy of Beverly Radkey and the Goodhue County Historical Society, Red Wing, Minnesota)

17

sight, Mrs. Cleveland threw the vase off the train.[2]

A Cleveland Vase on loan to the Goodhue County Historical Society of Red Wing is marked SAXON, RED WING, MINN. on the bottom and #105, the shape number, on the side. Red Wing's use of the mark Saxon is something of a puzzle. Most likely the name of Red Wing's first artware line, Saxon does not appear in any existing company records or advertising. Other *Brushed Ware* pieces so marked have been found, although rarely. The piece shown in Fig. 3–4 also is marked with both the word SAXON and a shape number, in this case #103. A 1901 article mentions a vase being made that was a copy of Mrs. Cleveland's.[3]

It seems reasonable to assume that pieces marked SAXON were made sometime after the production of the original

Fig. 3-4. One of very few **Saxon** pieces ever found *(right)*. The in-mold inscription is on the bottom *(above)*, and the shape number is impressed on the vase's side *(below right)*. The vase is 10" tall, unglazed and stained green.

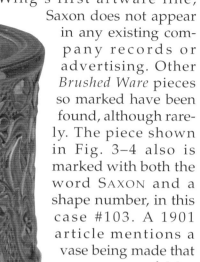

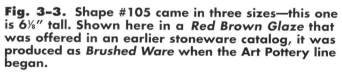

Fig. 3-3. Shape #105 came in three sizes—this one is 6⅛" tall. Shown here in a *Red Brown Glaze* that was offered in an earlier stoneware catalog, it was produced as *Brushed Ware* when the Art Pottery line began.

Cleveland Vase, that is after 1887, but as to when the usage of the term begins and ends, and to what extent it was used is unknown at the present time.

The earliest known documentation of shapes used in the *Brushed Ware* line is found in a company catalog dated about 1914. It showed a series of jardinieres decorated with floral patterns and glazed in a *Red Brown Glaze* (Fig. 3–3). Some time later they were produced as *Brushed Ware*.

As far as can be determined, the first use of the

Fig. 3-5. At least one independent company sold this item as a cemetery pot, offering to write the name of the deceased on the piece. The pot on the right has a plug hole (glazed) with cork and is marked RED WING ART POTTERY. The other two are marked with a circular RED WING UNION STONEWARE CO. stamp. All are 6¾" tall in *Dark Green* .

Fig. 3–6. This #144 with crane motif was offered in 8", 10" and 12" sizes in 1931. The 12" version shown here *(far right)* has a clear glaze, although others have been found glazed white. The 6" piece *(far left)* is unmarked, but has the same interior green glaze color. This size was not listed in any company literature, and possibly not a Red Wing piece.

phrase *Brushed Ware* in company literature appears in the August 1931 price list where it was one of two types of Art Pottery (the other being *Glazed Ware*). Today collectors refer to all the molded stoneware products of this type as *Brushed Ware*, and most people consider it a closer relative of stoneware than Art Pottery.

Early pieces were simple utilitarian shapes, most with floral and leaf designs. By 1931, there were seventy-four different shapes and sizes in the *Brushed Ware* line. These included pieces with scenes of cranes in a marsh (Fig. 3–6), a 12" urn with a cherub motif, and a lobby (or sand) jar showing deer grazing in a woodland setting. The *Brushed Ware* style also was used on products categorized as flower pots, porch pots and gardenware.

Three stain colors were offered: *Dark Green*, *Light Green*, and *Bronze Tan* (Fig. 3–1). A fourth color—*Luster Green*—was offered on the deer lobby jar. Most of the simpler shapes were offered only in *Dark Green*.

Most pieces found are marked with either an oval or round RED WING UNION STONEWARE mark or the circular blue ink stamp RED WING ART POTTERY. The *Brushed Ware* line probably was made until the early 1930s, for after this time the products do not show up in company literature. It is possible—but doubtful—that Red Wing continued to make *Brushed Ware* flower pots and gardenware in later years. However, Red Wing did buy *Brushed Ware* for resale from the Robinson-Ransbottom company of Roseville, Ohio.[4]

As evidence of the appeal and longevity of *Brushed Ware*, note that Robinson-Ransbottom is still in business and still producing *Brushed Ware*.

Fig. 3–7. Offered as rustic pitcher and rustic mug in early stoneware catalogs, this same pitcher was sold by other companies such as Robinson-Ransbottom in Roseville, Ohio. The pitcher is 8¼", the mug is 4⅝".

Fig. 3–8. Most *Brushed Ware* motifs are based on natural forms, but this bulb bowl had a geometric pattern. It is 6½" across, and marked with a round RED WING UNION STONEWWARE CO. blue ink stamp.

Fig. 4-1. An 8" #200 vase in the *Nokomis* glaze. (Courtesy of Goodhue County Historical Society, Red Wing, Minnesota)

THE GLAZED WARE BEGINS

Having decided on Art Pottery as one of the alternatives to stoneware production, Red Wing spent $300,000 for a new tunnel kiln, as well as retooling and restructuring the plant.[1]

The company began promoting the new product in 1929. There was a small write-up in the August 21, 1929, *Red Wing Daily Eagle*: "*Only within the past few years it branched out into the Art Pottery field and here it has made a tremendous success. Demand for Art Pottery is growing rapidly and the Red Wing line, because of its early entrance into the field, is on the 'inside track.'*"[2]

The first trade publicity about this new line is found in an October 1929, trade journal, *Crockery and Glass Journal*:

RED WING ANNOUNCES LINE OF ART WARE
REPRESENTED IN CHICAGO, BY HELM & SOUKUP

The Red Wing Union Stoneware Co., Red Wing, Minn., is adding an extensive line of art ware to its already wide field of pottery products. This line of art pottery consists of vases in various shapes, sizes and colors, jardinieres, pedestals, bird baths, etc.

A continuous Harrop tunnel kiln was recently completed at a cost of over $300,000 at Red Wing. By this modern method in firing with a continuous car tunnel kiln, a car of

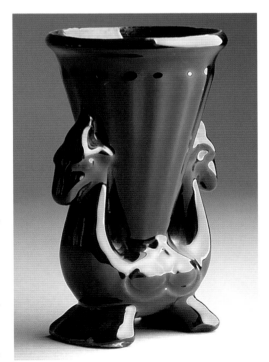

Fig. 4-2. #225-6½". This glaze is commonly referred to as cobalt by collectors, but the 1931 price list calls it DB— Dark Blue or Blue Black.

unfired ware is put into the charging end and a car of fired ware is taken out at the discharging end every 90 minutes, day and night, 365 days a year. The new tunnel is 385 feet long, the cars moving through at the rate of four and two-thirds feet per hour. The heat is applied midway between the ends, using oil for fuel. A maximum temperature of 2,390 degrees F. is maintained at this point for the maturing of the clay and glaze.

Helm and Soukup, 308 W. Randolph Street, have been chosen as the Chicago representatives of this art pottery division of the Red Wing

Fig. 4-3. Three *Nokomis* vases: (Left to right) #206-7⅜", #197-12½" and #201-6¼". The #197 is the tallest piece in the *Nokomis* line.

Union Stoneware Co. This line includes glazed and finished art pottery models and also unfinished lamp bases suitable for lamp manufacturers.

The company, profitable from the start, saw its luck begin to run out. The launch of its Art Pottery line was in the very same month the stock market crashed, beginning the country's worst depression ever. Old company income statements show that Red Wing's profitability, although on an almost steady, gradual decline for many years, dropped dramatically at about this time.

The Art Pottery Makers

Red Wing had a staff of craftsmen, potters, modelers and moldmakers. The chief moldmaker at the time was George J. Hehr. Hehr's father, Gottlieb—who learned designing and mold-making in Germany —was brought to Red Wing in 1883 from Canton, Ohio, to work as a moldmaker. George Hehr followed in his father's footsteps and seemed to have a flair for both designing and modeling. A Christmas Day, 1896, issue of the Red Wing Journal reports:

Fig. 4-6. (Left) #196-10½".
Fig. 4-7. (Right) #201-6". Because the glaze was hand-applied, subtle differences of color and texture are found on each piece of *Nokomis*. The two on either end have a more standard matte surface, while the second one from the left is a semi-matte and the third is glossy.

Fig. 4-4. (Top) #199-9¾".
Fig. 4-5. (Below) #236D-6⅜". A series of four elephants was offered in the 1931 price list, although not officially as *Nokomis*. This is the largest of the four offered, and like all the elephants, it is unmarked.

JERUSALEM IN CLAY
GEORGE J. HEHR AN ARTIST AT THE POTTERIES PRODUCES A UNIQUE SET PIECE

George J. Hehr, Molder for the Red Wing Stoneware Co. and well known in local pottery circles has completed a unique set piece. It represents the Birth of Christ and a number of events in the life of Jesus. The whole piece is about 8 by 12 on a slanting platform which represents the side of a mountain.

There are 76 figures in the piece including Mary and Joseph, the manger, the three wise men, Jesus, the babe, a shepherd and his flock of sheep, his dog, the 12 disciples, the 10 virgins, five wise and five foolish and a number of other figures. The disciples and the virgins have been arranged so that they work automatically revolving in their places.

All of the figures are of stoneware or plaster of paris. Mr. Hehr first modeled them in clay, the molds were made of plaster and in these the figures were cast. The entire work consumed five weeks during which time George Hehr was assisted a portion of the time by his brother. The piece is to be placed on exhibition in the center of the city. It is a credit to Mr. Hehr and indicates ability above the ordinary. It will be remembered that Mr. Hehr's father modeled a piece that was sent to the world's fair and that attracted considerable attention there.

George Hehr is reported to have designed and modeled many of the pieces of Red Wing's first line of glazed Art Pottery. It also can be assumed that other skilled turners, most notably Charles Lewis "Lou"

McGrew, turned some of the classic shapes from which the molds were made.

The initial Art Pottery shown in the catalog titled "The Red Wing Line" consisted of sixty *Glazed Ware* pieces along with forty-two *Brushed Ware* pieces. The shapes were an eclectic mix of classical, Art Nouveau, Arts and Crafts styles and Egyptian motifs, the latter popular at the time because of the touring King Tut's artifacts. The shapes were offered in colorful, high-gloss glazes and in the semi-matte glaze, *Nokomis*. The *Glazed Ware* line had expanded to 130 different styles or sizes by 1931. This line was produced into the early 1930s.

Nokomis

The most unique Red Wing glaze of this period is *Nokomis*. The company initially referred to it as "a semi-matte finish in blended tones." Later the glaze was described as "a metallic finish in gray and tan with a tint of copper." Other pieces have been seen to have blue tones. Although a few high-gloss versions have been found, *Nokomis* was primarily a matte finish, in fact, the only matte finish Red Wing made at this time (Fig. 4–7).

Nokomis was initially a line unto itself. A series of thirteen simple, classic shapes were offered only in this glaze. By 1931 the line was expanded to eighteen shapes. The *Nokomis* glaze also has been discovered on other shapes such as the elephant figurine (Fig. 4–5), lamp bases (Fig. 13–2), and other shapes not part of the official line. A couple of RumRill pieces have been found with the glaze as well (Fig. 4–15).

The scarcity of *Nokomis* today suggests that the line did not sell in great numbers. In a 1934 trade magazine, what might have been the opinion of the day was expressed in a somewhat disparaging reference to *Nokomis* as "an ashen gray-green coloring, made to resemble the weather-beaten face of Hiawatha's grandmother." (In Longfellow's "Song of Hiawatha," Nokomis is the name of Hiawatha's grandmother.)[3]

Today, *Nokomis* is one of the most sought-after of Red Wing's glazes. Ideally

Fig. 4–8. #209–9⅛" in *Yellow*, the high-gloss style of this era.

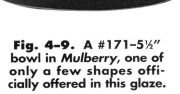

Fig. 4–9. A #171–5½" bowl in *Mulberry*, one of only a few shapes officially offered in this glaze.

one hopes to find examples that exhibit a rich blending of colors. Pieces usually are marked with the circular blue ink stamp RED WING ART POTTERY. Generally, there is a shape number on each piece that is usually in relief but sometimes impressed, possibly hand-incised.

Nokomis was a very time consuming glaze to apply. Gary Tefft wrote that *"My uncle, who worked at the pottery in the lab where the glazes were fritted, was L. 'Pinky' Paulson. His job was to mix the ingredients for the glazes and to melt them into a glass, which was broken up and pulverized in a ball mill. This is done to keep the individual constituents from segregating after they mixed with water and are ready to be applied. It also makes the glazes less toxic to those applying them, as it ties up the lead in the glass. Of course, because the lab personnel dealt with the raw lead compounds, they were much more susceptible to lead poisoning. That is exactly what forced Paulson to leave the pottery: he suffered acute lead poisoning and became quite ill.*

When asked about the Nokomis glaze, Paulson noted that it had been a 'special,' variegated glaze that they worked with at that time. He remembered that it had been difficult to work with and get uniform results. His impression was that it was abandoned due to the cost involved."

The Lion Vase

Another glaze, a *Combination of Gray and Tan* that is similar to and often mistaken for *Nokomis*, was used exclusively on what is now referred to as the Lion Vase, a shape that came in two sizes (Fig. 1–1). The vase also was done in a *Light Green* glaze and others have been found with gray/tan coloration on the top portion and light blue beneath.

Dark Blue

Another sought after glaze is *Dark Blue*, a high-gloss glaze that appears black (Fig. 4–2 and 4–14). With close inspection along the edges of a piece (where the glaze is not as thick) one can distinctly see a blue cast. In the 1931 price list, the glaze is listed as *"DB—Dark Blue or Blue Black."* Commonly

Fig. 4-10. #186-9⅜" in a crackle version of the *Yellow* glaze.

referred to as cobalt, the glaze was offered on a variety of shapes and sizes.

Yellow and Light Green

The most frequently used glazes were the high-gloss glazes *Yellow* and *Light Green* (Fig. 4–12). By 1931 over 80 percent of the Art Pottery shapes were offered in one or both of these colors. These glass-like finishes from this period were unique throughout the remainder of Red Wing's Art Pottery production.

Crackle Version

One interesting variation of the high-gloss *Yellow* and *Light Green* reported to have been made was a crackle glaze. The crackle version gave a piece the appearance of having a web of overall crazing under the surface glaze. It was said to have been created by crazing the first coat via temperature extremes, not much

Fig. 4-11. Three non-standard colors: #155-12½" in a deep blue; #155-15¼" in a green (possibly the *Dark Green* offered on the 1931 Price List); and #155-9" in *Light Blue*, a glaze offered in the 1929 catalog.

different than the childhood trick of taking a glass marble from boiling water and dropping it into cold water. It then was overglazed with a second transparent glaze.

Sometimes high-gloss pieces are found with surface flaws or partial crazing which may be confused with the high-gloss crackle version. Such pieces are easily distinguished, however, for the crackle pieces have an evenly proportioned crazing overall (Fig. 4–10).

Other Colors

During this era, Red Wing officially offered other colors that included *Mulberry*, *Light Blue* and *Dark Green*. Another few styles had combinations of *Green and White* (Fig. 4–13). Since the chemicals for all the

Fig. 4-12. #252-12" in *Light Green.* A lid was added later, when it sold as RumRill pottery.

glazes were mixed from scratch, subtle variations appear in a lot of colors. In addition to these subtle variations of "officially offered" colors, many other colors of glazes were manufactured (Fig. 4–11).

Fig. 4-13. #159-15¼", 12½" and 9". An Egyptian motif vase in *GW-Combination Green and White.*

Fig. 4-14. #247-9" in *Dark Blue.*

Fig. 4-15.
#291-5⅛″
in a
Nokomis
glaze
marked
RumRill.

Fig. 5–1. From the *Athenian Group* in *Suntan–Green Lined.* The base is #572 and the separate bowl is #573. Together they are 11½" tall. This base also was offered with a shallow bowl (#574).

THE RUMRILL ERA
Red Wing from 1932–1937

During the Great Depression, Red Wing's profits were dropping each year. In 1932, the company lost money on its pottery operations for the first time. It is difficult to say if Art Pottery sales were a good thing for Red Wing during this era. The new kiln, retooling, and the expense of glazing material all were new burdens on the bottom line. Some have maintained that the repeal of the Volstead Act dealt the stoneware industry a fatal blow. With the passing of the 21st Amendment, there was little need for home brewing equipment.

Since very few company records are known to have survived from this era, it is not certain how George Rumrill and Red Wing began their business relationship. Press releases and advertisements published in trade magazines of the time provide some answers, but generally speaking, there is a paucity of documentation about George Rumrill and the firms that manufactured pottery in his name.

4 *Shown here are four of the new numbers from the Rumrill line of art pottery which is being introduced by the Arkansas Products Co., Little Rock, Ark. These things are being displayed in New York by Martin S. Breslauer & Co., Inc., 225 Fifth Ave.*

Fig. 5–3. First documentation of the RumRill line as seen in *The Gift and Art Shop*, August 1932.

What is known is that he was a terrific salesman. He began in the pottery business in about 1929 by nationally distributing the products of two Arkansas firms: Camark pottery—made by the Camden Art Tile

Fig. 5–2. George Djalma Rumrill (Photo courtesy of Georgine R. Mickler)

Mary Ellen Stratton set this attractive table for the Rumrill Pottery exhibit at the recent china and glass show in New York's Hotel Pennsylvania. Miss Stratton used a brown linen background for blue wares. This is a candid camera photograph.

the Art Pottery market, Red Wing's expertise had been selling utilitarian farm products, so it is easy to conclude that the company welcomed the opportunity to enter into an alliance with a successful Art Pottery distributor. In August 1932, Red Wing introduced a "new" line of Art Pottery that bore the name RumRill. Much of

Ivanhoe is the name of this new pattern on a shape reminiscent of Old England, at Rumrill Pottery Co. It has a matt glaze finish in ivory, suntan, Alpine blue, and ocean green.

Fig. 5–4 *(Upper left)* and **Fig. 5–5** *(above)* are reproductions from two magazines.[2]

and Pottery Company of Camden, Arkansas—and Hywood, produced by the Niloak Company of Benton, Arkansas.[1] Rumrill's sales and distribution company was called the Arkansas Products Company.

At some point around 1932, Rumrill ceased distributing Camark and Hywood and entered into arrangements with the Red Wing Union Stoneware Company to produce pottery for his company. Newly entered into

the RumRill line consisted of shapes previously produced by Red Wing. [Note that the Rumrill name—when applied to pottery products—was spelled variously Rum Rill, RumRill and RUMRILL. For consistency's sake, this text will use the RumRill spelling when referring to the pottery, and Rumrill when referring to the person.]

Between 1932 and 1937 all RumRill pottery was made exclusively by Red Wing, while at the same time Red Wing marketed Art Pottery, lamps and stoneware under the Red Wing name.

Rumrill, along with a partner—Alfred Leymer—started RumRill Potteries. Leymer was manager and secretary-treasurer of a local funeral home, P. H. Ruebel & Company. It is assumed that Leymer put up the capital and that Rumrill ran the company, for Leymer's name never again appears in any documentation until he made a claim against Rumrill's estate (for $4,006). Certainly Rumrill was having financial problems before starting RumRill Potteries, as he made several court appearances for non-payment of child support.

Rumrill was essentially a broker, wholesaling the products made by others. RumRill Potteries in Little Rock, Arkansas, was never more than just office space where he would coordinate his sales agents and their order fulfillment. His sister, Frances, oversaw

Fig. 5–6. #570–10" in *Suntan*— *Seal Brown Lined* from the *Athenian Group.*

the day-to-day operations of the company. Only one other staff person was ever known to have worked there. There may have been some warehousing space, but Rumrill's stepdaughter—who was a teenager during the five years she lived with Rumrill—remembers very specific details. She related that Rumrill and his sister would coordinate the orders and have Red Wing ship the pottery FOB (Freight On Board, i.e., freight from where the product was shipped, in this case Red Wing, Minnesota). Rumrill was on the road frequently, exhibiting at trade shows, hiring salesmen, selling pottery and garnering new accounts. He purchased a new Buick every other year. According to one of his salesman, "Buicks could handle being on the road all the time, Rummy thought."[3]

Despite Rumrill's best efforts, the 1930s was a bad decade for Red Wing. The company shut down for periods during most of the summers. Although Red Wing's pottery operations were showing profits again by 1933, the company would never reach the profitability it had during its stoneware heyday. By 1937, Japanese dinnerware imports had peaked to a level of "*5 million dozen*,"[4] a level that would be surpassed after the Second World War, and a trend that contributed heavily to the demise of the company.

RumRill Pottery

No handicraftsman's art
Can to our art compare,
We potters make our pots
Of what we potters are.

This short poem was printed on the front cover of the 1933 catalog "RumRill Art Pottery Produced by Red Wing Potteries."[5] The first actual documentation of RumRill Pottery was in an August 1932 *The Gift and Art Shop* feature that showed four pieces of the new line (Fig. 5–3). The line shown in the 1933 catalog had 192 shapes, thirty-seven of which formerly were produced by Red Wing. There were also many variations of Red Wing pieces, not to mention many other close similarities to wares made by other pottery companies such as Camark, American Encaustic Tile, and Brush McCoy, as well as to products made by certain glass manufacturers. The line was a mix of modern, Art Deco, Art Nouveau, and classic shapes. Twelve new glazes were offered, including several two-tone color schemes (Fig. 5–13), such as *Dutch Blue—Blue, White Stippled* (Fig. 5–10).

In addition to the shapes picked up from the 1931 Red Wing line, other groupings included a series of Art Deco angular vases (Fig. 5–8) and a grouping of pieces with swan handles (Fig. 5–17).

RumRill Pottery Co. trade advertisements at first make no mention of Red Wing as a producer of its pottery. Indeed, trade publication advertisements and articles mention trade shows at which either or both Red

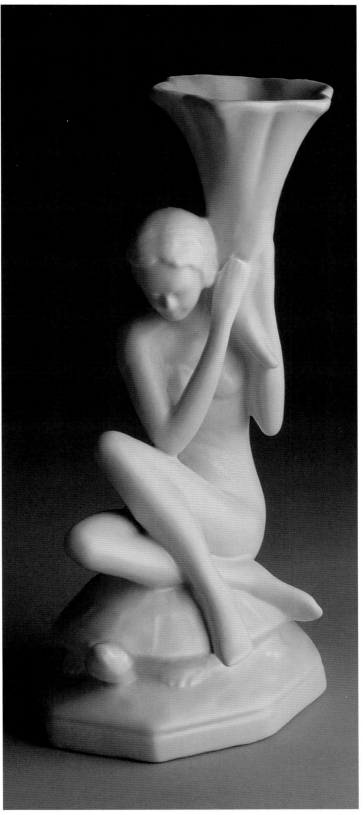

Fig. 5-7. #576–10½" in *Suntan—Green Lined* from the *Athenian Group.*

Wing Potteries, RumRill Potteries, or their various sales representatives exhibited. But by February 1935, both company names appeared in RumRill's ads.

In the fall of 1934 additional pieces were added to the line. The first was an antique finish (*Pompeian*) (Fig. 5–9), said to have been "*excellently done with* under-glaze work so that the finish cannot be washed off, as has been the difficulty with similar finishes."[6] This same finish was continued for several years: in 1936 it was used on vases with a grape motif, and later (renamed *Eggshell Ivory–Antiqued With Brown*) on Red Wing's *Magnolia Group*, where molded magnolia flowers were the motif.

What was initially referred to by a trade magazine as the Nude Series (Fig. 5–1, 5–6, 5–7, and 5–16) premiered in July 1935. The series was based on Red Wing's #249 vase that had been produced earlier (Fig. 1–2). Later named the *Athenian Group*, the line consisted of ten vases, bowls, and candleholders, all with Art Deco-styled nudes. These nudes —as they currently are referred to—are now some of the most sought-after pieces Red Wing made.

Introduced in 1936 was the *Trumpet Flower Group* (Fig. 5–11), a labor-intensive line that did not last long probably due to the handwork required to apply the flowers.

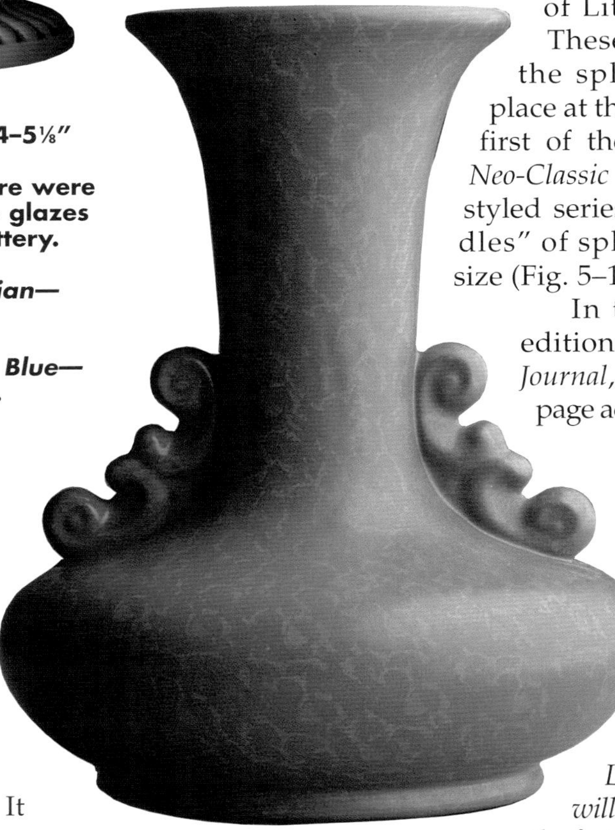

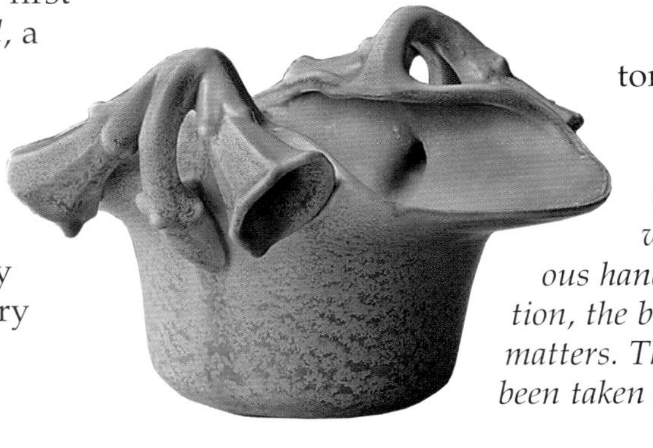

RumRill Dinnerware

In December 1935 the *Gypsy Trail* line of dinnerware was introduced (and listed as trademarked to RumRill Potteries) (Fig. 5-4). It appears that George Rumrill and his agents were the sole distributors of Red Wing's first attempt at dinnerware.[7] *Gypsy Trail*, a brightly-colored dinnerware in the California style, initially consisted of the *Reed* and *Plain* patterns; later *Chevron* was added. Another dinnerware line, *Ivanhoe*, was introduced by RumRill Pottery in February 1937 (Fig. 5–5). It is very scarce.

Fig. 5–8. *(Top)* #314–5⅛" in a dark blue. Very unusual because there were no known dark blue glazes listed for RumRill pottery. **Fig. 5–9.** *(Above)* #339–4½" in *Pompeian— Antiqued Ivory.* **Fig. 5–10.** *(Right)* #308–10¼" in *Dutch Blue— Blue, White Stippled.* **Fig. 5–11.** *(Below)* #493–5½" *Trumpet Flower Group* in White and Green Blend.

Ownership of the RumRill Name

In the fall of 1935, both Red Wing and George Rumrill applied for a trademark for the name RumRill. It appears that Rumrill was awarded the right because on June 8, 1936, an agreement was reached between George Rumrill and Red Wing Potteries:

whereas George Rumrill ("as a member of said co-partnership") signed away "the entire right, title, and interest in and to the said trademark and the registration thereof, No. 330010, together with the good will of the business in connection with which the said mark is used.[8]

The 1937 trade advertisements featured RumRill Pottery, but included prominent listings for both Red Wing Potteries of Red Wing, Minnesota, and for the RumRill Pottery Co. of Little Rock, Arkansas. These ads foreshadowed the split that was to take place at the end of the year. The first of these ads featured the *Neo-Classic Group*, an Art Deco styled series that featured "handles" of spheres in descending size (Fig. 5–15).

In the December 1937 edition of *Crockery and Glass Journal*, Red Wing ran a full-page ad (Fig. 5–12) that stated:

Starting January 1, 1938, RumRill Art Pottery and Gypsy Trail Hostess Ware, always manufactured by Red Wing Potteries and formerly sold through the RumRill Pottery Co., Little Rock, Arkansas, will be offered directly from the factory.

From the company's board of directors meeting on December 20, 1937:

Mr. Hoyt reported the necessity of changing our plan of sales. To continue with the Rumrill Pottery Co. was a serious handicap owing to increased cost of production, the burden of a heavy credit risk, and other matters. The greater part of their sales force has been taken over by the company.

Starting January 1, 1938, RumRill Art Pottery and Gypsy Trail Hostess Ware, always manufactured by Red Wing Potteries and formerly sold through the RumRill Pottery Co., Little Rock, Arkansas, will be offered directly from factory.

This arrangement will guarantee better service for you, a much greater range of merchandise and for the present, a maintenance of 1937 prices.

Under the new arrangement, all shows will be covered, as before.

See the complete line at the Glass and Pottery Exhibit

ROOM 705—WM. PENN HOTEL
JAN. 10th-18th, 1938—PITTSBURGH

Fig. 5-12. Red Wing advertisement in the December 1937 *Crockery and Glass Journal*.

Red Wing hired four new salesmen who had worked for Rumrill: Ralph Lumb (who had been with Rumrill eight years), Ralph Gunschel, Lee R. Manchester and C. E. Carlstrom. The other two sales agents on Red Wing's staff at the time, J. F. Quinn and Harvey L. Johnson, had been with them for at least ten years.

For the next few months both companies ran advertisements in the trade magazines. Small notices appear about George Rumrill's new pottery line being produced in Zanesville, Ohio, and in April 1938 this article ran in the *Crockery and Glass Journal*:

George D. Rumrill Announces Policy, Staff

Following certain confusion in recent months in connection with Rumrill Pottery Company since its ceasing of operations as part of the Red Wing Potteries, George D. Rumrill, sales manager of the Rumrill Pottery Company, now functioning in Little Rock, Ark., and making ware in Zanesville,

Ohio, wrote this letter to Crockery and Glass Journal on April 2, 1938, in explanation of the confusion about Rumrill ware, which came from the fact that Red Wing Potteries, Inc. owned the name RumRill. In the December Directory Issue of Crockery and Glass Journal the listing of Rumrill Pottery Company at that time was necessarily in connection with the Red Wing Potteries, Inc., since Red Wing Potteries still owned the RumRill name. George Rumrill's letter, in part, follows:

"The Rumrill Pottery Company has at no time discontinued business. . . and at no time were we ever out of business. . . . Our present representatives are: The Bates Co. Chicago and Middlewest; Fisk & Fisk, Inc., New York City and Eastern territory; A. C. Morris, Southwest; Hal Copeland, Southeast; George D. Rumrill, Sales Manager; and Albert Kessler & Co., San Francisco.

We are now the only manufacturers of Rumrill Pottery anyway you want to spell it. All rights, titles, interests, claims, and trademarks to the name Rumrill have been assigned to us. We have given permission to our former factory connection to dispose of all pottery in bisque or finished product which they may have on hand which has our name on it, but they cannot manufacture any more.

How George Rumrill got the trademark back is unknown. No relevant court records have been found. Red Wing did not challenge this assertion, so it can be presumed true.

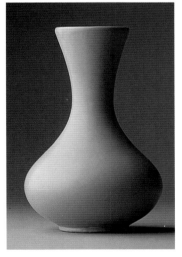

Fig. 5-13. *(Above)* **#183–8¼″ Lilac—Green over Lavender. One of the many RumRill shapes that was originally in the Red Wing line.**

Fig. 5-14. *(Left)* **This piece has a square RumRill sticker marked "Shape 230" even though that number never shows up in any RumRill catalog. A few pieces have been found with this glaze, most likely a "pink stipple."**

The Life of George Rumrill

George Djalma Rumrill (Fig. 5–2, 15–7 and 15–9) was born in Gainesville, Texas, in 1891; not much is known about his family or early life. As a young man he was a traveling cigar salesman, and by 1916 he had married the first of his five wives. By 1923 he was living in Little Rock, Arkansas, where he was listed as a manager of the Pulaski Ice Company, and where his sister Frances was secretary-treasurer.[9] In 1924 he formed the Rumrill Brokerage Company, Inc. with his brother, M. D. Rumrill as vice president, and W. A. McDonnell, a banker, as partner. It was set up for "buying and selling

pany, Rumrill went to work managing the Louis Schneider Candy Company, again, a company where his sister worked. By this time he was married to his third wife, Mable Curtis Smith, who gave him his second son, George D. Rumrill, Jr.

In June 1930, George Rumrill married his fourth wife, Minnie Oliver, about the time he started selling pottery for both Camark and Niloak through the recently formed Arkansas Products Company.

He was involved solely with Red Wing between August 1932 and December 31, 1937.

Although there has been speculation that George Rumrill designed his pottery, there is no evidence to

Fig. 5–15. Neo-Classic Group: front left, #672–3" x 10" bowl in *Seafoam—Ivory, Nile Green Lined*; front right, #673–3¼" in *Nile Green*; rear left, #663–8¼" vase in *Nile Green*; and #664–9⅛" vase in *Eggshell—Ivory, Semi-Matt.*

candy, confections, groceries and merchandise of every kind and description; and acting as agent or broker for manufacturers of same."[10] The company was dissolved two years later.

His second wife had died in childbirth bearing his first son, Jack, whom his sister Frances adopted in 1923. His stepdaughter from this marriage, Gretchen Wilson, was adopted by her maternal grandparents. She married a son of the publisher William Randolph Hearst in 1933, and later was married to the dime store heir Woolworth Donohue.[11]

After the dissolution of the Rumrill Brokerage Com-

support this. Minnie Oliver Rumrill did claim to be a pottery designer, however. In their September 1937 divorce records she stated that she traveled with him, assisted in sales, and designed and styled the line of pottery sold by his firm, for which she received no salary.

After Rumrill's involvement with Red Wing ended, he was known to hire designers, either having them create sketches that he would choose from or bringing in competitors' pieces—if not to be directly imitated, then to serve as a strong guideline for reinterpretation. The majority of post-Red Wing RumRill Art Pottery seems to have been designed by Louise Bauer, a Zanesville, Ohio designer who had worked at the Shawnee Pottery Company, and who later became the main designer for Hull Pottery.

According to Bauer, Rumrill would never bring in sketches, instead asking her to draw sketches, sometimes based on pieces that he brought in for "inspiration." Rumrill was involved in the design process only insofar as when he visited her father's pottery shop, he would sit on an old car seat and direct her to "take a little off here and a little off there."[12] Clearly, Rumrill had an opinion about what would sell.

In the fall of 1937, he married his fifth wife, Edith Layfield. Through his stepdaughter from this marriage, Ann Bates, it is known that her mother designed a couple pieces of pottery after RumRill had left Red Wing.

When Red Wing severed its ties with Rumrill, he went to the newly-formed Shawnee Pottery Co., a company that was set up to produce inexpensive pottery. It was at this time that American pottery interests had taken up a war of words against Japanese imports, declaring a boycott, with a "Buy American" campaign. Shawnee was set up as a model of efficiency with assembly line techniques, using clay and glaze combinations that would require only one firing instead of the more usual two. Shawnee produced pottery for many of the major department stores of the time including Woolworth, Sears Roebuck and Co., Montgomery Ward, Kresge, McCrory, and many others.[13]

Although articles mention Rumrill having his pottery made at a new Zanesville, Ohio, plant as early as January 1938, a Rumrill worker recalls problems with Shawnee getting the products right.[14] Rumrill did very little advertising or attending of trade shows during the first part of 1938. And again, lack of any definite sales records makes this period sketchy at best.

Fig. 5-16. *Athenian Group #571–8¾" x 11" Eggshell–Ivory, Semi-Matt.*

One researcher noted that he had talked to the gentleman who had been in charge of the mold vault. That gentleman tells about George Rumrill coming into Shawnee, after less than six months of production, to remove all of his molds in a fit of anger. They never saw him at the plant again.[15]

In December, 1938, it was announced that Rumrill pottery was going to be made exclusively at the Florence Pottery Company in Mt. Gilead, Ohio.[16] This factory had been in and out of operation since the late 1800s, and just prior to 1938 it was operating strictly as a manufacturer of flower pots and drain tiles. RumRill pottery was made there exclusively for the next three years.

Although his mainstay was Art Pottery, Rumrill tried various other products, including art glass. A series of hand-blown water sets in shaded colors retailed for $3.00, and the Rumrill Wood Co. produced unusual letter boxes, towel racks, and smoking articles.[17] Later he hired a glass blower who made small glass animals that were briefly marketed as *"Rumrill Treasures in Crystal by Beam."*[18] According to one of his salesman, the majority of pieces would arrive broken.[19] In January 1941, he premiered a new dinnerware line called *Sherry Louise*. It too was unsuccessful and short-lived, according to various sources.

Florence Pottery

A very interesting web of circumstances has been related by the Florence Pottery Co. plant foreman, Harold "Dutch" West.[20] According to West, J. Ewart Bruce, the son of the chairman of the board, had come before the board with a proposal to start making Art Pottery for Rumrill. Lawton Gonder (later to start his own pottery), a drinking buddy of Bruce, was to manage it. The board was reluctant to accept the proposal because they were in the black for the first time in many years. Later, when the senior Bruce died and the son took over, the company was completely retooled to make Art Pottery. Gonder was given a three-year contract. The company was never profitable, yet production continued on the pottery until it was stacked up and had to be warehoused wherever room could be found at the plant.

On October 16, 1941, a fire destroyed the entire plant. The fire started in the warehouse section, not near the kiln where pottery factory fires predictably start. The fire was found to have begun with a round blaze in the middle of the building as if started with gas. There was no city waterline to the building. The fire engine sat within three feet of a cistern that for some reason was not used. As the factory burned, people ran in and took the pottery out.

West relates that the fire chief and his wife ran into the factory. While he held his long coat out, his wife would load him up with pottery. On their second trip out to the car he had a heart attack and died. West also said that the FBI investigated for three years, but never found enough conclusive evidence to charge anyone.

The local newspaper carried the story as follows:[21]

Fig. 5–17. A variety of swan-handled vases from the *Swan Group:* (clockwise from left front) #440–4⅛" *Saffron;* #283–5⅛" *Matt Pink;* #298–9¼" a glossy black; #279–4½" *Apple Blossom-Green over Rose;* #442–10⅜" *Eggshell-Cream Matt* and #441–5" *Turquoise.*

Fire Destroys Pottery Plant Here

Early Morning Fire Totally Destroys Village's Second Largest Industrial Plant; Origin Unknown; Chief Dies

One-Hundred and Fifty Men And Women Thrown Out Of Work; Company Officials Uncertain About Plans For Future

LACK OF CITY WATER HAMPERS FIREMEN

All Of Buildings, All Equipment And Largest Stock Of Art Pottery Ever On Hand Are Included In The Estimated $200,000 Loss.

In the most destructive fire here in the last 25 years the plant of the Florence Pottery Co. in the west part of Mt. Gilead was totally destroyed by fire early this morning, Thursday, with the damage estimated at least $200,000 and possibly more.

H. C. Johnstone, Mt. Gilead fire chief, died of a heart attack at the fire.

One-hundred and fifty employees of the pottery, one-half of them women, will be thrown out of work by the destructive fire.

Smoke from the third floor was first noticed by D. R. Brown, one of three kiln burners on duty, shortly before 1:00 a.m. He immediately called H. E. West, plant foreman, while Willard Gardner, another kiln burner, called the fire department. F. L. Cover was the third kiln burner on duty.

Smoke Hinders

West arrived in a few minutes and immediately attempted to reach the blaze on the roof of the third floor. He was carrying a large fire extinguisher, but was driven back by billowing smoke without being able to use it.

West said that C. E. Alkire, a janitor, had been on duty in the third floor, until midnight, less than an hour before the fire broke out and that he had not seen anything unusual on the floor at that time.

There was no city water available for the firemen to use when they arrived as the plant is located in a section just added to the corporation in the last year. No water mains had yet been laid there and difficulty was experienced in using water from two fire-water cisterns.

Total Loss

The loss included the main building, a three-story brick structure 100 by 100 feet, several smaller buildings, the entire stock of art pottery on hand, and all the raw material and equipment.

According to Lawton Gondor, the General Manager, not a single piece of equipment or any or the finished stock could be salvaged.

The loss is partially covered by Insurance but company officials stated that the insurance will not cover a large part of the loss.

The company was organized in 1927 to take over and

modernize an old pottery plant which had been in use at various times. A large modern continuous kiln was installed and manufacture of flower pots and drain tile was begun.

Manufactured Art Ware

This business was continued until 1939 when the company abandoned the manufacture of flower pots and drain tile and began to make art ware. The business has expanded and the largest stock they have had was on hand yesterday as a busy season was just starting for the company.

The officials of the company are J. Ewart Bruce, president, W. H. Holland, vice president, Howard Kline, secretary and treasurer; and Lawton Gondor, general manager.

This morning, Thursday, the company officials were indefinite about plans for the future of the company.

"We know nothing at this time about the possibility of rebuilding," Mr. Holland said.

Fig. 5-18. #541-6" in a glaze called *Red Wing—Scarlet and Bay.*

Although the company was offered free space from at least two different cities, and local communities organizations lobbied and organized help, on December 4, 1941, the Florence Pottery Co. officials announced that they would not rebuild and that the corporation would be dissolved as quickly as possible. In a newspaper article,[22] the company officers stated that:

they have, in investigation, discovered that it would be practically impossible to obtain necessary building material and that it would also be impossible, at least for a long time, to get the necessary equipment and raw materials for operation of a new plant.

The same day, in another newspaper, this article appeared:[23]

Florence Pottery Manager to Head Zanesville Firm

Announcement of the incorporation of the Gonder Ceramic Arts, Inc. pottery to be established in South Zanesville was made last week. The company was incorporated for $95,000 with 1200 shares of stock.

Lawton Gonder, general manager of the Florence Pottery Co. at Mt. Gilead, will be the general manager of the new company.

Fig. 5-19. #600-6" in Ocean Green.

He formerly resided in Zanesville, being the superintendent of the old Fraunfelter China Co.

Gonder Ceramic Arts, Inc. made pottery for Rumrill for the next year until January 1943, when Gonder announced that Gonder Ceramic Arts, Inc. would henceforth devote all its plant facilities to an artware line to be merchandised under its own name.[24] Both company's catalogs from that era show that the RumRill line became the initial Gonder line, hence many pieces show up marked both ways.

Toward the end of his life, George Rumrill's daughter by his first wife rediscovered her father.[25] She had seen the name Rumrill at a trade show and upon tracking down the manufacturer discovered it was her own father, whom her mother had told her had been lost during the First World War.

Rumrill's daughter corresponded with him during the last year of his life. Rumrill told her of problems; the fire, obtaining shipping space, and getting materials as most of the glazing components were metals needed for the war effort.

Another problem was that Florence pottery had won a $5,668 judgment against Rumrill. Although court records did not specify the details, the sum was probably for pottery delivered but never paid for.[26]

By December 1942, under his doctor's recommendation, Rumrill checked into the Arkansas TB Sanitarium in Booneville, Arkansas (now the Booneville Human Development Center). In his letters to his daughter he was optimistic about getting back into the pottery business, and wrote about going to Sapulpa, Oklahoma, to look over the pottery facility there (presumably, Frankoma). But in January 1943, it was announced that Rumrill Pottery Company was ceasing operations due to the illness of the owner, George Rumrill.[27]

George Rumrill died on May 20, 1943, of tuberculosis.

Fig. 6–1.
A vase
from the
Belle
Kogan
100.
#762–7½"
in Copper.

The Belle Kogan 100
1938–1940

By 1938 the pottery business was recovering. Sales were up and production was on the rise at most factories across the country. The trades anti-import boycott worked, for in 1938 Japanese imports began to decline. Red Wing was on an upswing and profitable once again, but the Depression and questionable investments had depleted its $273,000 cash reserves to $66,500. On January 14, 1940, Elmore Sherman Hoyt—the president of Red Wing Potteries for forty-eight years—resigned three days after the losses were summarized at a board meeting.

The Belle Kogan 100

After the official separation of Red Wing and Rumrill, Red Wing commissioned prominent New York industrial designer Belle Kogan to design approximately 150 pieces, from which the company would choose 100 for production. Kogan had written articles and designed glass for the Federal Glass Company, designed silver for Reed & Barton, and designed products for numerous other companies. She was a founder and long-time chairperson of the New York Chapter of the Industrial Designers' Institute (later Society). She received many design awards throughout her life.

In the summer of 1939, Red Wing promoted these 100 new shapes by proclaiming them as UNPRECE-DENTED in bold type across its full-page ad for the July China, Glass and Housewares show in New York. A related mention came in the

Fig. 6-2. *(Above)* Lou McGrew creating the ridges on a *Terra-Craft* piece #963–10⅜" *(left)*. This series had ridges applied by hand to each piece after it came out of the mold. It looks as if McGrew is using a tableware fork to create the ridges! (Photo courtesy of Minnesota Historical Society)

The minutes of Red Wing Potteries January 11, 1940 board meeting highlighted the company losses:

	Ledger Value	Real Value
Red Wing Advertising Co. (stock)	20,000.00	none
Farm Lands (10,862 acres)*	80,062.20	11,099.45
R.W. Sewer Pipe Corporation	152,196.80	43,472.00
Mortgage Loans	20,730.63	12,000.00
Depreciation	0.00	206,418.18
TOTAL	272,989.63	272,989.63

*large amounts of land that had been purchased earlier already had been sold during the Depression, sometimes for pennies on the dollar.

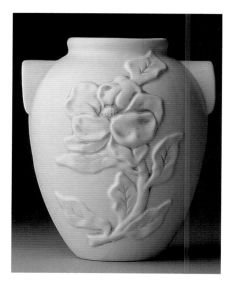

Fig. 6–3. *(Below)* **A vase from the *Magnolia Group* #1217–10".**
Fig. 6–4. *(Below left)* **A bowl from the *Terra-Craft* line #966–3⅞" x 10¼" Green Outside—Luster Green Lined.**

Newsnotes section of *Crockery and Glass Journal*:
"Newsworthy this month in the art pottery field is the fact that perhaps for the first time in the history of the art pottery business—although this is not confirmed—a pottery is producing at one time and for one show presentation, 100 entirely original shapes. These shapes had both modern and classical styling."

Kogan wrote an article prior to the 1939 New York's World Fair in which she described how every great fair or exposition in the past had left some outstanding mark on cultural or industrial progress. She said:
"The theme of the New York World's Fair is 'Building the World of Tomorrow with the Tools of Today.' It need scarcely

be pointed out that the underlying keynote of such a theme is Modern—Modern design, Modern architecture, Modern coloring, Modern sculpture and art, Modern materials."[1]

Red Wing's 1938 fall catalog featured these 100 pieces (Fig. 6–1) numbered 745–849 (with a few exceptions), as well as approximately 240 former RumRill pieces now marked as Red Wing, including four nudes and nine miniature vases. Red Wing added four new colors to eight of the glazes that had been used on RumRill.

It should be noted that Red Wing workers such as hand-turner Lou McGrew probably also were designing pieces at this time. There were many talented craftsman working at Red Wing during the entire Art Pottery era who were capable of designing salable Art Pottery. It was the job of the modelers and mold makers to bring to life the sketches and drawings brought in by designers, so it is likely that modelers with such talent—namely George Hehr and Russel "Teddy" Hutchson—were the creators of many of the unattributed pieces of this period.

1939

In the summer of 1939, the featured new line was *Terra-Craft Pottery*. These fourteen new vases and bowls designed by Kogan were said to combine *"simple classic lines with handwork and tooling."*[2] Though some of the pieces appear to be hand-thrown, they were slip-cast molded and then tiny ridges were scribed all over the exterior of the piece (Fig. 6–2). They came in *Terra Cotta, Adobe*, and *Green* (Fig. 6–4).

Red Wing also released a series of nineteen figurines in 1939, including the six now commonly referred to as ash receivers (Fig. 6–5, 6–6, and 6–7). Impractical in size for such use, they were never called ash receivers in any company literature. However, at least one other company produced similar items with much wider openings and a cigarette rest.

"New outstanding pottery colors" advertised that year included *Ox Blood, Ivory Antique, Celadon Green*, and *Williamsburg Blue*.[3]

Other pieces were added to the Art Pottery line every year, such as the two classical shapes added in 1939 that featured hand-turned styling (Fig. 6–8).

The Magnolia Group

In 1940 Red Wing asked Kogan to design a line similar to a previously popular RumRill line that was glazed *Pompeian—Antiqued Ivory*. Ornately decorated with magnolia blossoms in relief (Fig. 6–3), the original twenty-four shapes came in *Matt Ivory*, *Brown Antiqued Ivory*, *Green Antiqued Ivory* and *Oxblood*.

Also new in 1940 was a series of low bowls and flower arrangers. These flower arrangers came in shapes of fish, seahorses, and cranes. Eleven new figurines were produced, as well as a series of fruit-shaped bowls that were part of the *Hostess Ware* line (Fig. 11–9, 11–13 and 11–24).

Fig. 6-8. *(Right)* Two vases in *Luster Dubonnet* #901–8⅛" and #902–10".

(Top to bottom) Animal novelties in *Matt Green*. **Fig. 6-5.** #877–5" and #878–4¾". **Fig. 6-6.** #880–5¾" and #879–5". **Fig. 6-7.** #875–5" and #876–4¾".

Fig. 7-1.
#1147–11¾"
Gray Engobe
with Solid
Turquoise.

THE MURPHY ERA
Red Wing in the 1940s

Within the company changes were happening: E. S. Hoyt had retired as president, handing over the reigns to his nephew, Herbert Haddon Varney. Business was good, but it seems as though Red Wing was not fully prepared for it because—at the December 6, 1941, board meeting—the new president noted that *"a loss in volume was experienced to the extent of 150,000 to 200,000 dollars entirely due to the lack of kiln capacity. This condition caused considerable embarrassment as well, in giving our customers service."* This cold appraisal convinced the board to allocate $25,000 for construction of another kiln using recycled materials.

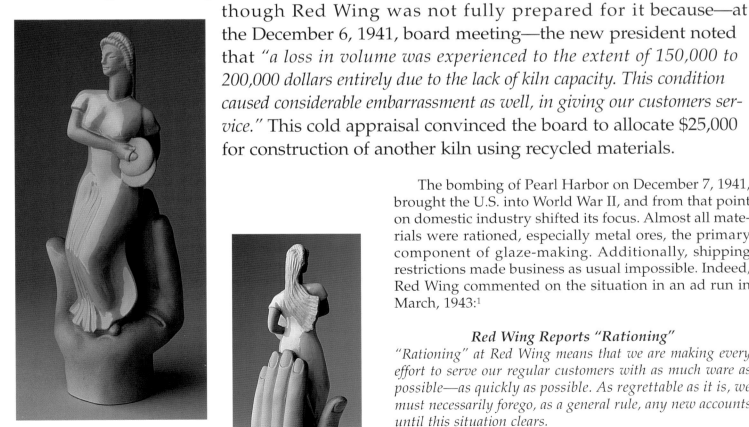

Fig. 7-2 and Fig. 7-3.
#1178-13" *Gray Engobe with Solid Turquoise.*

The bombing of Pearl Harbor on December 7, 1941, brought the U.S. into World War II, and from that point on domestic industry shifted its focus. Almost all materials were rationed, especially metal ores, the primary component of glaze-making. Additionally, shipping restrictions made business as usual impossible. Indeed, Red Wing commented on the situation in an ad run in March, 1943:[1]

Red Wing Reports "Rationing"
"Rationing" at Red Wing means that we are making every effort to serve our regular customers with as much ware as possible—as quickly as possible. As regrettable as it is, we must necessarily forego, as a general rule, any new accounts until this situation clears.

In fact, Red Wing ran no more advertisements (at least in the trade magazines) until after the war in January 1947, when it announced new dinnerware designed by

Fig. 7–4. Reproduction of Red Wing Potteries ad from the July 1941 *Crockery and Glass Journal*. With war raging in Europe, Red Wing tried to fill the demand caused by a lack of European pottery. Charles Murphy's cookie jars became some of Red Wing's best sellers.

Eva Zeisel and artware designed by Charles Murphy. Both product lines premiered at the Chicago Gift Show that same year. The January 1947 advertisement of Art Pottery was one of the last times Red Wing featured its artware in advertising to the trade—from that point on, dinnerware became the primary product line advertised and promoted.

The End of Stoneware Production

At the close of the war, America was the only industrialized nation whose industrial base and infrastructure had not suffered destruction. American industries were king, and the economy was stronger than it had been since the 1920s. Red Wing also was experiencing a boom in business.

When the Red Wing plant was remodeled in 1947, the last of the old draft kilns was removed, and it is assumed that stoneware production stopped that year. The last sale noted in existing company records shows the Chicago office selling a shipment of stoneware jugs in 1947. The stoneware era had come to an end after sixty-nine years of production.

When Red Wing President H. H. Varney died in 1949, Harry John Barghusen—an accountant and Red Wing board member—was appointed president. Red Wing's dinnerware now was selling well and the company concentrated its energy on it. Art Pottery and kitchenware were just sidelines.

Charles Murphy Arrives

In 1940, Red Wing sought to expand into decorated pottery and dinnerware and it found success with talented artist and designer Charles Murphy.

Charles Murphy, whose father had worked in the pottery industry, had studied fine arts—not ceramic arts—at the Cleveland Art Institute. While a student there he worked at R. Guy Cowan's renowned pottery on the weekends. Another noteworthy connection was the fact that during this period he roomed with Victor Schreckengost, who later became one of the most prominent designers at the Cowan pottery. He first went to the Homer Laughlin Company as a designer, and later worked at a decal company designing dinnerware decoration. In 1939, Murphy designed the decal for Homer Laughlin's commemorative plate for the 1939 New York

Fig. 7–5. Premiering in 1947, this series was offered in three different crackle glazes: *Eggshell Crackle—Bronze Footed and Lined* (shown below), *Turquoise Crackle* and *Chartreuse Crackle*. #1335–14⅛" and #1325–12⅜".

World's Fair, a noteworthy accomplishment considering that Frederick Rhead was the head of Homer Laughlin's art department at the time. Murphy also painted the large mural at the pottery exhibit in the Home Furnishings Buildings at the fair.

In 1940, Red Wing hired him as design director. Although initially his focus was on setting up production methods and designs for the new hand-painted dinnerware lines, he also was designer for all the new Art Pottery. One of the first things he wanted to do was to create a more expensive Art Pottery line to sell in jewelry stores and other more exclusive retail stores. The 1942 catalog featured twelve of these new pieces. Six were modern art figurals described in the catalog as *Gray Engobe with Turquoise* (or *Turquoise and White*) and a *Bronze Tan Engobe with Turquoise* (or *Turquoise and White*) (Fig. 7–1, 7–2 and 7–3). The other six were hand-painted figurines, ranging in size from a peasant couple standing 15" (Fig. 7–11), to a pair of baseball players at about 8". All were short-lived products.

Featured in 1941 advertisements were the Pierre, Katrina and Friar Monk cookie jars —also designed by Murphy—and the new *Provincial Luncheon Ware* and several pieces of Art Pottery with hand painted floral designs, all having a provincial Dutch motif that resembled products unavailable due to the war in Europe (Fig. 7–4).

The 1942 catalog showed a series of high-relief vases with Art Deco styled figures. One of these, shape #1148 (Fig. 7–7), was included in a 1984 exhibition featuring American Art Pottery from the Newark Museum of Art.[2] The catalog described the vase and commented on Red

Fig. 7–6. #1140–8½" Eggshell Ivory— Luster Elfin Green Lined.

Wing's products:

Light earthenware body, cylindrical form tapered at both ends, molded with stylized Art Deco relief of figures and plants; overall burgundy-red glaze[3] with gray-green interior glaze. Even the mass-market artware producers turned out high-quality design and fine glazes as evidenced by this example of Red Wing. The vase demonstrates the continued if diluted effort to produce affordable art wares that nevertheless maintained standards of quality and design.

The 1947 Red Wing Art Pottery catalog featured a new crackle glaze on modernistic forms (Fig. 7–5). This effect was created by using a glaze that would craze during firing. After firing, the crazing was filled in with India ink. Shape #1336 (See the photo in the Foreword of this book) was included in the "Art Pottery of the Midwest" exhibition at the Walker Art Center in Minneapolis in 1988. In his catalog commentary, curator Marion Nelson described the piece as:

. . .semi-matt fine crackle glaze on exterior and black semi-gloss glaze on interior with brown glaze . . . this organic vessel in soft white on a high-gloss dark brown square base is the best example of modernism known by an American commercial art pottery.[4]

This line included three vases on square bases ranging in height from 9" to 14", two bowls and a pair of candlestick holders. Another series of five vases, starting with shape #1300 (which was later used as part of the 2300 "anniversary series") had a similar look and was available in the special finishes of *Crackled White, Crackled Turquoise,* or *Crackled Chartreuse.*

Four new figurines were introduced in 1947 that were available in standard glazes, or (for nearly double the cost) in the special finishes.

Fig. 7–7. #1148–10¼" Luster Tan—Luster Green Lined.

Fig. 7–8.
Candleholder
#1365–9" in
Luster Gray;
#1350–10" in
Luster Pink and
#1349–9" in
Como Blue.

Finishing off the host of new styles and glazes was a six-piece series with bold brown and white lines; three of the pieces have African figures as handles (Fig. 7–9). The line was discontinued in 1949.

In 1949 Charles Murphy had serious disagreements with president Varney and he left Red Wing to work for the Stetson China Company in Illinois. There is little

Fig. 7–9.
In front,
#1329–18½"D
long bowl;
#1327–7½"D
covered bowl
and #1328–10"
vase. All in
*Brown Engobe
with Bright
White Over-
glaze.*

documentation available about who may have contributed to Red Wing's designs after Murphy's departure, but we may presume that staff members were actively designing Art Pottery.

In 1948 the latest in a series of figurine planters was introduced (shapes #1337–#1346), eight new animals and a boy and girl each holding flowers. Also introduced that year were the Chinese figures and the figure referred to as the gay 90s gent (Fig. 7–8). The latter two were also available in either the special crackle glazes or standard glazes.

1949

Although Red Wing shape numbers are explained in greater detail in Chapter 16, note that at this time—although the company had numbered its pottery in

Fig. 7–10. #1161–9" *Matt Lily Green—Eggshell Ivory Lined.*

ascending numerical order over the years—the January 1949 catalog introduces a series numbered out of sequence. Shapes #6001–#6008 were the start of a numbering trend that gave special, premier finishes a completely separate series of shape numbers. Shapes #6001–#6008 supposedly were offered in three special glazes, a *Chinese Amber—Chocolate Overlaid with White, Opal—Dove Gray Overlaid with White* and a *Quartz—Dubonnet Overlaid with White* none of which the author has ever seen any examples. All were discontinued by the fall of the same year.

Fig. 7-11.
#1125–15¼"
and
#1124–14¾"
both *Hand
Painted.*
(Courtesy of
Goodhue County
Historical
Society, Red
Wing,
Minnesota)

Fig. 8-1.
#B1433–10¼"
Chartreuse—
Luster Gray.

$\mathcal{T}$HE 1950s

"$\mathcal{P}$ottery Makers Suffer From Inroads of Plastic, Imports From Japan" reports the October 1, 1951, *Wall Street Journal*. "*A flood of dinnerware imports from Japan is pounding them. Makers of plastic dishes are biting at their business. And they're still plagued by the slow-down aftermath of last year's consumer scare-buying.*"

"*A depression in the midst of a booming economy*" is the way their plight is described by a spokesman of the U.S. Pottery Association.

The article goes on to report that most dinnerware sales were down by half from the previous year. Most potteries in East Liverpool, Ohio—the mecca of American-made dinnerware—were running at fifty percent capacity. One pottery president had this to say about why the industry was losing sales:

There's the new "Sloppy Joe" generation of realistic kids not interested in formalities . . . or thinking of dinnerware as heirlooms. It's getting harder to sell them earthenware. They might even buy plastics.[1]

The American government was accused of selling the U.S. pottery industry down the river by some people in the industry. A May 24, 1957, *Red Wing Daily Republican Eagle* article stated:

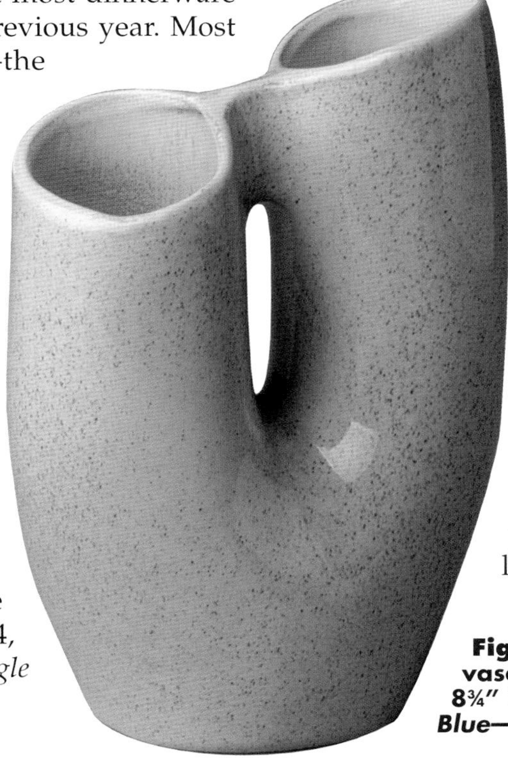

Fig. 8–2. Tree vase #M1508–8¾" in *Fleck Nile Blue—Colonial Buff.*

. . . Red Wing . . . Potteries people understand that American tariffs against Japanese pottery are low for a reason. They used to be fairly high, but they were lowered through reciprocal tariff agreements under the Franklin Roosevelt administrations and they've been kept low under President Eisenhower because the United States wants Japan to trade with America rather than with Communist China, which might lead to a growth of Communist influence in Japan.

In addition to help from lower tariffs, Japan learned how to increase product quality using methods largely untried in the U.S. In 1950, W. Edwards Deming, the manufacturing efficiency guru, was invited to Japan.

Fig. 8-3. *Tropicana* line by Belle Kogan. From the left: Desert Flower #B2002-8" in *Citron Yellow—Woodland Green*, Bird of Paradise #B2003-10⅛" in *Citron Yellow—Luster Gray*, and Shell Ginger #B2001-8⅛" in *Ming Green—Citron Yellow.*

For the next two decades he helped to redesign and motivate the industries of Japan. Deming's "Total Quality Management" techniques became popular in the U.S. only after American electronics, automobiles, and other products began to be perceived as inferior to their Japanese counterparts.

When America entered the Korean conflict, consumers reacted with what was referred to as scare-buying. As a guard against inflation, the Office of Price Stabilization was created. This federal agency required Red Wing to file reports every six months for approval on all retail price limits for its entire product line. Whether this requirement had a detrimental effect on Red Wing's business is not known, but it certainly was another headache for management.

Upon the death of H. H. Varney in 1949, Harry John Barghusen became Red Wing's president in January, 1950. He encountered problems from the beginning. Besides the general pottery industry

problems, Red Wing employees were unhappy with both their union and the company.

Additionally, for the first time since it was formed, the company had to borrow money.

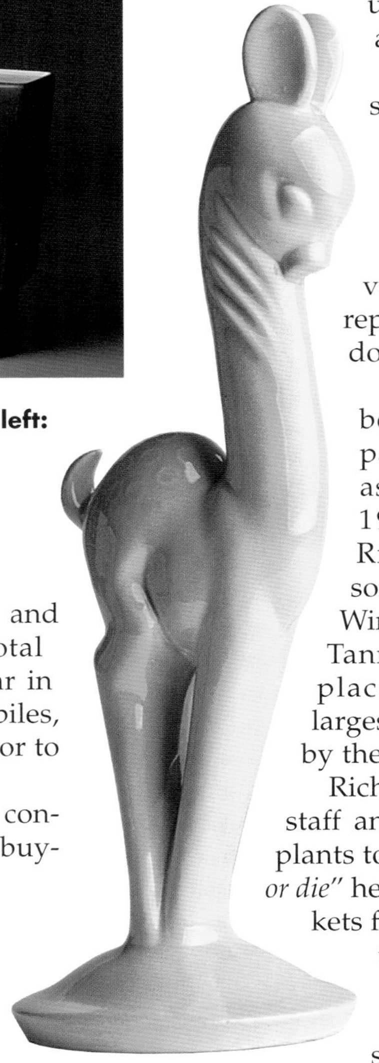

Diversify or Die

In January 1950, the employees voted a new union in—the CIO—to replace the AFL. In May, a strike shut down the plant for eight weeks.

In the 1950s, company profits began to erode. In 1955 the company lost $27,000, and—probably as a result of this loss—in October 1955 the board named Forest Richardson as president. Richardson came "from the tannery," as Red Wing natives called the F. B. Foot Tanning Company, which had replaced Red Wing Potteries as the largest area employer (and now owned by the Red Wing Shoe Company).

Richardson expanded the engineering staff and brought in experts from other plants to diversify the products. "*Diversify or die*" he said, as he looked at the new markets for clay in building materials, electronics, atomic energy, aircraft and guided missiles.[2]

Richardson got off to a rocky start, however, when, in January 1956, he tried to cut back the number of men required for kiln firing from thirteen to eight. This started a series of walkouts, slowdowns and disciplinary layoffs. It was six weeks before the factory was operating again at full capacity.[3]

In 1956 and 1957, even though sales were up, Red Wing was still losing money. Again the board changed presidents, this time appointing Richard A. Gillmer, a former Red Wing sales representative in Chicago and a vice-president of the company. He remained president until the Red Wing Potteries closed in 1967.

Fig. 8-4. *(Above)* #1364-12½" figurine in *Chartreuse.*
Fig. 8-5. *(Left)* #2315-10¼ Over-lay glaze *White-Luster Black.*
Fig. 8-6. *(Right) Textura* line by Belle Kogan: *Luster Pink—Luster Gray* and *Luster Gray—Luster Coral* clockwise from front, #B2101-4", #B2100-8¼", #B2107-12⅜" and a pair of #B2113-7⅛".

Fig. 8-7. *(Left)* Nestling pair of vases: the larger is **#B1418-7"** and the smaller is **#B1418A-5"** in *Travertine—Citron Yellow*.
Fig. 8-8. *(Below)* Two *Cypress Green* vases **#1632-8"** and **#1509-7¼"**; in the front a small vase from the *Garden Club Pottery* line **#5016-3½"** in *Green*.

By 1958, due to heavy cuts in the staff, Red Wing was in the black again and paid dividends for the first time in three-and-a-half years. In fact, in 1958 Red Wing was reported to be the strongest prospect for buying Vernon Kilns, a Los Angeles-based dinnerware manufacturer.[4] Red Wing ended the decade on a high note, again showing profits in 1959 and initiated planning for a new retail store in Rapid City, South Dakota, that opened August 1, 1960.

The Art Pottery of the 1950s

During this decade, there were many new lines, shapes and totally new styles, in addition to special items made for the company's seventy-fifth anniversary in 1953. The decade was modernism, functionalism, amorphism, and just plain stylistic.

With the departure of Charles Murphy, Red Wing again turned to Belle Kogan for a brand-new series for the new decade. Two new series, *Tropicana* (starting at shape #2000) and *Textura* (starting at shape #2100) sported the new prefix "B", fulfilling Kogan's request for some sort of designation on her designs. In 1953,

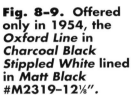

Fig. 8-10. Part of the *DeLuxe Line,* "The Muse" in *Mulberry* **#B2507-7¼" x 13¾"**.

when Charles Murphy returned to Red Wing, his new designs where marked with the letter "M." Another prefix, "H", appeared on a series of *Hand Painted* vases that premiered in 1952. It has been reported that the "H" designated moldmaker Teddy Hutchson, but because the "H" is found only on *Hand Painted* vases (or on the shapes that started as *Hand Painted* vases), it could be assumed that the letter denotes the line name. Hutchson designed many pieces, and he, Kogan

Fig. 8-9. Offered only in 1954, the *Oxford Line* in *Charcoal Black Stippled White* lined in *Matt Black* **#M2319-12⅛"**.

and Murphy all designed pieces that were not marked with their initials. (Note that "B" and "H" are not followed by a hyphen whereas "M" usually is.)

The *Tropicana* line had three different relief patterns: Bird of Paradise, Shell Ginger, and Desert Flower (Fig. 8–3). In addition to vases, window boxes and bowls were produced.

Textura was comprised of eight different vases (Fig. 8–6) that had three differently textured exteriors, either a rough stucco-like surface, rough vertical lines or a grid texture. Both *Tropicana* and *Textura* came in new colors.

Another grouping designed by Kogan was called the *Deluxe Line* (#B2500–#B2509), and it featured The Nymphs and The Muse (Fig. 8–10) along with The Ducks, The Parrots, and centerpieces of swans and jumping dolphins to go along with decorative bowls and candleholders.

In 1952, a line of *Hand Painted* vases carried the designs of three of the then-current dinnerware lines: *Lotus*, *Magnolia* (not to be confused with the Art Pottery line of the same name) and *Blossom Time*.

Fig. 8–11. **#M1472–8½"** in *Colonial Buff*, *Matt White* and *Cinnamon*.

The 75th Anniversary

To celebrate its 75th year in business in 1953, Red Wing came out with a new series having shape numbers beginning with the number 2300. Thus, the line is now referred to as the "2300 series" by collectors. This line was originally offered in two new *Over-lay* glazes, *Gray* over *Luster Burgundy* and *White* over *Luster Black*, the latter appearing blue where the two colors blend (Fig. 8–5

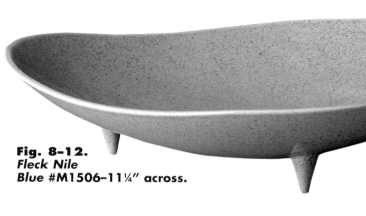

Fig. 8–12. *Fleck Nile Blue* #M1506–11¼" across.

and 8–20). Most of the 2300 shapes had been used previously (although with different shape numbers), but there were three new shapes by Belle Kogan: #B2315, #B2316, and #B2317. All three were offered in both 10" and 12" sizes.

The following year, 1954, another glaze was used on the 2300 series shapes: a white stippling over a charcoal-black body. Called the *Oxford Line* (Fig. 8–9), it was offered until 1955.

Another glaze that was offered only during this two-year period was a glaze named *Travertine* (Fig. 8–7). Pieces with this exceptionally thick glaze often required grinding on their base in order for them to sit flat.

Charles Murphy Returns

After the death of Varney—with whom Murphy had not seen eye-to-eye—Murphy returned to Red Wing in 1953.

Two of his new designs are seen in the July 1953 sales sheets, #M2318 and #M2319 in the new *Over-lay* glazes.

In the early part of the 1950s, instead of printing new catalogs twice a year as had been the norm, the company used individual sales sheets that collectively made up the Red Wing catalog in a folder provided by the company. After Murphy's return, a redesigned catalog in a new format was issued in 1955. It showed almost exclusively new Murphy designs with the exception of a few Kogan-designed proven sellers. The January 1953 price list had seventy-eight "B" shapes, eight "H" shapes and no "M" shapes. (Even though there were some Murphy designs included, his earlier designs had not been marked in this way.) The 1955 catalog, however, had seventy-one "M" shapes and only ten "B" shapes.

The Flecks

A whole new series of glazes (new for Red Wing anyway), the Flecks were featured in the new 1955 catalog. However, a *Fleck Gray* (with a *Light Gray* interior) appeared in January 1954, and later that year the *Fleck Zephyr*

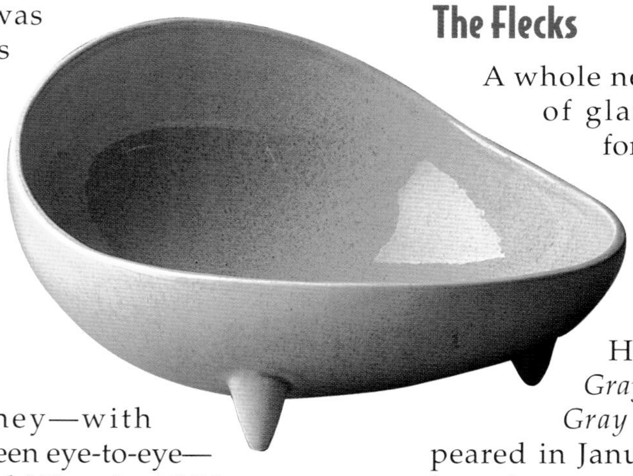

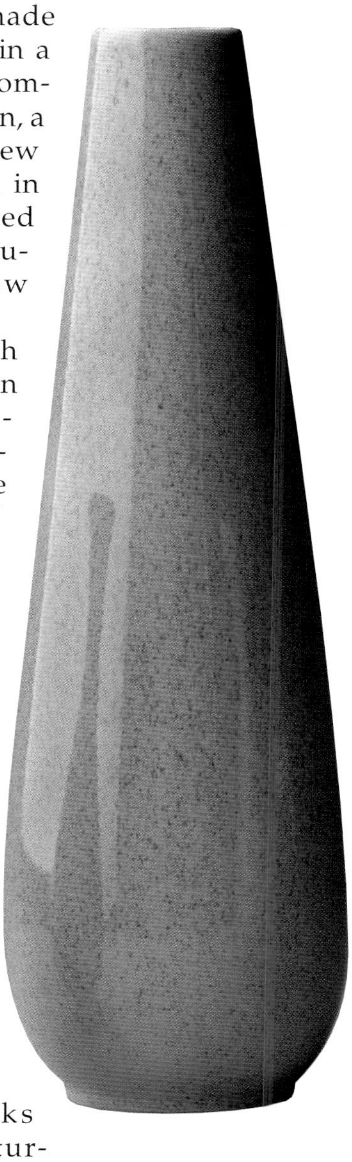

Fig. 8–13. (Left) *Yellow Fleck* footed bowl #M1494–9" across.
Fig. 8–14. (Above) *Fleck Zephyr Pink* #1554–11⅞".

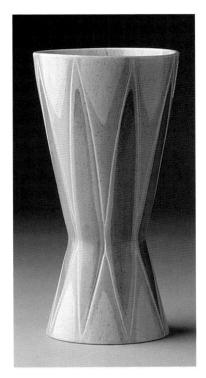

Fig. 8-15. One of the *Sgraffito* line which came out in 1955 and was out of production by 1956. #M4005–10⅛" *Hand Painted with Tan Speckle Overglaze.*

Pink (also with a *Light Gray* interior) was offered. *Fleck Gray* was short-lived and was not used as part of the 1955 catalog that featured Flecks. In fact, other than the *Sgraffito* line, the only colors offered in 1955 were *Luster Black, Matt White— Matt Green*, and the four *Fleck* colors: *Fleck Zephyr Pink—Light Gray, Fleck Nile Blue—Colonial Buff, Fleck Green—Colonial Buff*, and *Fleck Yellow— Light Celadon*. These light colors with tiny flecks of dark brown would continue to be the dominant glaze for the rest of the 1950s. In the spring of 1960, the last two Flecks, *Fleck Zephyr Pink* and *Fleck Nile Blue* appear in the catalog for the final time.

1955 to 1959

New in 1955 was the premier glaze/line called *Sgraffito* (Fig. 8–15), named for the age-old decorating technique wherein the unfired glaze is scraped away in part to reveal the different colored clay underneath. The name *Sgraffito* was used in 1941 (on three shapes: #1129, #1130 and #1131), but that version was more of a decorated

Fig. 8-16. *(Above)* Chessmen vases in *Luster Black* #M1464–12¼" (King) and #M1465–12¼" (Queen).

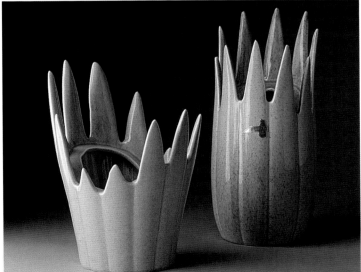

Fig. 8-17. *Fleck Green* #M1480–9" and *Fleck Nile Blue* #M1481–11".

pottery than a design that used true sgraffito technique.

Murphy designed a whole new series of amorphous-shaped vases (Fig. 8–2), a group of five wildly spiked vases and bowls (Fig. 8–17), and other interesting pieces such as the 12" king and queen chess-piece vases (Fig. 8–16). Also offered during this period were various bowls, planters, jardinieres and ashtrays.

What Did They Put in All Those Bowls Anyway?

In general, the shapes that were new for the mid-50s were bowls, and lots of them. There were regular bowls, footed bowls, ring bowls, oblong bowls, square bowls, round bowls, triangular bowls—as well as deep triangular and deep square bowls— five-compartment nut bowls, console bowls with legs, leaf bowls, long leaf bowls, footed leaf bowls, bowls with leaf designs, a bowl with handles and an Old English bowl. All these bowls were offered in one catalog (1956)!

Also offered at this time—along with a variety of plain planters and jardinieres— were planters in such shapes as a cart, piano, violin, and swans.

1957 Garden Club Pottery

A new series, called *Garden Club Pottery* appeared in a catalog supplement in 1957. It started with shape #M5000—as well as previously used shapes #600–#605. This line is made up of simple shapes available in matte glazes of *Black, Brown, Gray, Pink, Blue* and *Green*.

Ashtrays

During the mid-1950s, Red Wing made many different ashtrays such as the horse-head ashtray designed by Murphy (Fig. 8–11), and the wing-shaped ashtrays in red. By 1957 ashtrays had their own page in the catalog, and in

Fig. 8-19. *Jolly Jars: Mosaic 8", Sweet Shot 7",* and *Sierra 5".* **According to the company catalog, suggested usages were as snack jars, bathroom jars, canister sets, cookie jars, candy jars, dresser sets and munch jars.**

1958 an entire line of *Hobnail* ashtrays, also designed by Murphy, was *the* new line for the year. Originally also marketed as candy and nut dishes, this line was named after the thick-headed nail used on the soles of shoes and boots. *Hobnail* pieces have shape numbers #M2000– #M2007.

Jolly Jars

Finishing out the decade were *Jolly Jars*, a series of lidded jars in three abstract patterns (Fig. 8–19). Although their hand-painted designs were more like Red Wing kitchenware or dinnerware, the jars were offered in the Art Pottery catalogs. Each of the three finishes were offered in three sizes. *Sweet Shop* and *Mosaic* shared the same shape; *Sierra* is a somewhat more bulbous shape and has a larger lid handle.

Fig. 8-18. **#B1427-8" in Woodland Green—Luster Light Yellow.**

Fig. 8-20. From the "2300" series, *Over-lay glaze Luster Burgundy-Gray*: Vase #2302–10⅛" and pair of candle-holders #2311–8¼" and 7¾". Sizes on pieces varied subtly due to drying times, how the pieces were finished off, and the making of the molds.

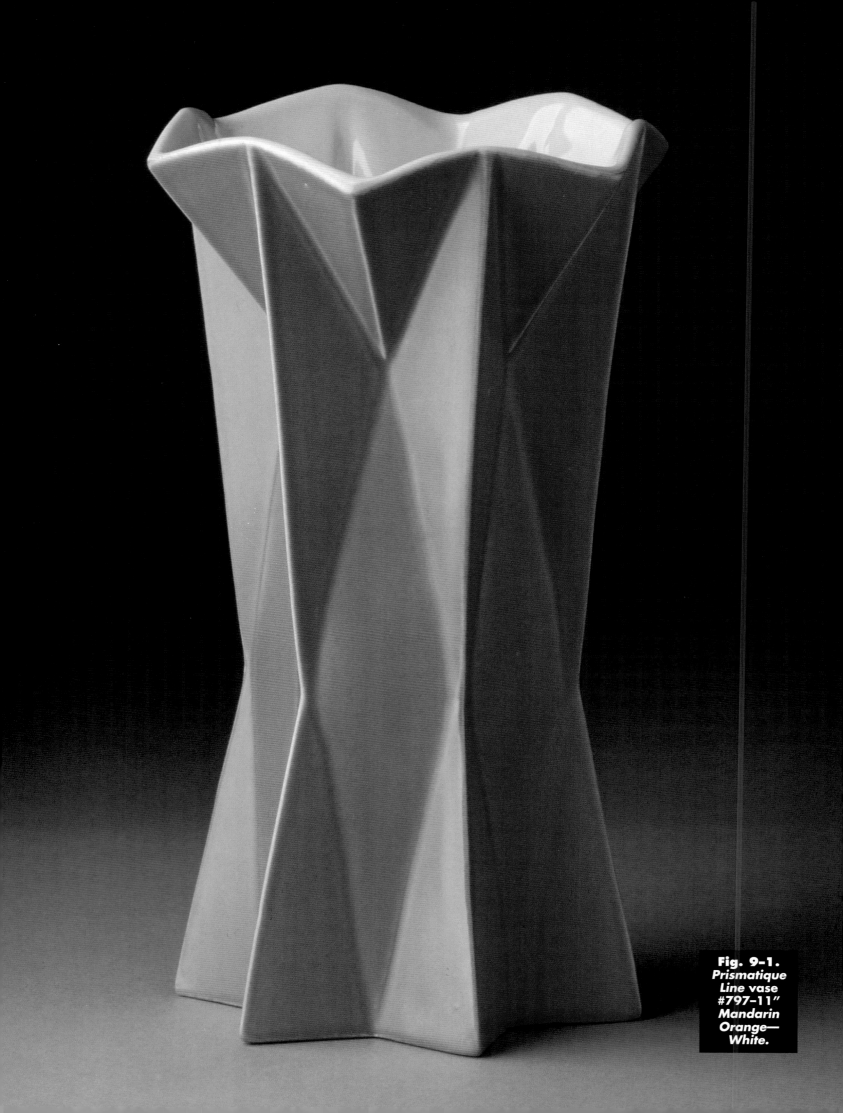

Fig. 9-1.
*Prismatique
Line vase
#797–11″
Mandarin
Orange—
White.*

$\mathcal{T}$HE 1960s

In 1950 only 10 percent of a department store's dinnerware was imported; by 1967 the number was nearly 90 percent. This often-cited figure pretty much says it all. In addition to the pottery industry's problems of the 1950s (plastics, less demand for formal dinnerware, etc.), there was also the fact that the facilities were old and run-down. Red Wing was no exception. In *Death of a Business*[1] this is how the physical plant was described:

Built in the nineteenth century, the plant was an industrial engineer's nightmare. Comprising four floors, this manufacturing facility was a maze of narrow aisles, posts, ramps and walls. As the need arose for more space over years, an additional section would be "tacked on" to the existing facility, leaving the problem of a ramp to a new level, narrow doorways and obstructing walls. A smooth flow of production was wishful thinking in the Red Wing plant; excessive handling and trucking of in-process ware sent costs rocketing. Storage facilities were inadequate, and in-process ware and finished goods were stored where space could be found—along aisles, in niches and crannies along the kilns, on the fourth floor, and in quonset huts outside the plant. Without any system or space for storage, time-consuming long-distance

Fig. 9-2. (Left) 1960s original cardboard mock-up of *Prismatique Line* piece #798. (Photo courtesy of Belle Kogan)

Fig. 9-3. (Below) #M3012-10" *Decorator Line* by Charles Murphy in the three *Crystalline Glazes* offered: (left to right) *Burnt Orange, Silver Green* and *Blue.*

trucking was necessary and quantities of ware were "lost" indefinitely in the little-traveled corners of the plant.

Red Wing's profits through the 1960s were marginal at best, averaging about $30,000 per year. Total sales slowly declined nearly every year of the decade. The exception was 1966 when there was an increase in profits, a direct result of selling *Bob White* and *Pepe* dinnerware in supermarkets.

The company again tried to diversify: making ceramic tile, more specialty items, developing

Fig. 9-4. *Doric Ensemble* line: *Riviera Blue #666–6"*, *Bittersweet #662–11"* and *Butterscotch #667–10⅛".*

less formal dinnerware, and selling dinnerware as supermarket premiums. The one bright spot was the Red Wing Potteries Salesroom. By 1966 it accounted for nearly 25 percent of the total company sales.

The spring of 1967 brought uncertainty among the supermarket premium buyers. Red Wing built up its stock in anticipation of more deals with supermarket chains, but by April the company had failed to make a single sale in this market, and record-breaking losses of $90,000 had been posted for the year. This loss, coupled with strong union demands, hurt the company dramatically. After a bitter three-month strike, the shareholders voted to liquidate the company on August 24, 1967.

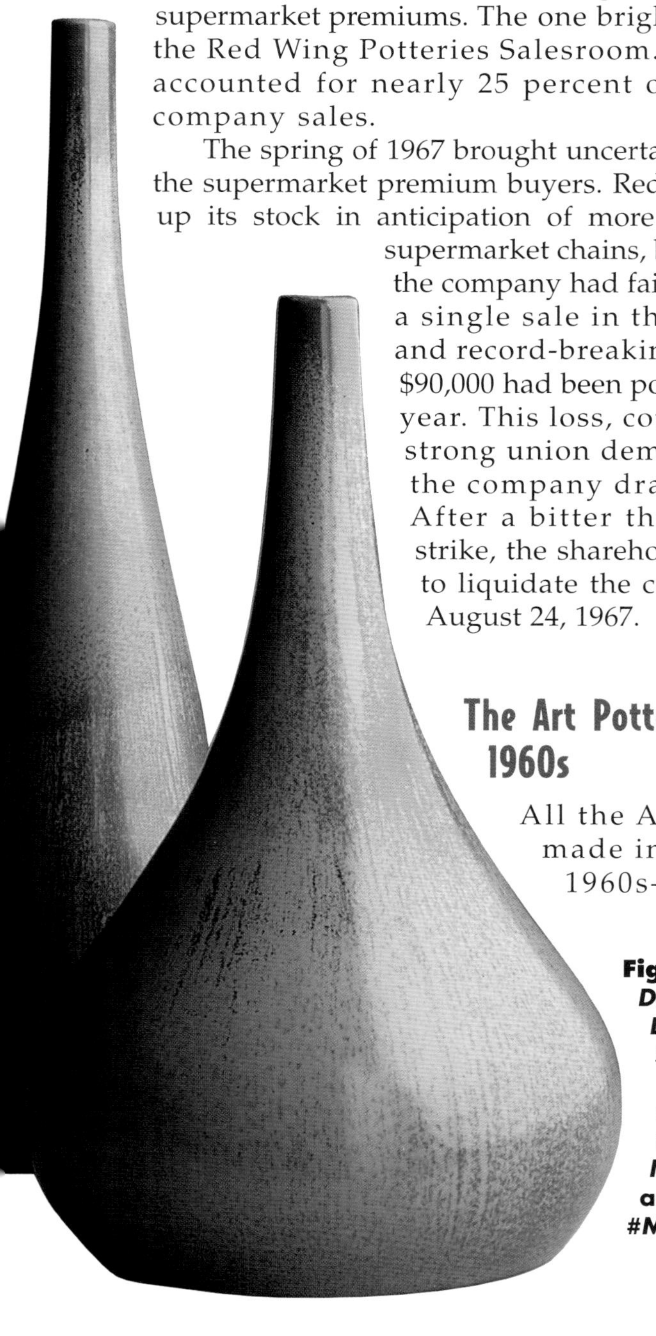

The Art Pottery of the 1960s

All the Art Pottery made in the early 1960s—whether

Fig. 9-6. *Decorator Line* in *Silver Green Crystalline Glaze M3006–16"* and *#M3007–12".*

new designs or proven sellers— were lumped into two separate categories: *Floraline*, which had ninety-one pieces, and *Stereoline* with twenty-seven. *Floraline* used standard glazes previously offered: *Cypress Green*, *Mat White*, *Cinnamon* and *Black. Stereoline* used new glazes called *Sagebrush*, *Hyacinth*, *Butterscotch* and *Bronze Green*. This categorization lasted only a couple of years.

The first prestige line associated with the 1960s actually debuted in 1959. Designed by Charles Murphy, it was called the *Decorator Line* with *Crystalline Glazes*. The high-relief designs range from geometric to the offbeat #M3013 (Fig. 9–18).

The initial fourteen shapes included eight tall, narrownecked/wide-bodied vases (Fig. 9–6)—some with high-relief designs—and six ashtrays. The three different mottled glaze colors were iden-

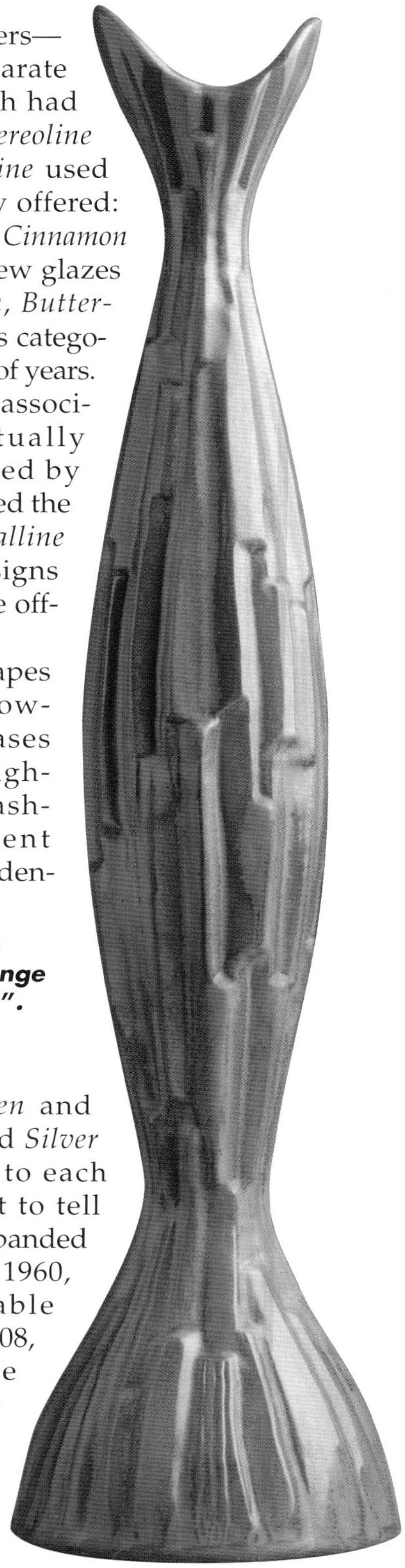

Fig. 9-5. The tallest of the *Decorator Line* in *Burnt Orange Crystalline Glaze #3018–21".*

tified as *Blue, Silver Green* and *Burnt Orange*. The *Blue* and *Silver Green* glazes are similar to each other and can be difficult to tell apart (Fig. 9–3). This line expanded to twenty-four shapes by 1960, with a jardiniere available in three sizes (shapes #808, #810, and #812). These three jardinieres also were offered in the new *Stereoline* colors. The *Decorator Line* was short-lived. The vases appeared last in the

Fig. 9-7. The *Monarch* line had two finishes: *Gothic Green* (shown) and *Contemporary Blue*. Clockwise from front: oval low bowl #938–2¼" x 6½", round low bowl #940–2¼" x 10½", oval planter #939–3¾" x 8½" and #941–2¼" x 8" round low bowl.

Fig. 9-8. (Above) *Chromoline Handpainted*: left rear, #682–13⅛" and #M3006–16⅛" in *Blue and Yellow Combination*; others in *Rust and Green Combination*. Standing up in right rear is bowl #681–10¼"D. In front; compote #675–6"D, compote #676–8"D and a pair of candleholders #678–6".

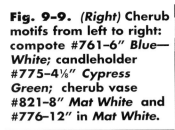

Fig. 9-9. *(Right)* Cherub motifs from left to right: compote #761–6" *Blue— White*; candleholder #775–4⅛" *Cypress Green*; cherub vase #821–8" *Mat White* and #776–12" in *Mat White*.

Fig. 9-10. *(Left)* The *Belle Line* in *Chocolate—White Overlay (Chrome Yellow Lining)* #845–8¼" and #880–2¾" x 6⅜".

Fig. 9-11 and Fig. 9-12. (Above) Probably the rarest of the figural pieces made by Red Wing, named *Cowboy A*, *(left)*, #43, and *Cowboy B*, *(right)* #44, both 22".

spring 1961 catalog, although the jardinieres appeared until 1962 and the ashtrays until 1965 (except for #3005 which continued through 1967). Many collectors refer to these as "Modernism" pieces.

The spring 1960 premier line was *Doric Ensemble* (Fig. 9-4) in new, brighter colors of deep reddish-orange (*Bittersweet*), bright purple (*Amethyst*), and *Riviera Blue*. A total of seven different shapes were offered as candleholders, compotes and a bowl.

In the fall of 1960, there were two new lines. The first was the *Chromoline Handpainted* (Fig. 9–8), a line of fifteen cylinder-shaped vases, bowls, candy dishes, compotes, ashtrays and candlesticks. The pieces have the appearance of being hand-turned, and are hand-painted with encircling stripes in two color-combinations, *Rust and Green*, and *Blue and Yellow*. The other new offering

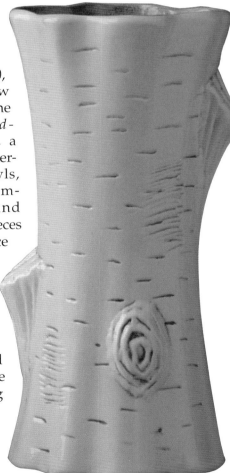

Fig. 9-13. *(Left)* The *Birch Bark Line* smaller canoe is #734–9⅜" long; the larger canoe is #735–11⅞" long.
Fig. 9-14. *(Above)* *Birch Bark Line* vase #732–7⅝".

was the *Birch Bark Line* (Fig. 9–13 and 9–14), a line of only six pieces with a glaze made to resemble the bark of a white birch tree. The line consisted of a vase, two planters, and three different canoes of 10", 12" and 17". (Originally just two were offered—the 12" was added later).

In the fall of 1961, four figurals that are considered among Red Wing's rarest were produced. They were Cowboy A and Cowboy B, a pair of 22" full-figure wall plaques depicting bow-legged cowboys (Fig. 9–11 and 9–12). The other two were a pair of cherub-like figurals referred to on a production chart as Baby Standing and Kneeling Baby. The four figurals were only offered for two years and are considered very scarce.

In 1962, Red Wing again hired Kogan to design a line that became her biggest seller. Called the *Prismatique Line*, (Fig. 9–1) its sharp, angular lines were applied to fifteen different shapes in five different glaze colors. Kogan relates that the inspiration for her creation came to her one day while sitting in her dentist's chair. She saw a tooth with its angular-shaped roots. She rushed back to her design studio and sketched out designs for the *Prismatique Line*. The original cardboard mock-up (Fig. 9–2) was the prototype for shape #798, the 8" version of shape #797 (Fig. 9–1). This line was sold until 1965, with two of the shapes continuing until 1967.

In 1963, cherubs appear on several pieces: in the 14" high #776 vase, in the #761 console bowl and on the #775 candlestick. The spring 1963 catalog shows four vases and planters that have cherubic figures attached somewhat tenuously to their exteriors (Fig. 9–9). They were offered for only one season.

In fall of 1963, Kogan designed her last line for Red Wing, the *Belle Line*, offered in colors exclusive to this line (Fig. 9–10).

Fig. 9–15. Marked RED WING #914, this 11¾" *Bronze Line* piece never shows up in any known catalog.

Fig. 9–16. Introduced in July 1965, this lion planter is #917–13"D in *Tahitian Gold.*

In 1965, the premier line offered by Red Wing Potteries was the *Bronze Line*. It consisted of mostly classical shapes glazed in a rich, glossy bronze color with a bit of a crackle. Two pieces seem to stand out: a Polynesian-type figural candleholder (#913) and a nude female figure vase (#912). The scarcest of the *Bronze Line* pieces is the figure of a female centaur standing 11¾" tall (Fig. 9–15).

In 1966, the final premier line, the *Monarch* line was introduced. It came in eight shapes: one vase and seven bowls or planters. It was offered in two glazes called *Contemporary Blue* and *Gothic Green* (Fig. 9–7).

The regular line for the last few years was heavy on ashtrays, novelty planters and the usual assortment of vases, jardinieres and planters. Probably the most noteworthy novelty planter was the *Giraffe Planter* (shape #896), a design of which its creator, Charles Murphy, was personally fond.

Fig. 9–17. *Decorator* line #M3019–12" in *Burnt Orange Crystalline Glaze.*

Fig. 9–18.
Decorator Line #M3013–15" with a *Silver Green Crystalline* glaze.

Fig. 10–1. Salt and pepper shakers from the *Town and County* line designed by Eva Zeisel.

CHAPTER 10

DINNERWARE
ART POTTERY IN DISGUISE

Although this book is about the Art Pottery made by Red Wing, the artistic quality of much of the Red Wing dinnerware, especially notable in some serving pieces, merits attention by Art Pottery collectors. By the late 1940s Red Wing was primarily a dinnerware manufacturer and the majority of its marketing efforts promoted dinnerware. In fact, in July 1952, only 15 percent of Red Wing's output was Art Pottery.

The term "dinnerware," as used in this book, refers to all the various luncheonware, earthenware, dinnerware, and casual china that Red Wing Potteries produced. Initially, all the dishes Red Wing sold were considered luncheonware, such as the *Gypsy Trail* group (*Plain*, *Reed* and *Chevron*) and *Provincial Luncheon Ware*.

Gypsy Trail
In June 1935, Red Wing launched its first dinnerware line called *Gypsy Trail*. It was sold and marketed through the RumRill Potteries (although seconds very likely were sold at the Red Wing Potteries Salesroom, the company's seconds shop in Red Wing). *Gypsy Trail* was offered in bright colors similar to those successfully used by various California potteries in the early thirties: *White*, *Turquoise*, *Blue*, *Yellow,* and *Orange.*

In the fall of 1935, Gypsy Trail became the series name for several lines. The initial line was renamed *Reed* (Fig. 10–5) and a new line called *Plain* (Fig. 10–3) was added. In the spring of 1936, Red Wing introduced a third line—*Chevron*—named for the edge treatment motif of repeated chevrons (Fig. 10–2). *Chevron* was produced until at least March 1939, and *Reed* and *Plain* show up in price lists until 1943.

A new line was introduced in the February

Fig. 10–2. *Chevron* dinnerware: *Orange* 5" Pitcher (32 oz.), *Blue* 3¾" pitcher (19 oz.), *Yellow* 3⅛" kettle candlestick and plates 6⅛", 7", 8¼", 10" and 12".

Fig. 10-4. Duck ashtray 2¾" x 4⅜" in *Royal Blue* from the *Plain* dinnerware.

Fig. 10-5. (Below) Reed dinnerware: 5¼" *Orange* 6 cup teapot (also available in 8 cup); 6" *Turquoise* ball pitcher (24 oz.—also available in 8 oz., 11oz., 16oz. and 32oz.); 5⅞" *Yellow* syrup pitcher (19 oz.); 3½" *Blue* creamer; 9¾" *Orange* dinner plate; and two *Orange* mixing bowls, 10¼"D and 9"D.

Fig. 10-3. *Plain* dinnerware: Left rear, *Blue* 3½" fluted mug with wood handle (7 oz.); *Orange* 4¾" mug (10 oz.); *Yellow* 5" mug; *Orange* 7½" swirl pitcher (64 oz.) marked RED WING #735; *Orange* 7⅛" jug with ice stop (64 oz.) marked RED WING #547. In front, creamers *Yellow and Royal Blue* 2⅜"; salt and pepper shakers *Turquoise and Yellow* 2⅞"; *Royal Blue* creamer 2⅜" and sugar 2"; *Orange* chocolate cup 4" and plate (with cup ring) 7¼".

1937 *Crockery and Glass Journal:*

Ivanhoe is the name of this new pattern on a shape reminiscent of Old England, at RumRill Pottery Co. It has a matt glaze finish in ivory, suntan, Alpine blue, and ocean green.

No catalog or any other promotional material is known that documents this line, and few examples of the pottery itself exist (Fig. 10–7). With the split of Red Wing and Rumrill just a few months later, and Red Wing's subsequent introduction of *Fondoso*, most likely very little *Ivanhoe* was ever made.

Fondoso, another Gypsy Trail line (Fig. 10–8, 10–9 and 10–10), was designed in 1938 by Belle Kogan after she had designed her 100 Art Pottery pieces. Red Wing aggressively advertised this line with its new pastel colors.

In April 1941, *Provincial Cooking Ware* (Fig. 10–11) was introduced. This line included containers with terra cotta exteriors and dark brown lids and interiors. When this line was reintroduced with almost exactly the same shapes in the 1960s, the color was renamed *Bittersweet Red*.

When Red Wing hired Charles Murphy to set up hand-decorated dinnerware production in 1940, he introduced a new policy of creating several lines using the same molds. The first was *Provincial Luncheon Ware* decorated in a French Provincial style. It premiered in February

Fig. 10-6. A *Chevron* cocktail set in *Orange.* 6 pint pitcher 11½", originally sold with a wooden dash. Cups are 4 oz.

Fig. 10-7. *Ivanhoe* salt and pepper shaker in *Alpine Blue.*

1941. The four lines based on this shape were named after the French provinces *Orleans, Normandy, Brittany* and *Ardennes*.

Dinnerware lines had glazes applied—using artist brushes—by women set up on an assembly line with a conveyor belt running down the middle to carry dishes. A decorator would apply strokes on top of a light stencil mark and send the plate down the line to the next hand-painter, who would apply different strokes. The more strokes a pattern had, the higher the production cost.

In response to a successful Russell Wright dinnerware line, in August 1941, Red Wing introduced what would be its most prolific shape, Concord; its first pattern was *Harvest* (Fig. 10–31). The next design (premiering in February 1942) was *Lexington*, which used a rose pattern. Red Wing would go on to make at least a dozen different lines through the late 1950s using the Concord shape.

In 1942 Charles Murphy designed a new line initially called *Labriego Ware*. "Reminiscent of the Spanish hacienda,"[1] *Labriego Ware* was offered in *Dark Brown* with either a *Chartreuse* or *Orange* lining or *Gray* with either a *Maroon* or *Turquoise* lining. It was reintroduced in January 1948 as *Hospitality Ware* (Fig. 10–15 and 10–16). The colors offered were *Blue—White Lined, Yellow—White Lined, Green—Dark Brown Lined* and *Beige—*

Fig. 10–8. *Fondoso:* in rear *Orange* chop plate 13¾", *Pastel Green* oval plate 12⅛", little sugar 2¾" and little creamer 4", and *Orange* covered casserole 9¼"D.

Fig. 10–9. (*Right*) *Fondoso Powder Blue* coffee with wood handle 9¾".
Fig. 10–10. (*Below*) *Fondoso Turquoise* compartment tray or fruit and vegetable baker 10⅞".
Fig. 10–11. (*Bottom*) *Provincial Ware—Glossy Brown* lid and inside, *Bisque* outside 3¼".

Dark Brown Lined.

In 1943 Red Wing produced a new line of dinnerware called the *Bakeware Line* (Fig. 10–13). This is often called "oomph ware" because of a sales flyer that announced:

Red Wing Puts
"Oomph"
into Earthenware.
The New Bakeware Line
A lifetime cooking ware. . . . Smart . . . Colorful . . . Sanitary and Tough . . . Easily Cleaned and will withstand hard usage.

Bakeware Line came in many different shapes and sizes, from a large meat roaster (Fig. 10–14) to a variety of casseroles and bowls, in addition to plates, cups and saucers. It was referred to as Victory Ware,[2] probably because it replaced metal items that could be used for the war effort. Also, the brown glaze was "albany slip," using a clay from Albany, New York instead of metallic glazes. Albany slip glazing was used earlier by Red Wing during the stoneware era.

As quoted in the exhibition catalogue *Eva Zeisel: Designer for Industry*,[3] in 1946 Red Wing's president H. H. Varney:

. . . desired an informal, inexpensive, earthenware service. According to Zeisel, he wanted one that would be 'Greenwich Villagey;' that is, he wanted something colorful and boldly modern that would capture the fancy of the more adventurous members of mid-America. Certainly the com-

Fig. 10-12. Left, *Bakeware* mug and *Village Green* mug on right, both 4¾".

mercial success of Russel Wright's *American Modern* had proven that there was a demand for modern, informal dinnerware. Once the war was over and domestic production resumed, many potteries moved into this market.

Apparently the Red Wing designs were ready by the spring of 1946, but the product was not presented commercially until the spring of the following year. It was baptized *Town and Country*, like the name of the popular magazine, to emphasize its intended use for casual dining, informal family meals, and buffet parties. Thus there were beanpots, large and individual casseroles, and a profusion of serving platters; coffee mugs were the alternate cup form, not demitasses. The informality of *Town and Country* was also underscored by its color. Offered in five different combinations with a range of blues and greens or yellows and browns, some glazes mat, others glossy, the set was a colorful potpourri. Even the

Fig. 10-15. *(Above) Hospitality Ware:* in front, creamer 3⅛" and sugar 4¼"; in rear, oval bean pot, six cup coffee server 10⅛" with cover, and oven casserole all in *Yellow—Lined in White*.
Fig. 10-16. *(Right) Hospitality Ware* pitcher 9¼" in *Green—Dark Brown* (48 oz.).

lids could be a different color than the vessel.

In her designs Zeisel sought a sturdiness appropriate for informal meals. Because the ceramic body is not particularly refined, the walls are intentionally thick. The handles on the casseroles are robust stumps, modeled to fit the hand. Unlike the classic calm and refined elegance of the Castleton service, *Town and Country* was meant to be humorous and even

Fig. 10-13. *(Above) Bakeware:* Clockwise from front, small nappy 2" x 8¾"; large casserole (lid missing) 3" x 11⅛"; deep casserole 3¾" x 10⅛"; large mixing bowl 4⅞" x 10¼" and medium casserole (with lid) 4" x 9¾".

Fig. 10-14. *(Left)* meat roaster 6⅞" x 15".

eccentric. The dinner plates and saucers depart from the norm of circular symmetry; the central depressions are off center and one side is higher than the other. Serving platters are tear shaped. Perhaps the most daring components are the pitchers and the salt and pepper shakers. The flaring, sculpted handle of the pitcher responds to the contour of the spout and creates a sensation of a young bird opening its beak. Zeisel's zoomorphic impulses are clearly registered in the amusing salt and pepper shakers.

Red Wing continued to make *Town and Country* for at least seven years.

In August 1951, Red Wing came out with *Village Green*, the first pattern of about six to use this new shape. Similar in appearance to the *Bakeware Line*, there are distinct differences between the two (Fig. 10—12): the browns on *Village Green* have a ribbed look and all the shapes were different, the dinner plates are solid green, whereas *Bakeware* plates have a brown bottom. The line also was offered in *Village Brown*.

Another major shape—introduced in 1953 to celebrate Red Wing's 75th anniversary—was Anniversary.

In the 1950s Red Wing introduced the Casual shape with the *Smart Set* line (Fig. 10–21), a classic 1950s pattern. Another pattern based on the Casual shape, *Bob White* (Fig. 10–23), was Red Wing's biggest seller, produced

Fig. 10–17. *(Right)* Artist palette-shaped plate 13" in *Mulberry*. This shape called *Patio Supper Service*.

Fig. 10–18.
Called the *Festive Supper Set* and sold as one of four shapes under the *Provincial Luncheon Ware* line, this shape, along with *Patio Supper Service*, was available in the *Quartette* dinnerware line colors: *Ming Green*, *Chartreuse*, *Copper* and *Mulberry*. The other two shapes were offered in hand-painted patterns from the Concord lines.

until the company closed in 1967. It has even been suggested that the line's popularity was insured when a February 1956 *Playboy* magazine centerfold model was shown holding a *Bob White* cup.

RoundUp (Fig. 10–30) premiered for Red Wing in January 1958. Initially it was named *Chuck Wagon* and sold exclusively through the mail by The MAL Company based in Red Wing. MAL was owned by F. Lyle Carlson who took the first name initial of his wife, daughter and his own (Muriel, Annette and Lyle) to form the name of the company.

Many of the *Chuck Wagon* and *RoundUp* pieces are alike, for they both used the same cowboy motif, but sub-

Fig. 10–19. From the *Town and Country* line: left rear, *Metallic Brown* mixing bowl 9¾", *Rust* 3 pint pitcher 8¼", *Rust* sauce dish 7"D, *Gray* sugar with cover and creamer, *Chartreuse* salt 4⅜" and *Dusk Blue* pepper 3".

tle differences exist between the two. For example, the *RoundUp* plate had a chuck wagon and the *Chuck Wagon* line did not.

In the mid-1950s, the Futura shape was introduced. In 1956, *Tampico*—designed by Charles Murphy—won top prize at the National China, Pottery and Glass show. Another shape, called Contemporary, was offered in two patterns: *White and Turquoise* and *Spruce*. A short-lived, limited pattern made during the 1950s called *Kermis* (Fig. 10–24), came decorated with a clown.

Sensing a need to fulfill a market for fine china in addition to more casual earthenware, in 1960 Red Wing introduced True China shape from a clay formula of its own devising. It was offered in eight different patterns.

Red Wing continued to make other shapes such as a line commonly referred to as "Cylinder,"[4] as well as Like China, and Ceramastone (Fig. 10–26) all made in a variety of patterns. It also went after the industrial market with a line called *Hotel or Restaurant China*.

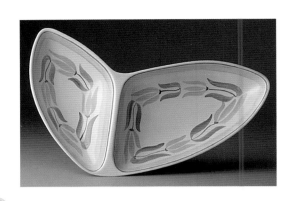

Fig. 10–20. *(Above) Tip Toe* divided vegetable dish 14"D.

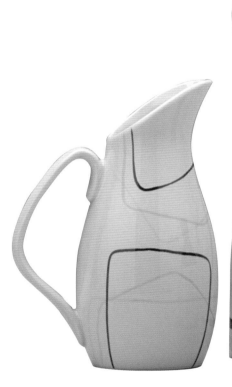

Fig. 10–21. *(Left) Smart Set:* creamer 7"; cruet with stopper 9½"; sugar and cover 5⅜" and water pitcher 14¼".
Fig. 10–22. *(Below) Tampico* pattern of the Futura shape cup 2¾".

Fig. 10–23. *(Left) Bob White* pattern: divided vegetable dish 14¼"D, small bird salt (upright 4⅛") and pepper shaker, hors d'oeuvre bird 8⅜" and tall salt and pepper shakers 6".

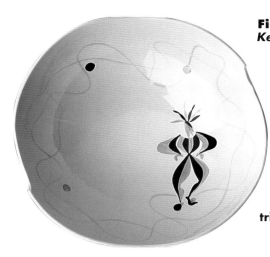

Fig. 10-24. *(Left)* *Kermis* salad bowl.

Fig. 10-25. *(Right)* ashtray 3⅝"D offered in the True China shapes, this pattern called *Merrileaf*. Ashtrays from this line were given away, which is probably why these have the unusual triangular mark on the back.

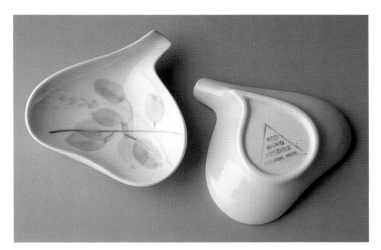

Fig. 10-26. *(Above)* A shape called Ceramastone offered in various patterns and colors. This was Red Wing's last series. Figural candleholder 7", cup 2¾", plates 10" and 7¼".

Fig. 10-27. *(Above)* *Flight* pattern divided vegetable dish 12⅜"D.

Fig. 10-28. *(Left)* Two *Village Green* pieces: 3¾" x 12" large salad bowl and 2½ quart fondue casserole that has a total width of 12½". The salad bowl is marked U.S.A. and the fondue is marked RED WING U.S.A.

Fig. 10-29. *(Left)* *Northern Lights* pattern in Futura shape pitcher 12⅞".

Fig. 10-30. *(Right)* *RoundUp* cup and saucer and fruit dish.

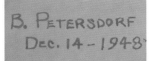

Fig. 10–31. *(Above)* From the August 1941 *Crockery and Glass Journal,* announcing the new *Harvest pattern,* the first mention of what was to be called the Concord shape. *(Above left)* "Lunch-hour" piece on a shape from the *Party Ware* line, an informal line of twelve shapes hand-decorated with fruit. *(Above right)* Sample plate by Charles Murphy.

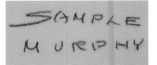

These two rows show some of the various dinnerware marks Red Wing used over the years.

    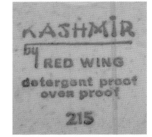

Brittany 10″ plate (Provincial shape)

Orleans 10⅛″ plate (Provincial shape)

Lexington 6¼″ plate (Concord shape)

Magnolia 10½″ plate (Concord shape)

Iris 10½″ plate (Concord shape)

Lotus 10½″ plate (Concord shape)

Lotus 10⅜″ plate. Notice the subtle differences between the two *Lotus* plates.

Willow Wind 10½″ plate (Concord shape)

Blossom Time 7⅜″ plate
(Concord shape)

Capistrano 13⅜″ platter
(Anniversary shape)

Driftwood 11″ plate
(Anniversary shape)

Picardy 10¼″ plate

Provincial 10¼″ plate

Hearthside 6½″ plate
(Casual shape)

Northern Lights 6½″ x 7″
oval plate (Futura shape)

Lupine 10¾″ x 10″ oval
plate (Futura shape)

Vintage 10⅜″ plate
(True China shape)

Daisy Chain 5⅞″ plate
(True China shape)

Granada 6″ plate
(True China shape)

Lute Song 10⅜″ plate
(True China shape)

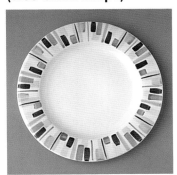

Desert Sun 7¾″ plate

Tahitian Gold 10¼″ plate
("Cylinder" shape)

Pompeii 10⅜″ plate
("Cylinder" shape)

Turtle Dove 7½″ plate
("Cylinder" shape)

Brocade 10⅜″ plate
(Like China shape)

Kashmir 10¼″ plate
(Like China shape)

Hotel or Restaurant China
7⅜″ plate

10½″ plate finished in a
Tan Fleck.

Fig. 11-1. King of Tarts heavily decorated. Usually offered *Hand Decorated Fleck Pink Overglaze* or *Fleck Blue Overglaze*. (Courtesy of Goodhue County Historical Society, Red Wing, Minnesota)

$\mathcal{K}$ITCHENWARE
Cookie Jars and Other Items

During many years of the Art Pottery era, Red Wing Potteries produced another kind of ware in addition to stoneware, artware, gardenware and dinnerware: kitchenware— items, as the name implies, for the kitchen. These items were marketed separately from Art Pottery and dinnerware. A few had shape numbers on their base; most had only the words Red Wing in various forms.

Red Wing always had produced items that could be categorized as kitchenware: stoneware items such as bowls and pitchers, which have been covered thoroughly in books on Red Wing stoneware. This text will concentrate on the ware that was made beginning in the late 1930s.

Gypsy Trail Hostess Ware

Gypsy Trail initially was the trade name for Red Wing's new dinnerware lines that came out in June 1935: *Plain, Reed, Chevron*, and eventually—in 1939— *Fondoso*. The name *Gypsy Trail* was soon to include *Hostess Ware*, a line that consisted of cookie jars, water pitchers, bowls, marmalades, and many other items. Eventually the term *Gypsy Trail Hostess Ware* was used to categorize the items not part of the dinnerware lines.

As part of this series, Belle Kogan designed five fruit-shaped cookie jars:

Fig. 11-2. Cabbage cookie jar 8½" in *Blue*, probably the rarest of all Red Wing's cookie jars.

the apple, pineapple, pear, bananas and grapes (Fig. 11–11). Later a cabbage that she did not design was included briefly in this group (Fig. 11–2). The cabbage was soon discontinued, and because of its short life it is the scarcest of the group.

Other items offered were salad and berry bowls, marmalades, and covered casseroles, all in apple, pear, or pineapple shapes. They were made in the bright, popular colors *Orange, Blue, Yellow, Turquoise, Pink* and *Green*.

Also offered were salad sets, bowl sets, teapots, pitchers, jugs and a variety of other items. More interesting to the collector today are the figural teapots such as the rooster #257 (Fig. 11– 20), and a peasant girl #260. Also popular with collectors of figurals are the rooster and fish-shaped marmites and casseroles (Fig. 11–20).

Fig. 11-3. *(Far Left)* Friar Tuck in *Blue.* The legend reads: "Thou Shalt Not Steal" 10½". **Fig. 11-4.** *(Middle)* Katrina "The Dutch Girl" 11" in *Yellow-Brown Highlights.* **Fig. 11-5.** *(Right)* Pierre "Chef" in *Green.* All three marked RED WING POTTERY HAND PAINTED with the raised wing ink stamp, but Pierre also lists three patent numbers.

Katrina, Pierre and Friar Tuck

The most popular Red Wing cookie jars ever produced were Charles Murphy's three figurals called Katrina the Dutch Girl, Pierre the Chef, and Friar Tuck—who bears the legend "Thou Shalt Not Steal" (Fig. 11-3, 11-4 and 11-5). Premiering in 1941, these three cookie jars were immediate successes; sales for Katrina alone are estimated at 200,000 per year. Schraffts, a store in New York City, sold them full of cookies. It is not certain how long these cookie jars were in production. A 1956 price list includes *The Chef* cookie jar, but whether it had been in continual production since the time of its introduction or whether it was revived to go with the *Carousel* and *King of Tarts* cookie jars is not known.

Fig. 11-7. *(Left)* Commonly referred to as Jack Frost, these cookie jars were officially called Pumpkin, large 12", and Pumpkin, small 8½".

Hand Painted Pottery

Beginning in 1942 Red Wing produced a series called *Hand Painted Pottery* using heavier stoneware clay. Three different designs—*Incised Peasant, Rose,* and *Fruit*— were offered in three shapes: cookie jar, munch jar and salad bowl (Fig. 11-14, 11-15, 11-17 and 11-18). All were offered in three different background colors: *Brown, Green,* and *White.*

What made these unique for Red Wing

Fig. 11-6. Drum cookie jar 9½" unmarked, commonly called drummer boy.

Fig. 11-8. *(Above)* Carousel 8½" x 8" marked RED WING POTTERY HAND PAINTED with the raised wing ink stamp.

Fig. 11-9. *(Left)* **Part of the *Hostess Ware* group, *Pastel Pink* pineapple marmalade with attached stand 5" and marmalade jar 2¾" without its cover in *Green*.**

Fig. 11-10. *Yellow* 6 cup teapot 5⅞".

was that instead of the decorations being under the glaze, these designs were cold painted, i.e., enamel paints applied onto the already glazed surface. For this reason, collectors have difficulty finding examples with their decoration completely intact.

Other Cookie Jars

In a January 1938 *Crockery and Glass Journal* article, the Roly-poly cookie jar was introduced as *"capacious enough to hold large batches of goodies, and comes in vivid colors."* Later it was referred to as the Ball Cookie Jar. Sometime around 1955 the King of Tarts (Fig. 11–1) and Chef were offered as *Hand Decorated* under either a *Fleck Pink* or *Fleck Blue Overglaze*. Carousel is *Hand Decorated with a Fleck Green Overglaze* (Fig. 11–8).

In the fall of 1959, Jolly Jars were introduced in the Art Pottery catalogs (Fig. 8–19).

The fall 1962 Art Pottery catalog started carrying six new cookie jars. Three of these were in the same shape: two were decorated to accompany the dinnerware patterns

RoundUp and *Bob White,* while a third, referred to as Happy, had a little verse written on the front. The *RoundUp* version was dropped in 1966 and the other two remained in production until the company closed. From the fall of 1962 until the fall of 1964 the last new cookie jar designs were produced: Drum (Fig. 11–6), Pumpkin large and Pumpkin small (Fig. 11–7).

Fig. 11-11. *(Above)* *Yellow* pineapple 8½"; *Turquoise* apple 8"; *Royal Blue* grape 10" and *Pink* pear 9".

Fig. 11-12. (Left) *Pink* 7¾" pitcher (64oz) marked #251.
Fig. 11-13. *(Right) Orange* 5"D apple individual salad or berry bowl (with optional 6¼"D stand); *Blue* 5" pear covered marmalade (with optional stand) and *Yellow* 5½"D pear covered marmite.

Fig. 11-14. Two cookie jars from the *Hand Painted Pottery* series. (Left) *Rose Design* 10½" in *Green* and *Fruit Design* 9¾" in *Brown*.

Fig. 11-15. *Incised Peasant Design* munch jars in *Brown* 6½".

Fig. 11-16. *(Right) RoundUp, Bob White,* and *Happy* cookie jars. *Happy* was reported to have originally been a Pillsbury premium, later sold in the regular Red Wing line. Poem reads: Happy the children/wherever they are/who live in a house/with a full cookie jar.

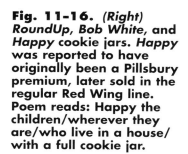

Fig. 11-17. (Above) Three salad bowls from the *Hand Painted Pottery* series with *Incised Peasant Design*. The bowls are 11¼"D.
Fig. 11-18. Salad bowl in *Rose Design* 11⅛".

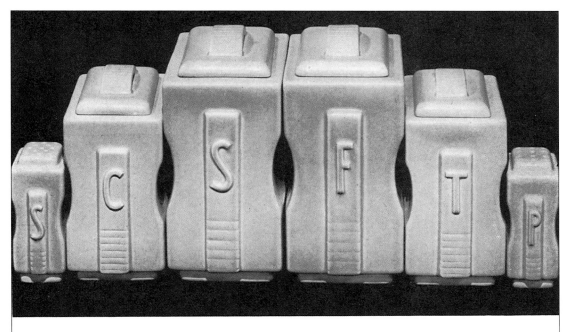

RED WING *presents*

A NEW CANISTER SET!

Bright, modern, this novel set will sell quickly and profitably for you. Every piece is moulded to fit the hand—**easy to hold**—easy to get at. Available in assorted colors—to retail at $4.75.

Fig. 11-21. (Above) Covered apple marmite in *Turquoise*.
Fig. 11-22. (Below) #984-4" *Luster Mazarin Blue* pepper (which strongly resembles the #982 apple in Fig. 11-23), both sold as Art Pottery.

Fig. 11-19. (Above) Ad from the July 1940 Crockery and Glass Journal. The set was available in *Orange, Blue, Yellow, Turquoise, Green* and *Pink*.

Fig. 11-20. Three pieces in the shape of animals: *Green* rooster casserole marked with shape #249-9", *Blue* rooster teapot (missing lid) #257-7" and *Yellow* fish casserole #248-5¾".

Fig. 11-23. (Right) Luster Mazarin Blue #913-6¼" pear and #982-4" apple.

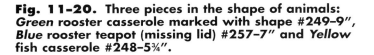

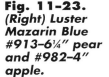

Fig. 11–24. Pieces from the *Gypsy Trail Hostess Ware* line. The same bases were sold either as berry bowls without lids or as covered casseroles with lids. Larger sizes listed as 12" were sold without lids as salad bowls. Pear covered casserole 10½"D, apple berry bowl 9⅛"D and pineapple covered casserole 10¼"D. All three in *Blue.*

Fig. 11–25. *Orange* wide-mouth pitcher 8¾", sold as a batter pitcher, and 3½" mugs.

Fig. 11-26. These water pitchers were sold as part of the Art Pottery line (from the first RumRill catalog in 1933 until about 1939). All marked with a RumRill ink stamp, either #50 or #A.50, except the *Nokomis* glaze in front which is marked with the circular blue ink stamp RED WING ART POTTERY. All were sold with ceramic stoppers.

Fig. 11-27. Initially sold as *Plain* dinnerware coffee servers in the *Gypsy Trail* line. Although other companies sold similar items, Red Wing's were marked with only the number 565, most of the time. The black and dark green ones shown here are also marked with the RED WING POTTERIES circular blue ink stamp with a star in the center.

Fig. 11-28. These pitchers actually sold as Art Pottery, first appearing in the 1936 RumRill catalog, and listed in Red Wing catalogs until 1940. Page 117 shows the bottoms of all these pieces with their various markings. This pitcher is commonly called a ball pitcher; as with the #565 pitcher above, similar shapes also were made by other companies.

Fig. 12-1. "PRETTY RED WING" is inscribed on the back of this 9½" long ashtray.

SPECIALTY ITEMS

Throughout its Art Pottery era, Red Wing produced items this book will generically refer to as "specialty items." This category can be subdivided into Red Wing company products (sold or given away by Red Wing) and items made for other companies. Note that almost from its beginning, Red Wing produced stoneware with other companies' advertising, as well as little novelty and giveaway pieces. This text, however, will concentrate on promotional items made from the 1930s on.

Red Wing Company Promotional Items

What distinguishes Red Wing's promotional items from its regular production Art Pottery lines is the fact that promotional items never show up in company catalogs. These were sold mostly through the company's retail salesroom and given away to tour groups and at promotional events.

Century of Progress

Red Wing produced a set with the 1933 *Century of Progress* World's Fair theme on it (Fig. 12–25). Commonly referred to as the "transportation set," it consisted of a pitcher and mugs.

Fig. 12-2. Initially produced to comemorate Red Wing's 75th anniversary in 1953. Although these 7⅜" ashtrays have been found in at least four colors, the red one shown here was the standard color.

Badgers and Gophers

Red Wing produced a series of small badger and gopher figurines. Both animals were represented on a football (Fig. 12–3), and as a tree stump toothpick holder. The series was produced around 1939, as some have a 1939 copyright notification. There has always been an intense rivalry between the University of Minnesota Gophers and the University of Wisconsin Badgers football teams, and these figurines are reported to have been sold as souvenirs at the annual games between the two teams.

Wings

In 1953, Red Wing produced a series of wing-shaped ashtrays.

Fig. 12-3. Gopher (left) 2½", badger (right) 2⅜", both marked RED WING POTTERIES ©1939 RED WING, MINN.

One shape, in a red glaze, first appeared as a 75th anniversary commemorative (Fig. 12–6). In addition to the more commonly found red-glazed wings, the shape has been found in at least four other glazes. At least one wing was produced as an advertising piece for an insurance agent in Illinois.[1]

Today, the most sought-after wing is a larger wing ashtray that is marked "PRETTY RED WING," RED WING POTTERIES USA (Fig. 12–1). This wing has a relief of an Indian maiden. *Pretty Red Wing* was a song title, for which the sheet music showed an Indian maiden on the cover. Both the smaller and larger ashtray shapes were designed by Teddy Hutchson.[2]

Another ashtray, only seen in orange, was used to promote Red Wing's lamp division.

After Red Wing Potteries closed, Hutchson made an orange-glazed wing ashtray to promote his own

ceramic mold company. Albert Stenwick, a local artist who worked at Red Wing for a time, also produced ashtrays on his own using the words Red Wing.

Other Ashtrays

A round ashtray also was made to celebrate the company's 75th anniversary. The only examples found of this scarce piece are red.

A small butterfly-shaped ashtray (Fig. 12–4) was made for the Trader Vic's restaurant chain, marked TRADER VIC'S. Others, marked RED WING, were given as souvenirs to people who toured the factory.

When the Hiawatha Bridge across the Mississippi River at Red Wing was completed, President Eisenhower officiated at its opening in October 1960. Red Wing created an ashtray designed by Teddy Hutchson to commemorate the event (Fig. 12–5). It was sold by the Red Wing chapters of the Eastern Star and the Rosary Society. Approximately 3,000 were reported sold that day, but it is impossible to estimate how many additional ashtrays were made and sold later at Red Wing's Salesroom.

In 1958, for the occasion of the 100th anniversary of Minnesota's joining the Union, Red Wing produced a centennial trivet in several different colors (Fig. 12–7 and 12–8). There was also an arrowhead-shaped ashtray promoting the city of Red Wing.

Fig. 12-4. *White 6"D ashtray marked* TRADER VIC'S U.S.A.

Fig. 12-5. Hiawatha Bridge ashtray.

Fig. 12-6. Impressed on the bottom of these wings are the three legends offered. Left, has RED WING POTTERIES 75TH ANNIVERSARY 1878–1953. Wings produced after the 75th anniversary bare the impressed legend (center): RED WING POTTERIES USA RED WING MINNESOTA. Others have an abbreviated version in raised letters (right): RED WING POTTERIES, USA.

Fig. 12-7. *(Above)* Minnesota Centennial trivet 6⅝"D.
Fig. 12-8. *(Left)* Back side of trivet showing enlarged state of Minnesota.

Promotional Items Produced for Other Firms

Throughout its history, Red Wing Potteries always made special advertising and premium items. Stan Bougie, a former manager of the Red Wing's Twin Cities Branch, noted that if a person or firm was willing to pay the cost of making a mold, "we would make whatever they wanted."

The organizations that turned to Red Wing for promotional pieces ranged from as large as the Hamm's Brewing Company to as small as a local hospital in Mankato, Minnesota.

In addition to producing specialty items, some companies or

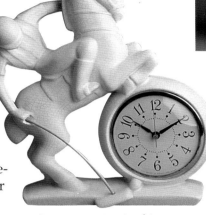

The five clocks made for the Mursen company.
Fig. 12-9. *(Left)* **Polo Player 11".**
Fig. 12-10. *(Above)* **Chef 10", Mammy 10", and Gretel 10".**
Fig. 12-11. *(Below)* **Tik Tok the Clown 11".**

Fig. 12-12. *(Left)* **Hamm's Krug Klub 4⅞" mug marked RED WING U.S.A. Fig. 12-13.** *(Below)* **Hamm's beer bear bank 11¾", unmarked.**

the Casual dinnerware shape. A few dinner plates have also been found. Mugs were made, embossed with the words HAMM'S KRUG KLUB (Fig. 12–12). Some ashtrays also were produced.

Mursen Clocks

George Jurgesen, owner of Red Wing's General Motors dealership, and Red Wing designer Charles Murphy formed a company called Mursen (which combined both of their names) to make clocks. The firm was founded in 1947 and lasted only a year, during which time it offered five different figural clocks (Fig. 12–9, 12–10 and 12–11).

Distillery Jug

In 1942, the Red Wing *Republican Eagle* ran a story headlined:

Little Brown Jugs for Distillery Now Being Made at Red Wing Pottery.
Manufacture of jugs to be used by a large Kentucky distillery as whiskey containers is now under way at the Red Wing Pottery Plant.

(Fig. 12–14). It is uncertain how long Red Wing continued to make these.

organizations commissioned Red Wing to place advertising messages on regular Art Pottery pieces. Only a few examples have been found (Fig. 12–29).

Hamm's Brewing Company

While it was based in St. Paul, Minnesota, the Hamm's Brewing Company had Red Wing make several items. The popular Hamm's bear mascot was made as a bank (Fig. 12–13). It was reported that 150 a day were produced for several months during the "land of sky blue waters" marketing campaign in the late 1950s. Red Wing produced limited numbers of a "popcorn set" for executives of Hamm's. It consisted of large and small bowls, a pitcher, and salt and pepper shakers, all in

Fig. 12-14.

Hankscraft

In the late 1940s, Hankscraft—a firm based at that time in Madison, Wisconsin —contracted with Red Wing to produce children's ware cups, bowls and specially designed plates that held hot water to keep food warm. Designed by Charles Murphy, some were decorated with nursery rhymes. One plate came in the

Fig. 12-15. Blue Hankscraft baby dishes. Hot water is put inside to keep food warm. The *Cat and the Fiddle* nursery rhyme is printed around the outside of this 10"D dish on left, and clown on right is 3½" x 9".
Fig. 12-16. *(Below left)* Cups 2¾", in a pastel pink and blue, and 3½" bowl in center in an unusual brown and blue mottled glaze.

restaurant supply store, Edward Don & Company (Fig. 12–19). Less common are the mugs without painted reliefs, and those that have a white field with much painted detail. The latter were said to be used only for displays at the restaurants.

E. Shon

Red Wing made a line of products for this New York area giftware store. The dishes came in yellow, brown and green and are marked E.S. USA (Fig. 12–17 and 12–18).

Fig. 12-17. *(Above) E. Shon* soup tureen, green lined with white 9¾".
Fig. 12-18. *(Left)* Marking on the E. Shon pieces.

shape of a clown. The products were made primarily in pastel pink and blue but other colors have been found (Fig. 12–16). Over the years other pottery companies made dishes for Hankscraft, but Red Wing's are marked with a telling script-style mark on the bottom (see page 115).

Trader Vic's

The famous island-cuisine restaurant chain based in San Francisco had many items made, among which are a mug with African figure (Fig. 12–22), coconut mugs, a 9" salad plate, a shell plate, a fish dish, a butterfly ashtray, and a mug specifically for its Fogcutter drink (Fig. 12–20). The Fogcutter mug has shown up in three different styles. The most commonly found example has painted reliefs on a *Tan Fleck* background. This version also was made for the Chicago-based

Fig. 12-19. *(Above)* 8¾" Marked Edward Don & Company.
Fig. 12-20. *(Below)* 8½" Marked Trader Vic's ©1963.

The Minnesota Twins

When pennant fever hit Minnesota in 1965, Red Wing made three different ashtrays. One said WIN TWINS; one celebrated the Twins' playing in the 1965 World Series (Fig. 12–23); and another—in the shape of home plate—commemorated the All Star game played in Minneapolis that year (Fig. 12–21).

Fig. 12-21. 10¾" X 10½".

Fig. 12-23. Ashtray on left, World Series 12⅝" across, marked Red Wing Potteries USA, and Win Twins ashtray, right, 6¼" across, marked Red Wing USA. Both are in the 60s color blend of *Green and Orange*.

Fig. 12-22. This 6⅛" mug is marked Trader Vic's © 1963 U.S.A.

Other Promotional Items

Considering how long Red Wing was in business, it should be no surprise if additional Red Wing promotional items are discovered in the future. Below is a list of some currently known items:

White Coffee Mug (Fig. 12–26): This mug was reportedly sold at a winter carnival held in Red Wing in 1963.
Shrimp and Butter Boats (Fig. 12–24): Others firms also produced these, but Red Wing's were marked RED WING U.S.A.
Mt. Rushmore: A souvenir ashtray depicting the monument.
St. Joseph Hospital (Fig. 12–28): An ashtray made for the Mankato, Minnesota hospital.
Thunderbird: A Bloomington, Minnesota hotel and convention center had Red Wing make a mug in a "totem pole" theme, along with a few other items on display in its coffee shop.
Windsor: A series of pieces were marked WINDSOR BY RED WING.

Other items that appeared on company production records include:
La Crosse Coffee Server and Creamer, Coleman Ashtray, Schlitz Mug, Reindfleisch (chick) Ashtray, Shrine Fez, Whittcrosse, Maico (ear) Ashtray and Old Mill Ashtray.

Fig. 12–24. Shrimp boat, 2¼" x 7" and butter boat 1½" x 5¼". Both marked RED WING U.S.A.

Fig. 12–25. *(Left) White mug 5¼",* depicting a 1933 Century of Progress theme, marked RED WING POTTERIES.
Fig. 12–26. *(Right) White mug 5⅞"* marked RED WING POTTERIES RED WING MINN.

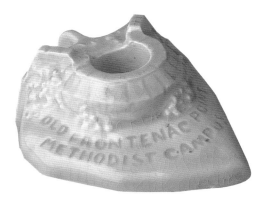

Fig. 12–27. This candleholder has the high gloss *Yellow* glaze of the early Art Pottery years—around 1930.

Fig. 12–28. Ashtray 8"D

Fig. 12–29. RumRill-era shape #297-5" in *Suntan—Seal Brown Lined* with advertising printed on the bottom.

Fig. 12–30. Left, BPOE 50 year anniversary ashtray 5⅜", and Lions ashtray 7".

Fig. 12–31. *(Right)* This 5" square ashtray depicts Minnesota's state theme: Land of 10,000 Lakes. It is marked #577 and also has the blue ink stamp RED WING POTTERIES with a star in the middle. It is in the *Pompeian* finish which premiered in February 1935.

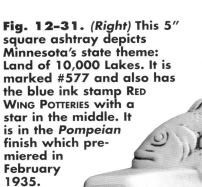

Fig. 13-1.
Three lamps,
left to right:
#1013–9⅛″ in a
glaze called *Red
Wing—Scarlet
and Bay;* a
lamp in *Apricot*
(shape number
unclear) 10¾″
and #969–9½″
in *Green.*

LAMPS

In the 1930s, rural electrification in America was becoming a reality, and with this came an expanded market for lamps. In 1929—according to its first notable national advertising campaign—Red Wing already was manufacturing and marketing electric lamp bases. A 1929 *Red Wing Daily Eagle* article noted that 2,000 were being made daily. Notes from a June 22, 1933, board of directors meeting mention that the company now was offering complete lamps. Almost all of Red Wing's standard Art Pottery vases could be adapted for lamp bases—most only required a hole to be drilled for a cord and the attachment of a metal cap to hold the light fixture.

Presumably because they were selling so well, in 1933 Red Wing opened a completely separate division based in Chicago called the Red Wing Lamp Division (The legal name was Red Wing Potteries of Chicago, Inc.). According to the company catalog, the lamps were manufactured in Chicago. From factory production notes it seems reasonable to assume that the ceramic bases were made in Red Wing and then shipped to Chicago where they were assembled, marketed and sold. For a short time Red Wing lamps were represented exclusively by Blank & Loewenthal, Inc., a manufacturer's representative located in a building heavily populated by pottery and glass lamp

Fig. 13-2. This 9½" lamp in the *Nokomis* glaze is marked #887 on the bottom.

wholesalers at 230 Fifth Avenue in New York City.

Problems with the lamp division were mentioned at the December 18, 1936, Red Wing board of directors meeting, but these problems were not specified. In Red Wing Potteries' annual reports, 1936 was one of the only year sales were broken down in a way that revealed revenues from lamp sales. In that year, there were $343,887 worth of total company sales on account, $22,207 cash sales, and $94,484 in lamps sales. Thus, in 1936 at least, lamps seem to account for about 20 percent of the company's total sales.

Fig. 13-3. *Yellow* lamp #951–8".

By the time Red Wing closed its lamp division, the company had been selling a wide variety of lamps, not only lamps with bases made in Red Wing. There were bases imported from China (that had more elaborate decoration), wooden bases, metal bases and floor lamps.

Minutes from a 1946 board of directors meeting note that it was "impossible to continue production of lamps." No further explanation of production problems was given, and with the 1947 liquidation of Red Wing Potteries of Chicago, Inc., Red Wing was out of the lamp manufacturing business. However, even after the lamp division closed, Red Wing occasionally would convert various Art Pottery vases into lamps to sell at its salesroom. Company records for 1951 show sales of $389,656 for dinnerware, $81,028 for artware, $16,621 for flowerpots and $653 for lamps.

Identifying Red Wing Lamps

The following pages show reproductions of catalog pages and original photographs featuring Red Wing lamp bases. However, because none of Red Wing's lamps were ever marked with the words RED WING, collectors may find the following useful in identifying Red Wing lamp bases.

1. All of the ceramic lamp bases seem to have a three- or four-digit shape number just like the Art Pottery of the same era.

2. The pieces were dry-bottomed, i.e., there was no glaze on the bottom. Additionally, there was always an outer ring upon which the lamp rested and a recessed inner ring where the shape number may be found.

3. The clay used was an off-white grayish color identical to the clay used for the Art Pottery of the 1930s and 1940s.

4. Many of the pieces were shapes from the regular Art Pottery lines. Collectors also should note that some lamps found may not have been production lamps. Vases of all types—including Red Wing's—were converted to electric lamps in great numbers by do-it-yourselfers and secondary lamp manufacturing firms—particularly in the 1920s and 1930s.

5. The similarity of glazes between a lamp of unknown manufacture and a known Red Wing Art Pottery vase is perhaps the least reliable means by which an identification can be made. Only a few glazes may be said with certainty to have been uniquely Red Wing's—*Nokomis*, for example.

6. Red Wing used Leviton brand light fixtures on many of its lamps. However, because other brands were also used and because secondary lamp manufacturers bought bases and attached their own hardware, finding a base with a Leviton fixture is no certain identifier.

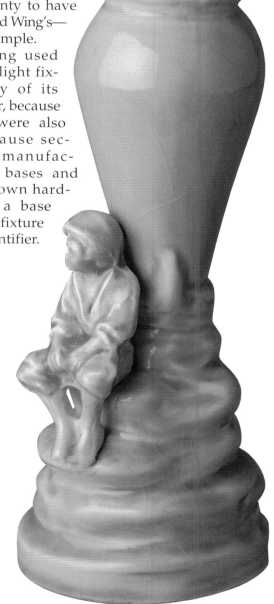

Fig. 13-4. *Yellow* 10¼" lamp base, unmarked. (Courtesy of Goodhue County Historical Society, Red Wing, Minnesota)

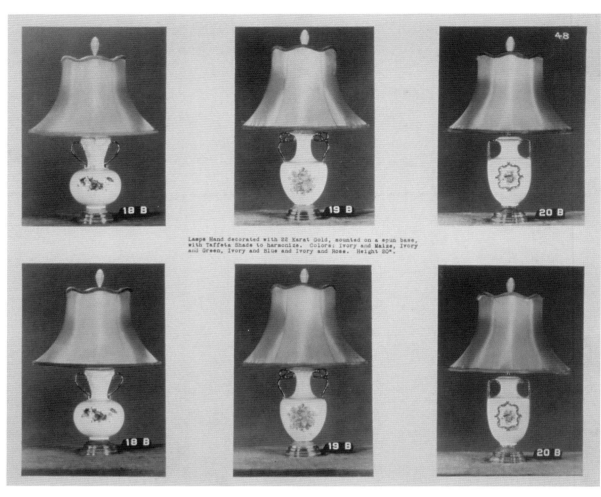

Lamps Hand decorated with 22 Karat Gold, mounted on a spun base, with Taffeta Shade to harmonize. Colors: Ivory and Maize, Ivory and Green, Ivory and Blue and Ivory and Rose. Height 20".

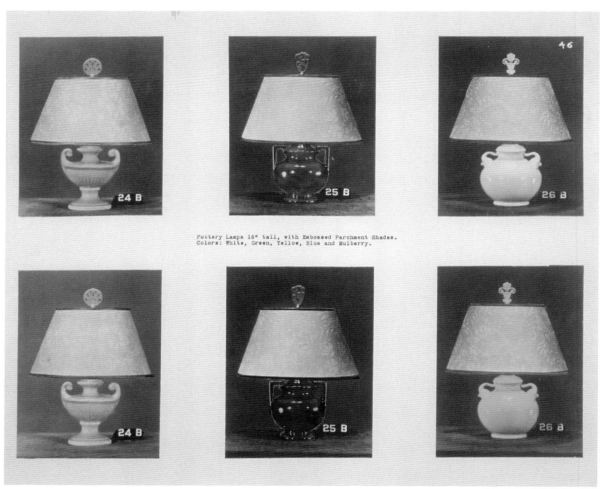

Pottery Lamps 16" tall, with Embossed Parchment Shades. Colors: White, Green, Yellow, Blue and Mulberry.

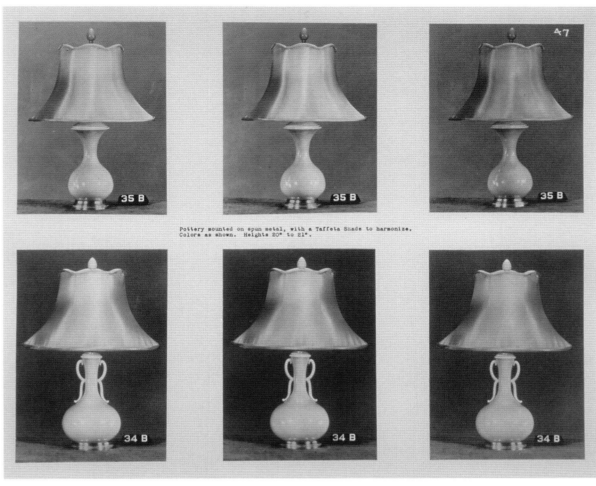

Pottery mounted on spun metal, with a Taffeta Shade to harmonize.
Colors as shown. Heights 20" to 21".

HT. 19½" TO TOP OF FINIAL. HAND DECORATED
TAFFETA SHADE. WHITE POTTERY BASE WITH
ANTIQUED LEAF DESIGN AND METAL MOUNTING.

HT. 19½" TO TOP OF FINIAL. TAFFETA SHADE.
BASE: POTTERY BIRD WITH METAL COMBINATION.
COLORS: WHITE - YELLOW - DUSTY PINK - BROWN.

HT. 21" TO TOP OF FINIAL. TAFFETA SHADE.
BASE AS SHOWN - HAND DECORATED POTTERY.

BOOKEND #17BE
POTTERY BIRD. COLORS: WHITE - YELLOW -
DUSTY PINK - BROWN.

BOOKEND #16BE
HT. 7". WOOD FINISHED IN GOLD OR MAPLE.

HT. 7". WOOD FINISHED IN GOLD OR MAPLE.
POTTERY BIRD. COLORS: WHITE - YELLOW -
DUSTY PINK - BROWN.

HT. 19½" TO TOP OF FINIAL. TAFFETA SHADE.
BASE: POTTERY BIRD WITH METAL COMBINATION.
COLORS: WHITE - YELLOW - DUSTY PINK - BROWN.

HT. 19½" TO TOP OF FINIAL. TAFFETA SHADE.
BASE: POTTERY BIRD WITH METAL COMBINATION.
COLORS: WHITE - YELLOW - DUSTY PINK - BROWN.

128A

HT. 19¼" TO TOP OF FINIAL. SHADE - HAND
DECORATED PARCHMENT. POTTERY BASE.
COLORS: WHITE - BLUE - YELLOW.

95   1020   30

129A

HT. 19½" TO TOP OF FINIAL. SHADE - HAND
DECORATED PARCHMENT. POTTERY BASE.
COLORS: WHITE - GREEN - YELLOW - MULBERRY.

130A

HT. 19¼" TO TOP OF FINIAL. SHADE - HAND
DECORATED PARCHMENT. POTTERY BASE.
COLORS: WHITE - GREEN - MULBERRY - YELLOW.

131A

HT. 17" TO TOP OF FINIAL. DECORATED PLEATED
PAPER SHADE. POTTERY BASE. COLORS: WHITE -
YELLOW - MULBERRY.

132A

HT. 17" TO TOP OF FINIAL. EMBOSSED PLEATED
PAPER SHADE. POTTERY BASE. COLORS: WHITE -
YELLOW - GREEN.

133A

HT. 17" TO TOP OF FINIAL. DECORATED PLEATED
PAPER SHADE. POTTERY BASE. COLORS: WHITE -
BLUE - YELLOW.

149A

HT. 22½" TO TOP OF FINIAL. SILK SHADE.
HAND DECORATED SUNTAN POTTERY BASE.

85A

HT. 24" TO TOP OF FINIAL. SHANTUNG SHADE.
BASE: POTTERY WITH METAL MOUNTING.
COLOR: TEAL BLUE.

148A

HT. 22½" TO TOP OF FINIAL. SILK SHADE.
POTTERY BASE AS SHOWN - OXBLOOD.

173A

HT. 23" TO TOP OF FINIAL. SHANTUNG SHADE.
IMPORTED CHINA BASE WITH METAL MOUNTING.

174A

HT. 24" TO TOP OF FINIAL. TAFFETA SHADE.
IMPORTED CHINA BASE WITH METAL MOUNTING.

179A

HT. 24" TO TOP OF FINIAL. BROCADED SILK SHADE.
IMPORTED CHINA BASE WITH METAL MOUNTING.

Ht. 21" to Top of Finial. Fabric over Parch. Shade. Pottery Base with metal mounting. Colors: White, Blue and Yellow.

Ht. 21½" to Top of Finial. Fabric over Parch. Shade. Pottery Base with metal mounting. Colors: White, Yellow and Mulberry.

Ht. 21" to Top of Finial. Fabric over Parch. Shade. Pottery Base with metal mounting. Colors: White, Yellow and Green.

Hand decorated Pottery on gold mounting, with Embossed Parchment Shades. Height 17".

22 Karat Gold Hand decorated Pottery, gold mounted, with Taffeta Shades to harmonize. Height 21".

Maple Lamp finished in Wheat and Gold, with a Fabric over Parchment Shade. Height 22".

Maple Lamp finished in Wheat and Gold, with a Fabric over Parchment Shade. Height 22".

Smart Pottery mounted on Wheat Base, with Fabric over Parchment Shade. Height 21".

Ht. 22½" to Top of Finial. Shantung Shade. Base. Hand decorated White Pottery with metal mounting.

Ht. 21" to Top of Finial. Taffeta Shade. Base: Moonex and Gold finished metal combination.

Ht. 20" to Top of Finial. Taffeta Shade. Base: Combination of Moonex, Crystal, Tenite and Gold finished metal.

Ht. 24" to Top of Finial. Silk Shade as shown. Base: Crystal and Glass. Colors: Crystal & Blue, Crystal & Ruby and Crystal & Green.

Ht. 17" to Top of Finial. Fabric over Parch. Shade. Suntan Pottery Base with metal mounting.

Glass Lamp with Decorated rayon Shade as shown. Ht. 22".

Distinctive Pottery Figures, mounted on a Wheat base with Taffeta Shades to harmonize. Height 25".

Fig. 14-1.
(Top) The Red Wing Potteries Salesroom about 1947. Woman at right is Eunice Horlitz.
Fig. 14-2. (Bottom) Also inside the salesroom, photo dated September 25, 1940. (Both photos courtesy of Mrs. Carol Berg, granddaughter of Eunice Horlitz. Top photo also courtesy of PPG.)

COMPANY STORES

Red Wing's main retail store, Red Wing Potteries Salesroom in Red Wing, Minnesota became a tourist attraction, where people from all over the Midwest and farther came to get a bargain on "seconds," pieces not perfect enough for sale through distributors. It is unknown exactly when seconds sales started, but in the 1921 annual statement, cash sales of $1,262 show up for the first time. Cash sales continued to rise every year thereafter (where records were available). By 1967 the outlet store had sales of $386,000, accounting for nearly 25 percent of Red Wing's gross sales.

Not much is known about the retail store's early years. It originally operated in an unheated section of Red Wing's warehouse. It is said that Andrew Selander, who was in charge of the sale of seconds for many years, fascinated customers because he kept money in his hat to make change.[1] Bartering for these seconds was a major part of the experience.

From a 1932 board meeting, *"Reference was made to cash sales at the factory and especially the tourist trade and Mr. Hoyt pointed out that it may become necessary to enlarge the office or make other arrangements."*

It seems as though management had a change of mind for a while about promoting the retail store. In the close of a 1947 newspaper article about Red Wing Potteries, president H. H. Varney makes a plea to *"Make it clear that we are a manufacturing plant only and not a retail outlet."*[2]

Some time after Varney died in 1949, the company obviously changed its mind again, because in 1953 a new 100' by 40' salesroom was built across the street from the factory. It was just off Highway 61, which at

Fig. 14-3. Built in 1953, the Red Wing Potteries Salesroom attracted people from throughout the Midwest. (Photo courtesy of Red Wing Pottery Sales)

that time ran in front of the factory. The seconds shop was complemented by a 15' by 30' gift shop that carried a large number of imported items. Later, a 30' by 48' garden shop was added for merchandising bird baths, planters and other gardenware. In 1959, Red Wing opened a 20′ by 30′ lunchroom. The final addition was a gift shop and country candy store in 1966. Although the retail outlet was only advertised with road signs and by word-of-mouth, it built up a large business; several thousand tourists visited on summer weekends.

When Red Wing Potteries closed, Richard Gillmer—the president and majority stockholder—bought the retail store business. Still operating and run by his family, pottery and gifts from all over the world may be purchased there.

The Twin Cities Branch Office

On December 20, 1929, Red Wing purchased 100′ of frontage at Carlton Street and University Avenue in St. Paul for an office, salesroom

Fig. 14–4. Stan Bougie was the manager of the Red Wing Twin Cities branch from 1961 until it closed in 1967.

and warehouse. By September, 1930, the building was completed and occupied. During its later years, Robinson-Ransbottom's products were sold also at the store. (Red Wing also bought gardenware from the Ohio firm to resell at the salesroom in Red Wing.) The store closed in 1967.

The Rapid City Factory Store

With increased sales of the seconds shop contributing to Red Wing's renewed profitable status in 1958 and 1959, the company decided to open an additional retail outlet. Called the Rapid City Factory Store, it opened on August 1, 1960 in Rapid City, South Dakota, at 3685 Sturgis Road (Fig. 14–6). Melvin L. Anderson, formerly in charge of Red Wing's main plant production scheduling, served as manager.

Chicago

Red Wing Potteries had a long history of operating in Chicago. A "Chicago Branch" is listed as being in existence in 1914. Very few records remain from this era, and Chicago is not mentioned again until 1921 when Red Wing started Union Stoneware of Chicago, later changed to Red Wing Potteries (of Illinois). Union Stoneware of Chicago was incorporated with $33,000 in capital stock; Red Wing

Fig. 14–5. In 1959 Red Wing expanded it salesroom to include a 20′ by 30′ lunchroom.

Fig. 14–6. *(Above)* With profits up in the late 1950s, Red Wing decided to open its second "factory store", this one in Rapid City, South Dakota. (Photo courtesy of Red Wing Pottery Sales)

Fig. 14–7. Although not a Red Wing Potteries company store, Andy's Pottery Shop and Red Wing Trading Post sold Red Wing pottery at the corner of 7th and Plum in Red Wing. (Photo courtesy of Helen Bell)

Union Stoneware Company was the sole owner.

By 1926, Red Wing had purchased property in Chicago. A three-story structure 84′ by 124′ eventually was constructed at a cost of $59,463. Primarily a warehouse and distribution center, it is not known if any retail sales were made out of this building (located at 2642 West Taylor Street).

Later Chicago addresses for the company were 817 West Wayman Street, 711 West Lake Street, 355 North Clark Street and finally, 341 North Clark Street.

In 1933, the Lamp Division was started in Chicago with $3,753 of capital. By 1936, the division had $94,484 in sales.

Early in 1947, Red Wing's Chicago cor-

Fig. 14-8, 14-9 and 14-10. Inside Red Wing's Potteries Salesroom from about 1965. Collectors should have fun looking through these photos finding items such as Charles Murphy's giraffe figurine in the right side of photo above. Also note the lamps in the sales-room, none of which show up in any catalog. Items not produced at Red Wing also were sold through the salesroom. (Photos courtesy of Red Wing Pottery Sales)

poration was liquidated by its sole stockholder, Red Wing Potteries. The assets were sold to the Chicago corporation's secretary-treasurer Richard P. White, who formed White's Artware-Gifts-Novelties at the 341 North Clark Street location.

In 1936, Red Wing opened a showroom in Chicago's famed Merchandise Mart, remaining there until around 1960.

Fig. 15-1. (Above) Teddy Hutchson, left, and Charles Murphy. (Photo courtesy of Marie Murphy)

Fig. 15-2. (Left) Belle Kogan on the Barbara Allen show in 1950. Barbara Allen is holding vase #B2107-12" from the *Textura* line, which Kogan had just designed. (Photo courtesy of Belle Kogan)

CHAPTER

15

RED WING DESIGNERS

Although not designers by trade, the early modelers and moldmakers were truly the first designers of the Art Pottery era. George J. Hehr followed in the footsteps of his father, Gottlieb—who was the first moldmaker at Red Wing. Hehr was brought in from Canton, Ohio. George Hehr was said to be responsible for the design of the first line of glazed Art Pottery.[1] But other craftsman and potters probably helped in the design and creation of pieces. Without company records or firsthand accounts, however, definite attribution is impossible. Once Belle Kogan and Charles Murphy were contracted, Red Wing prided itself in original designs.

After George Hehr retired, Teddy Hutchson was the chief modeler and moldmaker. A Red Wing resident, he is reported to be responsible for the design of many pieces such as the badger and gopher figurines, the wing-shaped ashtrays, the cherub series, as well as many others.

Red Wing did, however, eventually hire designers for its Art Pottery lines, and three of these are prominent in Red Wing's history. The first was hired out-of-house in 1938: industrial housewares designer Belle Kogan. The second was Red Wing's first design director and artist: Charles Murphy. The third prominent designer was Eva Zeisel. Although

Fig. 15–3. Belle Kogan in her New York design studio. (Photo courtesy of Belle Kogan)

Zeisel designed only one line of dinnerware for the company, that line is so noteworthy that she must be included as a Red Wing designer.

Belle Kogan

From the catalog of a retrospective exhibition of her work that was shown at The Center for Technological Education[2] we learn something about Kogan's professional life:

Belle Kogan is a retired industrial designer who worked and operated her own studio in New York City from 1930 to 1970. Miss Kogan specialized in the gift and housewares fields. She was one of the pioneers of this new profession. Her knowledge of packaging and merchandising techniques, along with her ability to design items, particularly three-dimensional, in a wide variety of materials, enabled her to offer practical and comprehensive design services to numerous clients. Miss Kogan has designed many lines in ceramics, glass, silver and all other metals, plastics and wood.

Miss Kogan states her design philosophy as follows: "I believe that good design should keep the consumer happy and the manufacturer in the black. The industrial designer not only must contribute new appliances to save time and work, but must satisfy the emotional and aesthetic needs of the consumer for color and form in the everyday things surrounding him. This means that the designer must be a business-man as well as an artist, and must accept the responsibility of his position as a liaison between management engineering and the consumer."

In 1906 when Belle Kogan was four, her family immigrated from Russia to the U.S. As a child she showed artistic talent. As she grew up she planned and studied to be a portrait painter. Later it was by pure chance that she became an industrial designer.

While working at her father's jewelry store she met manufacturers who recognized her ability and encouraged her to start designing.

At 27, after a summer course in design at New York University, she was retained as color consultant by a plastics company. That same year she joined the design staff of Quaker Silver Co., Attleboro, Massachusetts, designing cast metal merchandise. At the same time she continued her studies at the Rhode Island School of Design.

In 1930, her employer sent her to Germany for a course at the Pforzheim Kuntsgewerbe Schule and also to survey the field by visiting silver and glass factories in Germany, Czechoslovakia and France.

On her return to the U.S., Miss Kogan felt that

working for one company was too limiting. In 1931, in the depth of the economic depression, she opened her own industrial design studio in New York City. She had to work very hard to persuade some manufacturers that they would profit from investing in her designs. In those days and for many years industrial design was a field open to men only. But just two years later, Miss Kogan was able to show a variety of products of her design at the Art & Industry Exhibition in New York. She displayed two sets of china dinnerware, a child's duck-shaped clock of plastic, and a chrome toaster on a plastic base...

Pressed-glass items that she designed for Federal Glass Company were sold in the millions. Of those, her strawberry bottom nappy was chosen as the best product of its type in America in 1946...

Through her designs of plastic products, Belle Kogan revolutionized the use of this material, that had lost its appeal because of its technical short-comings. The melamine dinnerware she designed for the Boonton Company popularized the use of plastic on tables in millions of restaurants, army mess halls, homes and for outdoor picnics.

Ceramic products also gained status thanks to Belle Kogan. She preferred to create mass-produced quality items to enhance the general consumer's convenience and pleasure. Some of the ceramic companies she designed for include Red Wing Potteries, Brush Pottery Co., Fredricksburg Art Pottery Co., Haviland China Co., Ebeling & Reuss, Cameron Pottery, Cordey China & Lamp Co., and the Nelson McCoy Pottery.

... Miss Kogan has written many articles on design for a variety of publications. She has educated consumers, manufacturers and merchants through her presentations on past and present design processes and on the

Fig. 15–4. Charles Murphy, Red Wing's longtime staff designer. (Photo courtesy Marie Murphy)

trends in marketing and consumption. She expressed her opinion on many Radio and TV programs and in lectures throughout America.

In an article published in the October 1938 issue of China, Glass and Lamps, *Belle Kogan described her approach to designing vases for Red Wing. "Every piece in the whole line was created with thought for its decorative value independent of flowers. . . One more factor was strictly observed in working out the various shapes— a factor of importance from both the visual and the utilitarian points of view. This is the complete absence of any naturalistic flower forms in the modeling of the vases. In my opinion, such forms are definitely bad, competing as they do with the lovely colors and shapes of the real flowers. The very presence of such decoration subtracts some of the beauty from the ensemble.*

Kogan was a founder and long-time chair-person of the New York Chapter of the Industrial Designers' Institute (later Society). She was honored by the Institute with a testimonial dinner to mark her 25 year design career. In 1943 she was awarded a silver medal for excellence in the design of glassware. In 1946 the Philadelphia Art Alliance honored her with a "one man show of her products." In recognition of her professional and feminist achievements Miss Kogan was listed in *Who's Who in American Art* and in "Who's Who among American Women."

In 1970, Miss Kogan closed her office in New York and went to Israel to join K.V. Design, a subsidiary of the Koor Corp. In 1972 she retired and currently lives outside Tel Aviv.

Samples of her work are included in several museums including the National Museum of American Art (Smithsonian), Archives of American Art in Boston, and the Israel Museum in Jerusalem.

Charles Murphy

Charles Murphy was born in East Liverpool, Ohio, on August 9, 1909. At an early age the family moved to Sebring, Ohio, where his father was employed by Saxon Potteries. Murphy recalled that as a child he and his brother used clay and molds their father would bring home to make pottery in a tent in their backyard,

although they never fired any of it.[3] In the summers he would work at the potteries.

After graduating from high school in East Liverpool, he went to the Cleveland School of Art (now the Cleveland Art Institute), to study portraiture. While there, he worked weekends at Guy Cowan's pottery in Rocky River, Ohio, near Cleveland.

He received a Mattson Scholarship to study in Europe after graduating from the Cleveland School of Art.[4] He studied in Munich with Hungarian painter Peter Kalman. He also practiced painting: he and a roommate rented an apartment in Munich with a studio and hired their own models, paying them fifteen cents an hour.

After studying in Europe, Murphy returned to Sebring, painting portraits out of a studio, but because this was in the midst of the Great Depression, he earned little money. He was approached by Charles Sebring to start designing some pottery for the Sebring Pottery Company, which he did. Later, he also designed for Salem Pottery of Salem, Ohio.[5] Sometime in 1933–34 he began work as an assistant to the eminent designer Frederick Rhead at the Homer Laughlin Company. Later he created designs for the Commercial Decal Company of East Liverpool. These were produced as decals for application on china.

In 1936, Murphy married Marie Louise Gassner whom he had met while teaching at a local school.

At the American pottery industry exhibit of the 1939 New York World's Fair, Murphy was chosen to paint a 40' by 14' mural to depict the forty years of collective bargaining between the members of the United States Potters' Association and the National Brotherhood of Operative Potters. Murphy also designed the decal for the World's Fair commemorative plate produced by Homer Laughlin, a notable achievement when one remembers that Homer Laughlin's designer, Frederick Rhead, was considered the foremost designer in the industry at that time.

Red Wing's president H. H. Varney wrote to Rhead asking if he would recommend a designer for the firm. Subsequently, Varney approached Murphy, and by December 1940, Murphy was at Red Wing.

Although initially his focus was on setting up production methods and designs for the new hand-painted

Fig. 15-5. Charles Murphy photographed during an 1994 interview.

dinnerware lines, he also was the designer for all new Art Pottery. Another initial task led to the character cookie jars Katrina, The Chef, and Friar Tuck.

Murphy joined the Army Engineering Corps in the fall of 1943, where he sketched his comrades in the 29th Division. Word got to the division commander—General Gerhardt—who soon had Murphy with him sketching battle scenes in addition to his regular duty. Murphy was awarded a Bronze Star.[6]

Murphy returned to Red Wing after his military duty, where, after no longer "seeing eye-to-eye" with Varney, he left in 1947 to go work for the Stetson China Company in Lincoln, Illinois. After Varney died, his replacement, Harry Barghusen, was interested in Murphy's return to the company. Richard Gillmer, then the Chicago sales manager for Red Wing, helped talk Murphy into coming back.[7] Gillmer proposed that Murphy return on a freelance basis. Although not allowed to design for other potteries, Murphy could teach, paint, or pursue other projects. He returned to work at the Red Wing Pottery in 1953, and lived in Minneapolis until 1973.

While at the Red Wing Potteries, Murphy got involved with the Bureau of Engraving in Minneapolis. He designed a duck stamp for the bureau in the 1960s. After that he produced a successful series of nature studies illustrations for the Badger Paper Company (in Wisconsin), which in turn led to a series on butterflies and small animals.

Four of Murphy's paintings were used for a series of prints offered by Graphic Arts, Inc. in New York that were great sellers.[8] Later, he was represented by the wife of one of the Graphic Arts salesman who arranged for Murphy's original paintings to be shown and sold in galleries all across the country.

He also taught a class in industrial design at the Minneapolis School of Art for two years.

In 1973, Murphy and his wife moved to Sedona, Arizona, where he continued to paint wildlife until his death in 1994.

Eva Zeisel

Eva Polanyi Stricker was born November 11, 1906 in Budapest, Hungary. She spent much of her childhood painting. In 1923 she began study at the Royal Academy of Fine Arts in Budapest.[9] She apprenticed for a Hungarian potter for a short time and then started her own pottery in a converted hothouse on her parent's property.

Fig. 15–6. Salesman Harvey Johnson showing vase #1362 to customers. This photo was taken around 1948. (Photo courtesy Goodhue County Historical Society, Red Wing, Minnesota)

The Hungarian government asked her to send some work to the Philadelphia Sesquicentennial celebration in 1926, where she received honorable mention. After a short time with another potter in Hamburg, Germany, she applied for and received a position as ceramic designer at Schramberger Majolika Fabrik in Schramberger, Germany.

By 1930, she had opened her own studio in Berlin. In 1932, she went to the Soviet Union where she worked for several years in various ceramic factories.

In 1937, she left the Soviet Union for Vienna which she left the next year when the Nazis marched into Austria. Arriving in New York in 1938, she began design work for various companies.

In 1939, Zeisel began teaching ceramic design at the Pratt Institute, the prestigious industrial design school in Brooklyn. She published many articles in trade and design magazines promoting her views about modern design. She designed a line of dinnerware for Sears, Roebuck and Co. called *Stratoware*, a stylish and futuristic two-tone dinnerware. This led to design work for the Castleton China Company. In 1940 she was offered a position with Homer Laughlin by Frederick Rhead.

Sometime around 1945 she was approached by Red Wing's President Varney; his request for something "Greenwich Villagey" and her design lead to the *Town and Country* line (see page 65). This was the only line she design for Red Wing, who produced it for at least six years. Its daring, organic forms and quirky humor have made it a favorite with collectors.

By 1947, Zeisel had opened a studio in a basement apartment of the building in which she lived. Her career went into high gear, and she designed for such firms as Sears Roebuck and Co., United China and Glass, Hall China, Riverside Ceramic Company, General Mills, and Western Stoneware Co.

In the late 50s and early 60s most of her clients were German, Italian and Japanese. In the mid-60s she all but retired, only designing occasionally.

In 1983 she received a senior fellowship from the National Endowment for the Arts. In 1984 an exhibition of her work titled *Eva Zeisel: Designer For Industry* was organized by the Musée des Arts décoratifs de Montréal.

Other Designers

According to various secondary sources, each of the following people also designed Art Pottery for Red Wing. However, none of the individuals thus far have been documented as Red Wing designers.

Louise Palmer, of Minneapolis, is said to have designed the white-glazed figurines Baby Standing and Kneeling Baby (shapes #46 and #47).[10]

William G. Warr Jr., of Red Wing, is said to have designed dinnerware lines.[11]

Various candid photographs of salesmen reproduced in trade magazines.
Fig. 15-7. (Above) George Rumrill.
Fig. 15-8. (Right) Lee Manchester and Ralph Lumb.
Fig. 15-9. (Below) George Rumrill.
Fig. 15-10. (Below right) Ralph Gunschel.

A Mr. Lawton is said to have designed the Dynasty dinnerware shape.[12]

Someone named "Genter" shows up in 1939 company records as being paid $400 for design (compare this to the $2479.04 paid Belle Kogan for that year).[13] No other mention of this person or what they designed has been found.

Charles Murphy cites Betsy Bryant as doing some design work for Red Wing.[14]

Harold W. Darr designed some items for Red Wing.[15]

Ceramic Engineers

We would be doing an injustice if we did not mention the men whose work behind the scenes was a large contribution to Red Wing's Art Pottery. The ceramic engineers, besides being responsible for the overall technical aspects of pottery production, also were responsible for the creation of the glazes.

Ceramic engineers during the Art Pottery era were Karl Kayser (listed as glaze maker in company records), George Grady, G. L. Vincent and Tom Arnold.

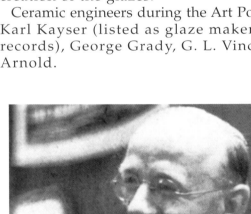

Fig. 16-1. The name of C. L. McGrew, a long-time turner at Red Wing, appears on this piece #174–4½" in an *albany slip* glaze.

IDENTIFYING
RED WING ART POTTERY

W hile the term "signed piece" often is used to describe any piece of Red Wing Pottery bearing the company name, the term traditionally denotes the application of a particular artist's signature. The term "marked piece" more accurately signifies the presence of the Red Wing name. As a normal operational procedure, Red Wing never had its employees sign any of its Art Pottery. The closest Red Wing got to having signed pieces was the use of the letters B and M to indicate Belle Kogan or Charles Murphy. Legitimate signed Red Wing will invariably prove to be lunch-hour pieces.

Nearly all of the alleged signed Red Wing Art Pottery the author has seen were pieces made at ceramic shops using discarded Red Wing molds. Red Wing had a policy of selling (or giving away) molds when an item was discontinued or when a mold was worn out. Most of these molds were bought by ceramic shops and schools that would use them to make cast pieces.

Some ceramic shops scratched the Red Wing name off the mold, others did not bother. This was not any attempt at deception, simply a cheap source for molds in relatively new and modern shapes. Many of the pieces cast from these discarded molds were used in classes given at ceramic shops. Students initialed their work to distinguish it from the similar pieces fired at

Fig. 16-2. This *Yellow* tumbler 2⅜" was sold as #53. It is dated Jan 20, 1930.
Fig. 16-3. Bottom view showing initials M. H.

the same time. The primary characteristic of these pieces is that they are distinctly lighter in weight than their Red Wing counterparts. Often the decorative glazing is crude and the initials or names are amateurishly scratched into the bottom.

Lunch-Hour Pieces

The term "lunch-hour" piece is used is used to describe work made by the factory employees on their own time, theoretically during their lunch hour, hence the term. This expression originated during

Fig. 16–4. This piece, displayed at the Goodhue County Historical Society, by Albert H. Olsen. (Courtesy Goodhue Historical Society, Red Wing, Minnesota)

Fig. 16–5. These vases probably were made during one of the Wednesday night art classes Red Wing offered in the late 1940s. This pair used shape #1300 blanks.

the stoneware era and is common throughout the pottery industry. During the Art Pottery era, workers made specially glazed pieces for family and friends. Most of these pieces were dinnerware.

Red Wing held Wednesday night art classes for a while around 1947. The factory would allow anyone to come in and use Red Wing glazes to "paint" on any blanks that the factory had on hand at the time. The author has seen only one pair that was likely done at one of these classes: a #1300 shape that is listed in catalogs as produced between 1947–49 (Fig. 16–5). These pieces, on a white field, have detailed drawings of flowers in many of the colors that Red Wing used at the time.

The Clay Body

Brushed Ware and other stoneware vases were very well suited to using local Red Wing clay. When Red Wing started making glazed Art Pottery, it was determined that a finer grade of clay was necessary. In 1934, company records indicate that an Indiana clay was used. Later, clay was brought in from Tennessee, Kentucky, North Carolina, Georgia, Florida and South Dakota.

There are no known pieces of Red Wing Art Pottery made with red clay (terra cotta) or yellow clay (the typical clay color of products made by the Ohio potteries).

The Look of the Bottoms

Earlier Red Wing Art Pottery used a "dry bottom" method, with an unglazed, molded ridge around the outside of the bottom (on which it would sit in the kiln). The area inside the ridge either was glazed or left

Fig. 16–6.

Fig. 16–7.

Fig. 16–8.

unglazed. Red Wing later would use kiln stilts, referred to as "crows feet." These small supports raise pottery off the shelf inside the kiln, thus allowing the bottom to be glazed. A piece thus fired will have three small unglazed dots on its bottom. The methods overlap chronologically: the stilt method was used as early as the mid-1930s, and some pieces still were being dry-bottomed up to the 1950s. Occasionally both bottom styles show up on the same shape.

Early Ink Stamps

Red Wing Union Stoneware Co.

Prior to the 1936 name change to Red Wing Potteries, the company used a variety of circular or oval ink stamps either blue or black that contained the words RED WING UNION STONEWARE CO. (Fig. 16–6, 16–7, 16–8 and 16–9).

Red Wing Ware

One stamp included the shape number and the phrase Red Wing Ware (Fig. 16–10). Ink stamp markings sometimes are not entirely legible, but this mark is illegible more often than others. It seems as though these stamps were used until at least 1929.

Fig. 16–9.

Red Wing Art Pottery

Sometime around 1929, Red Wing began to use a circular blue ink stamp containing the words Red Wing Art Pottery (Fig. 16–11). This mark was used at least until Red Wing began to produce pottery for George Rumrill, and possibly later.

Fig. 16–10.

Fig. 16–11.

RumRill

Red Wing produced pottery for George Rumrill from 1932–1937, after which time Rumrill had three other companies make pottery for him. Those manufactured by Red Wing show the word RUMRILL impressed into the bottom (Fig. 16–12). RUMRILL was usually written as one word with two upper case *R's*, but versions have been found with Rum Rill as two words, and some with all capital letters. The word RumRill was always accompanied by a three-digit shape number (with the exception of shape #50, #52, #53 and #54).

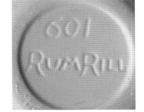

Fig. 16–12.

Fig. 16–13.

Shape Number Alone

During the time Red Wing produced RumRill pottery, it continued to manufacture and distribute its own Art Pottery. Many different shapes were marked with only the three-digit shape number (Fig. 16-13) (again with the exception of shape #50, #52, #53 and #54). Red Wing then would apply either a "Red Wing Art Pottery" or "RumRill Art Pottery" sticker. All other Red Wing Art Pottery is marked with the company name, except for a few pieces where there was not enough room to apply both the name and a shape number. In those instances a shape number alone was used, and in few cases, such as the four elephant figurines offered in 1931, not even their shape number was used.

Fig. 16–14.

Fig. 16–15.

RumRill Ink Stamp

This mark, either in blue or black ink, appears on the shape #50 water pitcher. This pitcher has also been found with the shape #A.50 (Fig. 16–14).

Red Wing Potteries With Blue Star

A few pieces have been found with an ink stamp bearing the words "Red Wing Potteries" in a circular pattern surrounding a blue star. The author presumes them to have been made during the mid-1930s because

Fig. 16–16.

the shape numbers on some pieces with this mark would have been used during this period. This mark is among Red Wing's rarest (Fig. 16–15).

Stickers

Square RumRill

The earliest sticker used on RumRill pottery is one-inch square. It has space for both the shape and glaze numbers, which were handwritten on the label (Fig. 16–16).

Wing-Shaped RumRill

During the Rumrill era, pieces had either this sticker with the words "RumRill Pottery" or a Red Wing Art Pottery sticker. Both stickers measured 1", and were red and gold metallic in color (Fig. 16–17).

Fig. 16–17.

Fig. 16–18.

Wing-Shaped Red Wing Art Pottery

Exactly like the sticker above except for the wording (Fig. 16–18).

Gypsy Trail

A triangular shape sticker was used on some of the earlier *Gypsy Trail*

Fig. 16–20.

during Red Wing's 75th Anniversary in 1953 and possibly for several years after (Fig. 16–20).

Raised Wing

Initiated after the 75th Anniversary sticker, this was used until the pottery closed in 1967 (Fig. 16–21).

Fig. 16–19.

pieces (Fig. 16–19). This example is the only one the author has ever seen.

75th Anniversary Raised Wing

This 1⅜" sticker was used

Fig. 16–21.

The Words Red Wing

As of 1938, Red Wing marked all its pieces with the in-mold impressed or raised lettering of "Red Wing" or "Red Wing Potteries" with or without "USA" and with a shape number (See pages 114–117).

Shape Numbers

To help in the production and ordering of products, Red Wing Potteries usually applied a number to every piece it produced. The number is called the shape number, though it is sometimes referred to as a mold number. This same number now aides in pottery identification and communication between collectors.

Except for a few pieces (and the RumRill-era pieces discussed previously), the shape numbers were almost always on the bottom and contained three- or four-dig-

its (although a handful of two-digit numbers were used). The shape numbers either were impressed or raised. Although there are many exceptions, the vast majority of Red Wing Art Pottery was marked in a systematic way. Numbers were assigned primarily in chronological order, but pottery with specialty glazes were sometimes assigned a different set of numbers such as the 4000 series assigned to the *Sgrafitto* line in 1955.

In 1951, starting at #400, Red Wing began to re-assign shape numbers, again assigning numbers in chronological order. There are *many* exceptions, however. In Appendix 2 there are two different shape number charts that go over all the numbers, including those exceptions, arranged both by shape number and by year.

Fig. 16–24. *(Right)* Little is known about this early mark.

Fig. 16–23. *(Above)* Mark used on early line of kitchenware products.

Fig. 16–22. *(Above)* Unusual wing ink stamp on the bottom of this circa 1931 piece.
Fig. 16–27. *(Below)* Swan planters marked differently from each other because this same shape was made at different times.

Fig. 16–25. *(Above)* Occasionally pieces surface with two different shape numbers.
Fig. 16–26. *(Right)* But the most unusual, has FOUR different shape numbers!

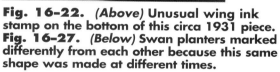

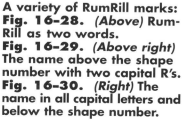

A variety of RumRill marks:
Fig. 16–28. *(Above)* RumRill as two words.
Fig. 16–29. *(Above right)* The name above the shape number with two capital R's.
Fig. 16–30. *(Right)* The name in all capital letters and below the shape number.

More RumRill marks:
Fig. 16–31. *(Above left)* A period after the shape number.
Fig. 16–32. *(Above right)* A more stylized R used.
Fig. 16–33. *(Below)* What is wrong with this picture?

Fig. 16–35. Mark used on the *Fondosa* dinnerware products around 1938.

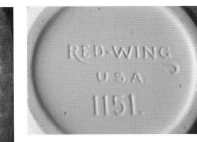

Fig. 16–34. *(Above)* Starting in 1938, pieces were marked RED WING with the shape number. Notice the backwards N in the mark above.

Fig. 16–39 and Fig. 16–40. *(Below)* Two more examples from this era.

Fig. 16–36 and Fig. 16–37. *(Above two)* Mark used circa 1939–1942.

Fig. 16–41. *(Below)* The mark used on Red Wing's *Hankscraft* pieces.

Fig. 16–38. *(Above)* During the late 1930s, the pottery trade was waging its own war against imports. For a short period beginning about 1940, Red Wing marked its pieces with MADE IN THE USA. This soon was shortened to simply USA.

Fig. 16–42. *(Right)* From around 1939 to 42, under the *Gypsy Trail* banner, some kitchenware was marked with shape numbers in the script style of the Art Pottery pieces of the same era.

Fig. 16–43. *(Above)* Although almost every piece was marked, sometimes the glaze was so heavy it is hard to read. Two #975 vases: the mark on the left is clearly visible, but the thick glazing of the piece on the right makes the number almost unreadable. **Fig. 16–44.** *(Right)* Sometimes the style of the bottom would change as the molds were remade. These two vases are identical except for the bottom variation.

Marks used for Red Wing's Art Pottery pieces from 1940 to 1967. Note the variety in styles, markings and bottoms.
(Above) Notice shape #19, which was the lowest shape number Red Wing used, coming out in 1963.

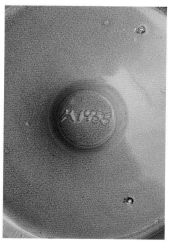

(*Above*) This pitcher was sold as Art Pottery, first appearing in the 1936 RumRill catalog. It was listed in Red Wing catalogs until 1940. The photograph above shows the bottoms of all these pieces with the various markings they used. Commonly called the ball pitcher, this was a popular shape during the 1930s. Similar shapes were made by a number of other companies.

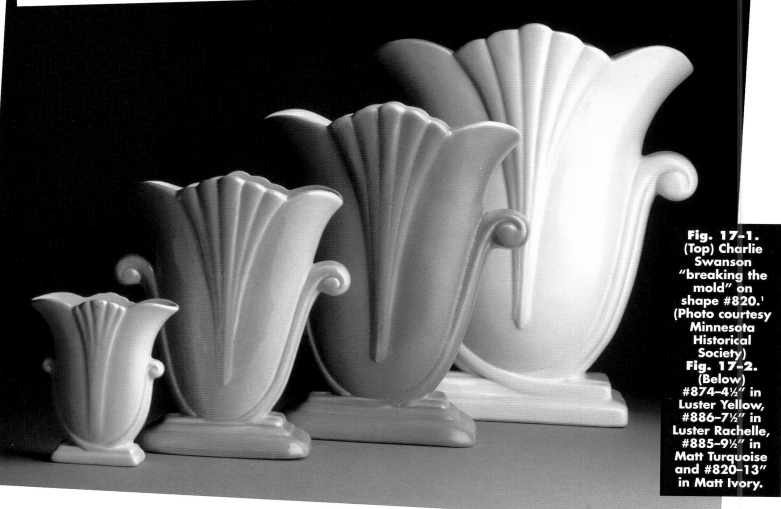

Fig. 17-1. (Top) Charlie Swanson "breaking the mold" on shape #820.[1] (Photo courtesy Minnesota Historical Society)

Fig. 17-2. (Below) #874-4½" in Luster Yellow, #886-7½" in Luster Rachelle, #885-9½" in Matt Turquoise and #820-13" in Matt Ivory.

How Red Wing Pottery Was Made
Manufacturing Techniques

Here, the basic manufacturing process of both Art Pottery and dinnerware will be described. This chapter is designed to give readers an overview of the entire process of taking a basic natural product—clay—and transforming it into something of beauty, both useful and durable.

Art Pottery

When Red Wing first started in the stoneware business, it dug its own clay from local clay fields. Over the years these fields were depleted. Red Wing started buying clay around the start of the Art Pottery era.

At the factory, clay was mixed with water to form a liquid clay referred to as "slip." This slip, resembling chocolate milk, would be poured into plaster molds and allowed to dry. This technique, now referred to as slip-casting, was how almost all of Red Wing's Art Pottery was made. A few pieces were ram pressed, a method that uses a machine to press a piece of firm clay into the correct shape.

Fig. 17-4. The first step in the production of a piece of Art Pottery was to create a model. These were either turned on a potter's wheel as Lou McGrew is doing here, or were hand-built. (Photo courtesy Minnesota Historical Society)

Fig. 17-3. Red Wing Potteries as it appeared during the Art Pottery era. The larger building in the rear exists today as a shopping center called Pottery Place. (Photo courtesy of Goodhue County Historical Society, Red Wing, Minnesota)

Here is a brief step-by-step process of how Red Wing's pottery was made:

First a model of the final piece had to be created. This was done by the modeler, usually the person in charge of the molds. Models were created by hand.

Whether turned on a wheel (Fig. 17–4) like the circular classic shapes of the *Nokomis* pieces, or modeled by hand as all the figural pieces obviously had to be, the modeler took the sketches or drawings by the designer, or the ideas of management, and created the model out of clay. From this model, the master mold would be made. (Fig. 17–5) Many actual production molds could be made from this master mold. A production mold could be used to make only about 100-200 pieces before the mold would start to wear out, creating large seams that were difficult to remove.

Depending on the design of each piece, two- or three-part molds were used. Two-part molds usually

5. Mold Making

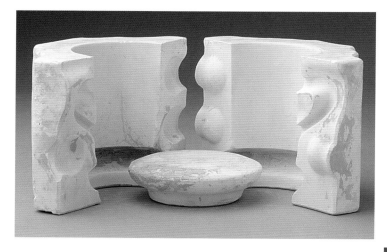

Fig. 17–5. *(Above)* Once the model was created, a master mold was made, from which many production molds could be made. (Photo courtesy of Goodhue County Historical Society, Red Wing, Minnesota)
Fig. 17–6. *(Left)* Red Wing used three-part molds for almost all of its Art Pottery and some of its dinnerware.
Fig. 17–7. *(Below)* This mold bottom would create the unique ridge characteristic of Red Wing's Art Pottery, along with any markings such as the shape number or the words Red Wing and USA.

would break right down the middle (Fig. 17–8), while three-part molds (Fig. 17–6) had a third section on the bottom (Fig. 17–7). The great majority of Red Wing's Art Pottery was made with three-part molds.

These molds were assembled and held together with a strong band of rubber. Slip was poured through an opening at the top. The mold then sat while the outside surface, next to the very porous plaster of the mold, started to harden. Once the slip reached the desired thickness (usually about twenty minutes, depending on the piece, the humidity, and the temperature), the excess was poured out. The piece then sat overnight so that it would be dry enough to easily come out of the mold. This process was referred to as "breaking the molds" (Fig. 17–9).

This greenware, as it called

Fig. 17–8. A two-piece mold that Red Wing used for some of its dinnerware.

at this stage, would then be "fettled" (Fig. 17–10). This is the process of using a wet sponge to smooth the mold seams. It was then allowed to completely dry; if any moisture remained in the piece when it went into the kiln, the piece would crack or break. It was then ready for the first firing.

The greenware was put onto specially devised kiln cars, about the size of railroad handcars, and rolled into the gas-fired kiln (Fig. 17–11). Those kilns could hold up to thirty-eight cars, taking about seventy-six hours for a car to go through. The process began with a gradual warming, and continued until temperatures exceeded 2000°F, and ended with a gradual cooling.

At this stage pottery was called bisque ware. Then to get the color and design, a chemical glaze was either sprayed on or the piece was dipped into a vat of glaze (Fig. 17–12, 17–13 and 17–14). If the piece had a decoration under the glaze such as the *Chromoline Hand Painted* or the *Jolly Jars*, the decoration was added before the glaze was applied using special chemicals that would, after firing in the kiln, come out the desired color.

The final firing (Fig. 17–15) or "glost" firing took only about seventeen hours with a top temperature of about 1950°F, allowing the glaze and any decoration to soften just

enough to join permanently, and creating a glass-like surface on the product. The final product then was taken to storage bins until pulled to fill orders (Fig. 17–16).

Making Dinnerware

Almost all of Red Wing's dinnerware (except for some True China patterns circa 1960) was semi-vitreous earthenware. Both earthenware and china use clay and flint in their mixtures, but this is where the similarity ends. The china mixture contains four times as much feldspar as earthenware, and it utilizes a softer variety. Also, china contains dolomite, while talc is used in earthenware.

Quoting from an old Red Wing Potteries handout, here is how Red Wing's semi-vitreous dinnerware is made:

Fig. 17–9. *(Above)* The molds are filled with a liquid clay called slip. While the pieces dry, the molds are held together with large bands of rubber. After the clay has dried to create the right thickness for the piece, the excess slip is poured out. The piece then is allowed to dry enough so that it can be pulled out of the mold. The worker then pulls the mold apart (referred to as "breaking the mold") and takes the piece out. (Above and right photos courtesy of Minnesota Historical Society)
Fig. 17–10. *(Right)* Once pieces are removed from the mold, the mold seams are "fettled," i.e., smoothed out, usually with a sponge.
Fig. 17–11. *(Bottom)* After the fettled piece has air dried, the first firing takes place, referred to as the bisque firing. (Photo courtesy of Goodhue County Historical Society, Red Wing, Minnesota)

The manufacturing process of Red Wing Semi-Vitreous dinnerware is most fascinating and revealing.

First, what is meant by "semi-vitreous?" Principal ingredients of the ware are clay, flint, and feldspar, and others in smaller amounts. In the extreme heat of the kiln at a pottery, the feldspar melts, partially dissolving the flint and clay, and cementing the particles together. Thus, it is semi-vitrified. If the heating process is extended sufficiently, the material becomes vitrified.

The process of making fine earthenware is essentially the same from one pottery to the next. But every manufacturer practices certain modifications in his formula for mixing ingredients and creating finished dinnerware—modifications he finds advantageous to his par-

ticular production. These are the typical steps in the manufacture of high-quality semi-vitreous dinnerware:

Raw materials, in finely powdered form, are mixed with exact proportions of water in huge vats to make a thin liquid "slip" of precise consistency. A close-meshed vibrating screen filters the milky slip, and an electro-

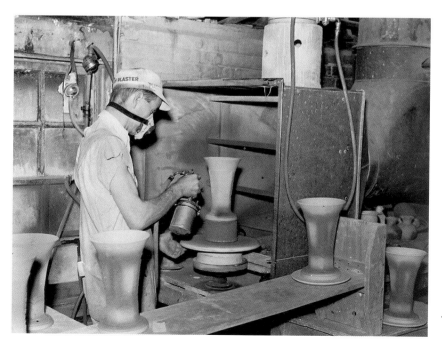

Fig. 17-12. *(Above)* The bisque ware is glazed either by dipping or spraying. Here a worker dips a piece. The process required him to stick his hand into this lead-based glaze. (Photo courtesy of Minnesota Historical Society)
Fig. 17-13. *(Right)* To make the lining a different color, Red Wing created a sprayer nozzle on a rod which was put inside the piece of pottery. The piece was then rotated to evenly spray the inside. A little cutting tool was used to create a fine line between the lining and the outside color. (Photo courtesy of Goodhue County Historical Society, Red Wing, Minnesota)
Fig. 17-14. *(Below)* This worker is spraying on a glaze. Sometimes the piece was sprayed more than once to get an even coating of glaze. (Photo courtesy of Minnesota Historical Society)

magnet is used to draw out any remaining metallic particles which would mar the finished product.

After most of the water is taken out of the mixture in filter presses, the putty-like material goes into the pug mill, where it is chopped and kneaded and all the air is removed. It is extruded from the pug mill as a dense, workable clay cylinder.

Plates and other regularly-shaped pieces are produced on a machine called a jigger. Fast-working operators flatten the correct amount of clay for one piece and place it on a mold which is shaped to form the inside of the piece. The mold is placed on the spinning jigger wheel, and a cutting tool is lowered to form the outside shape.

Hollow pieces, like sugar bowls and pitchers, are formed by casting, a process quite different from jiggering in that fluid slip, which has been prepared by adding a small amount of water to the filter-pressed material, is poured into a plaster mold which forms the outside contours of the ware. At this stage, before the pieces have received their first firing, they are called greenware.

When greenware has dried, it is ready for its first firing, called bisque firing. This is a

long journey through tunnel kilns, or ovens, lasting as much as 75 hours. Tunnel kilns may be straight, curved or circular-shaped, like a huge doughnut. During this trip the ware is subjected to heat gradually increasing to over 2100° and tapering to lower temperatures toward the end. It emerges white, hard, and ready for smoothing and glazing.

Glaze is a liquid mixture which is applied to the ware by dipping or spraying. The ingredients of glaze—lead oxide, whiting, borax, flint, feldspar—are such that, when the coated ware if fired again, the glaze melts into a hard,

permanently. Applying and protecting the design in this manner makes it impervious to detergents.

That, briefly, is the careful cycle through which kaolin clay and other important ingredients pass on the way to becoming the attractive and highly serviceable semi-vitreous dinnerware that is used every day on millions of American tables.

Fig. 17-15. *(Left)* After the glaze was applied, the pieces were put back into the kiln for the final firing, referred to as the "glost" firing. (Photo courtesy of Minnesota Historical Society)
Fig. 17-16. *(Below)* After firing, pieces were either stored or sorted to fulfill orders. (Photo courtesy of Minnesota Historical Society)

glass finish. This second, or "glost" firing, takes perhaps half as long as the first firing.

The beauty of our fine earthenware is enhanced by a decorating treatment applied through hand painting.

The bisque ware is taken to the decorating room where a design is stamped on the ware with vegetable dye. The ware is then taken to a decorating line. This line consists of any number of girls from 6 to 15. Each girl has a certain color to paint on the ware as indicated by the pattern previously stamped on the piece. The ware moves from one girl to the next and when the pieces reach the end of the line a complete decoration appears on the piece of ware. There is an inspector at the end of the line who determines whether the piece is satisfactory and, if so places the Red Wing back stamp on the item.

The hand painting is done previous to the glazing. The completely decorated plate is then given a shower of overglaze applied by an automatic spraying machine. The pattern painted on the piece is barely visible beneath the overglaze. However, after the piece has been fired through the glost kiln, at a 1950 degree temperature, the overglaze becomes transparent so that the design is plainly shown as if beneath a coating of glass.

During this 24 hour passage through the glost kiln the body decoration and glaze soften just enough to join

Fig. 17-17. *(Left)* Pottery was then shipped to retailers. This is a shipping box used for the *Bob White* water pitcher.

The Gypsy Trail

RED WING
POTTERIE

RED WING
MINNESOT

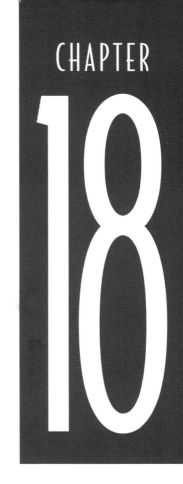

CHAPTER
18

ORIGINAL CATALOG REPRINTS

This chapter consists of many of Red Wing's company catalogs. Each new era at Red Wing is covered, including the 1931 price list, 1938 RumRill, 1942 Gypsy Trail kitchenware as well as Red Wing's 1938, 1942, 1947, 1954, 1956, 1963, and 1965 catalogs.

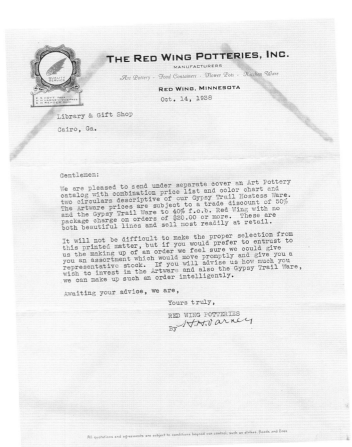

Price List -- August, 1931

Red Wing Pottery

GLAZED WARE

PRICES—
Are per dozen pieces. F. O. B. Red Wing, Minnesota. Crating charge on orders under $20.00.

IN ORDERING—
Specify colors wanted for each piece. Items can be furnished only in the colors noted.

SIZES GIVEN—
For bowls, flower pots and jardinieres are the diameters. For vases and all other pieces, the heights.

COLOR KEY

Y —Yellow.
M —Mulberry.
LG —Light Green.
DG —Dark Green.
LB —Light Blue.
DB —Dark Blue or Blue Black.
GT —Combination Green and Tan.
TG —Combination Gray and Tan.
GM —Combination Green and Mulberry.
GW —Combination Green and White.
MW —Combination Mulberry and White.
BW —Combination Blue and White.
N —Nokomis—a metallic finish in Gray and Tan with a tint of Copper.

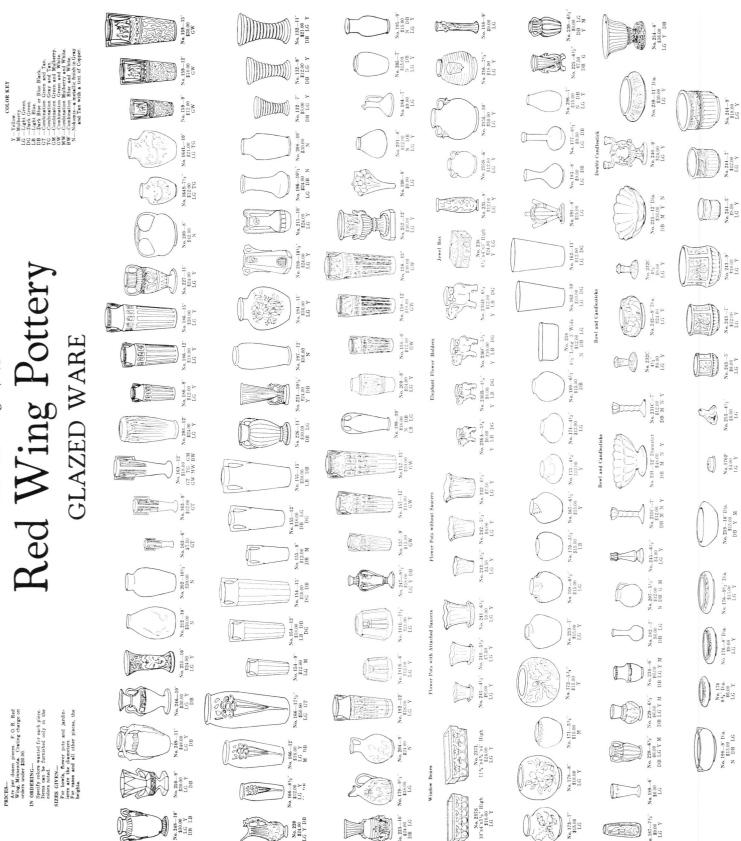

BRUSHED WARE

The outside surface of this ware is stained and not glazed. The stain is fired in and presents a soft, pastel effect. The inside has a luster glaze, in colors to blend with the outside.

COLOR KEY
DG—Dark Green
LG—Light Green
BT—Bronze Tan
LG—Luster Green

Bulb Pans

No. 115—8"
$5.00
DG

No. 115—7"
$4.00
DG

No. 115—6"
$3.50
DG

No. 115—5"
$3.50
DG

No. 121
$1.50
DG

Large Vases

No. 145—15"
$18.00
DG BG

No. 160—18"
$36.00
DG BG

No. 160—24"
$60.00
DG BG BT

Jardinieres with Pedestals

No. 161—33" High
$108.00
DG BG BT

No. 153—33½" High
$125.00
DG BG BT

Sand Jar or Umbrella Stand

No. 104
22" High, 10½" Dia.
$48.00
BT

Lobby or Sand Jar

No. 107
15" High, 12" Dia.
$48.00
DG BT LG

Small Urn

No. 131—12"
$30.00
DG BG

Bulb Bowls

No. 120—9½"
$8.00
DG

No. 120—8½"
$6.00
DG

No. 120—7½"
$5.00
DG

No. 120—6½"
$3.00
DG

No. 120—5½"
$2.00
DG

No. 106—16"
$45.00
DG

No. 106—14"
$33.00
DG

No. 106—12"
$18.00
DG

No. 106—10"
$11.00
DG

No. 106—8"
$8.00
DG

No. 108—16"
$57.00
DG

No. 108—14"
$41.00
DG BT

No. 108—12"
$23.00
DG

No. 108—10"
$15.00
DG

No. 108—8"
$11.00
DG

No. 126—7"
$7.00
DG

No. 147—4¼"
$3.50
DG

No. 127—6½"
$7.50
DG BG

No. 128—6½"
$7.50
DG

No. 150—7"
$5.50
DG BG

No. 148—7"
$9.00
DG BG

No. 119—7"
$8.00
DG BG

No. 105—9"
$8.00
DG BT LG

No. 105—7"
$6.00
DG BT LG

No. 105—5"
$4.00
DG BT LG

No. 152—12"
$17.00
DG BG BT

No. 124—10"
$11.00
DG BG

No. 139—11"
$15.00
DG BG

No. 144—12
$9.00
DG BG

No. 114—10"
With Chains
$9.40

No. 114—8"
With Chains
$8.10

No. 114—7"
With Chains
$7.20

No. 143—6½"
$7.00
DG BG

No. 146—7"
$7.50
DG BG

No. 133—11"
$15.00
DG BG

No. 133—10"
$12.00
DG BG

No. 133—8"
$10.00
DG BG

No. 132—11"
$15.00
BT

No. 132—9"
$6.00
BT

No. 132—7"
$4.00
DG BG BT

No. 137—11"
$15.00
DG BG

No. 123B—10"
$10.10
DG

No. 122B—9"
$7.40
DG

No. 122B—8"
$4.75
DG

No. 122A—10"
½ Size
$5.25
DG

No. 122A—9"
½ Size
$4.10
DG

No. 122A—8"
¾ Size
$4.75
DG

No. 122A—7"
¾ Size
$4.10
DG

No. 122—10"
$8.50
DG

No. 122—9"
$6.00
DG

No. 122—8"
$5.20
DG

No. 122—7"
$3.00
DG

No. 123—6"
$3.15
DG

No. 123—5"
$2.25
DG

No. 123—4"
$1.50
DG

Rose Design Fancy Flower Pots - Red Clay Body - Unglazed Inside - Stained Outside

No. 125—10"
$11.00
DG

No. 144—10"
$7.50
DG BG

No. 144—8"
$5.00
DG BG

No. 144—12"
$18.00
DG BG

RumRill Pottery

RED WING POTTERIES
RED WING, MINNESOTA

RumRill Pottery
Fluted Group

1938

267-9"   387-7½"   301-11"   258-8½"   497-7"

390-6½"   299-7"   395-14"   356-7"   296-8"

300-8½"   320-5½"   454-4½"   453-9½"   454-4½"   256-6"   294-5½"

RumRill Pottery
Grecian Group

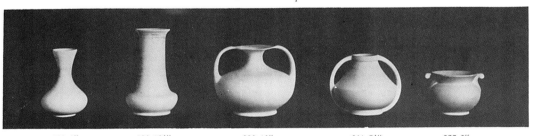

183-8"   196-10½"   200-10"   261-7½"   277-5"

307-10"   364-7"   368-7"   375-8½"   401-12"   506-7½"

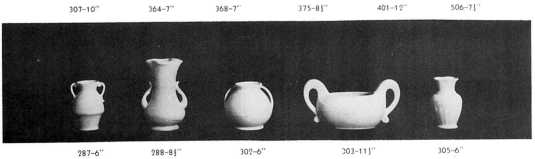

287-6"   288-8½"   302-6"   303-11½"   305-6"

RED WING

RumRill Pottery
Sylvan Group

PAGE THREE

448-9½"   449-11½"   450-5½"   455-8"   514-6"

438-8½"   439-7"   445-8"   446-11"   447-8"

397-5½"   433-3½"   435-12½"   436-9"   437-17"
           Candlestick

RumRill Pottery
Shell Group

PAGE FOUR

452-19"   459-4½"   460-4½"   461-8½"   545-8½"
           Sugar   Creamer

416-9½"   417-3½"   429-6½"   431-8½"   432-7½"
           Candlestick

412-8"   413-7½"   414-12"   415-12½"

Chapter 18

418–5"
Candlestick
440–10"
441–11"
442–10"
443–9"
444–8"

246–10"
248–10"
257–6½"
259–6"
260–9"
279–7½

282–8"
284–10½"
298–9"
352–11"
388–8½"

RumRill Pottery
Continental Group
PAGE SIX

220–10"
240–9"
252–14"
335–6"
337–8"
338–13"

339–6"
392–11"
393–14½"
410–10½"
419–19"

RumRill Pottery
Trumpet Flower Group

489–8½"   490–4½"   491–10"   492–8"   493–9"

485–13"   486–7"   487–12½"   488–9"

RumRill Pottery
Florentine Group

PAGE EIGHT

232–9"   237–10x4x3½"   247–9½"   308–10"   348–7"   360–5½"

362–9½"   365–5"   369–7½"   420–9½"   421–9½"   423–13"   427–6½"

RumRill Pottery
Miscellaneous Group

451–7″   499–5½″   502–7½″   503–7½″   504–7½″   505–7½″

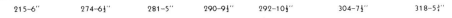

215–6″   274–6½″   281–5″   290–9½″   292–10½″   304–7½″   318–5½″

341–7″   354–4½″   355–6″   363–7½″   366–10″   370–7″   372–7½″

RumRill Pottery
Indian Group

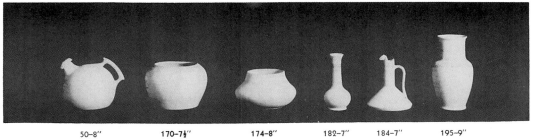

50–8″   170–7½″   174–8″   182–7″   184–7″   195–9″

198–9″   204–9″   207–5½″   219–10″   262–7½″

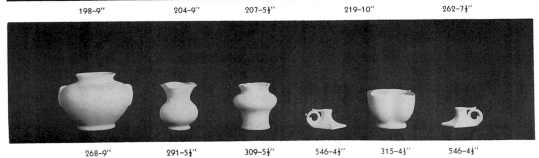

268–9″   291–5½″   309–5½″   546–4½″   315–4½″   546–4½″

Fern Group

376–7"   518–7½"   409–3"   377–12"   378–9½"   385–6"
Candlestick

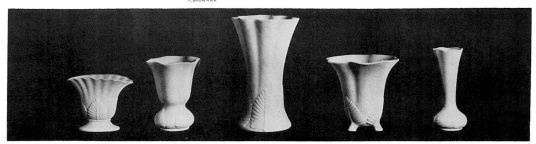

517–7"   515–9"   383–14"   382–9½"   516–10"

MEDIEVAL GROUP

406–8½"   407–5½"   397–5½"   398–9½"   397–5½"   389–7"   422–11"

RumRill Pottery
Classic Group

357–2½"   408–6½"   462–8½"   494–13½"   495–7½"   500–5½"

285–8"   344–6"   316–12"   342–9"   295–10"   278–9"

231–12"   231C–7"   233–12"   271–14½   273–8"   276–6"

Chapter 18

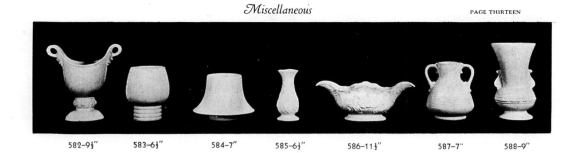

582-9½"   583-6½"   584-7"   585-6½"   586-11½"   587-7"   588-9"

589-7½"   590-7"   591-7"   592-7"   593-7"   594-8"   595-9"

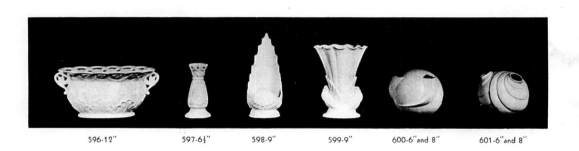

596-12"   597-6½"   598-9"   599-9"   600-6"and 8"   601-6"and 8"

RumRill Pottery
Mandarin Group   PAGE FOURTEEN

332-9"   310-7"   313-11"   314-6"   353-7"

297-5"   331-11"   311-4"   312-9"

RumRill Pottery
Novelties

PAGE FIFTEEN

54-4"   549-4"   386-6½"   53-2½"   52-8¾"   484-6½"   550-6½"   336-6"

430-6"   551-6"   329-6½"   510-8"   547-7½"   323-4"   324-4"   325-4"   326-4"   327-3"   557-3"   558-3"

396-7"   333-5½"   555-11"   391-6"   553-9"   428-5"

RumRill Pottery
Manhattan Group

PAGE SIXTEEN

544-10"   532-7½"   534-15½"   533-7½"   535-12½"

541-7"   543-7½"   539-14½"   554-3½"   542-7½"

507-7½"   536-9"   537-12"   538-8½"   501-8"

136

RumRill Pottery
Renaissance Group

496–6½"   519–7"   520–8"   521–12½"   522–6"

527–10½"   528–8"   529–6"   530–10½"   552–7"

523–7½"   524–9½"   525–7¾"   526 Bowl 12"   531 Inset 10"

Flower Pots

242–5½"   474–3"   474–4"   474–5"   474–6"   509–5"   509–7"

FLOOR VASES

145–15"   155–15"   166–17½"   374–20"   186–15"

RumRill Pottery
Jardinieres

123–10"   124–10"   152–12"

243–5, 7 and 9"   244–5, 7 and 9"   556–9"

Urns and Sand Jars

107–15" High   12" Diameter   131–12"

731–24'   104–22" High   10½" Diameter   717–24"

Chapter 18

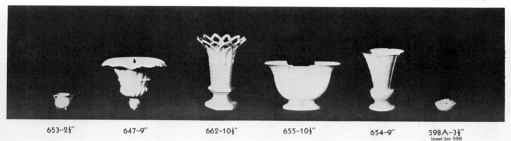

653-2½"   647-9"   662-10½"   655-10½"   654-9"   598A-3½"
Inset for 598

677-6½"   677-7½"   677-8½"   661-6"   661-5"   661-4"   661-3"
For 4" Flower Pot   For 5" Flower Pot   For 6" Flower Pot

COFFEE TABLE ENSEMBLE

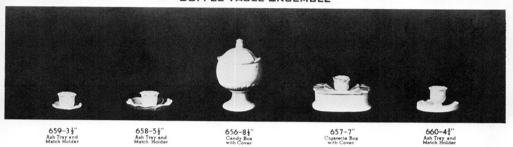

659-3½"   658-5½"   656-8½"   657-7"   660-4¾"
Ash Tray and   Ash Tray and   Candy Box   Cigarette Box   Ash Tray and
Match Holder   Match Holder   with Cover   with Cover   Match Holder

426-7"   319-6½"   483-6"   509 A-7"   367-6"   509 A-5"   272-6"

560-4"   559-4"   561-4½"   566-5½"   510-7¼"   575-7"   508-4½"   394-5"

480-7½"   482-8"   562-12½"   478-8"   343-7½"

RED WING

RumRill Pottery
Athenian Group

| 571–11″ | 568–11½″ | 563–10″ | 564–9″ | 567–8½″ |

| 576–9½″ | 572 - 574–11½″ | 572 - 573–10″ | 570–10″ | 569–11½″ |

Vintage Group

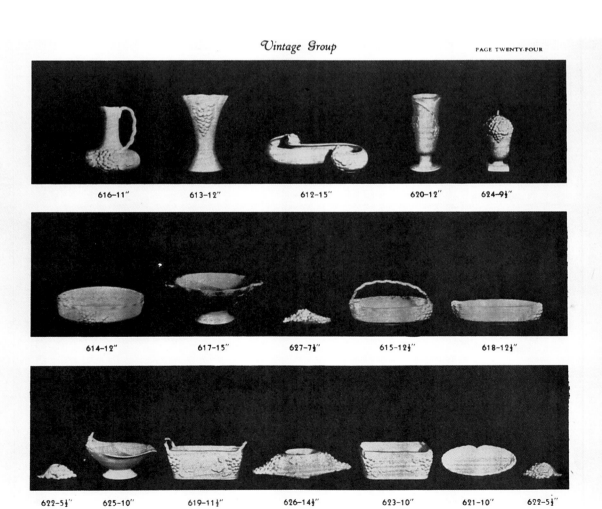

| 616–11″ | 613–12″ | 612–15″ | 620–12″ | 624–9½″ |

| 614–12″ | 617–15″ | 627–7½″ | 615–12½″ | 618–12½″ |

| 622–5½″ | 625–10″ | 619–11½″ | 626–14½″ | 623–10″ | 621–10″ | 622–5½″ |

140

Chapter 18

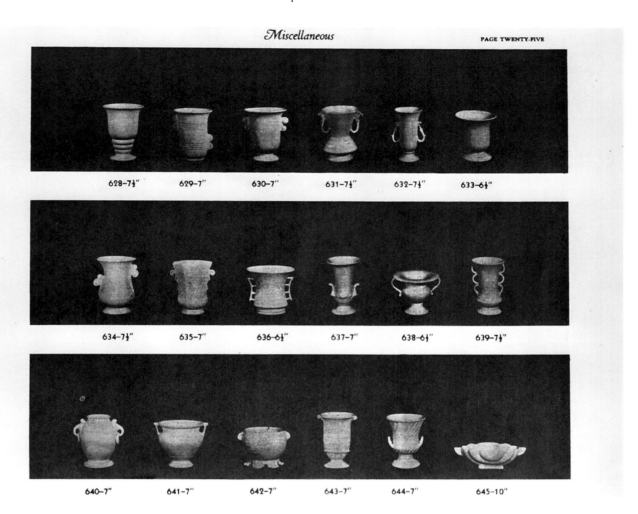

628—7½" 629—7" 630—7" 631—7½" 632—7½" 633—6½"

634—7½" 635—7" 636—6½" 637—7" 638—6½" 639—7½"

640—7" 641—7" 642—7" 643—7" 644—7" 645—10"

Neo-Classic Group

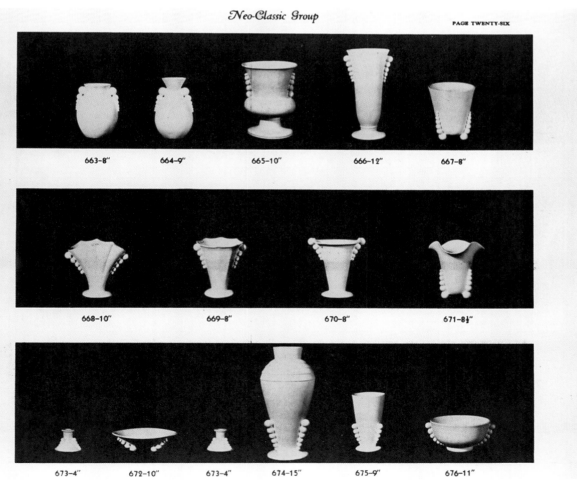

663—8" 664—9" 665—10" 666—12" 667—8"

668—10" 669—8" 670—8" 671—8½"

673—4" 672—10" 673—4" 674—15" 675—9" 676—11"

678 - 14"   679 - 8"   680 - 8"   681 - 10"   682 - 6½"   683 - 10"   684 - 11"   685 - 9½"

Miscellaneous

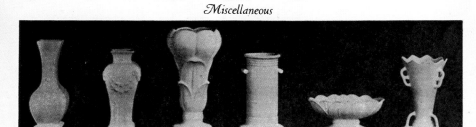

686 - 11"   687 - 10"   688 - 13"   689 - 9½"   690 - 9½"   691 - 9½"

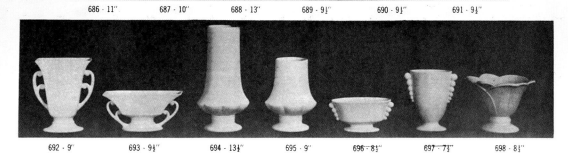

692 - 9"   693 - 9½"   694 - 13½"   695 - 9"   696 - 8½"   697 - 7½"   698 - 8½"

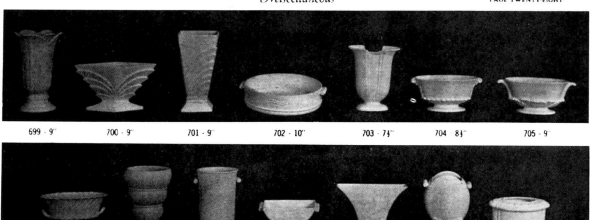

699 - 9"   700 - 9"   701 - 9"   702 - 10"   703 - 7½"   704 - 8½"   705 - 9"

706 - 7½"   707 - 7"   708 - 7"   709 - 7"   710 - 8"   711 - 7"   712 - 7"

Medallion Line -- Georgia Rose Group

170F - 7½"   174F - 8"   196F - 10½"   195F - 9"   200F - 10"   203F - 10½"   219F - 10"   463F - 11"

Chapter 18

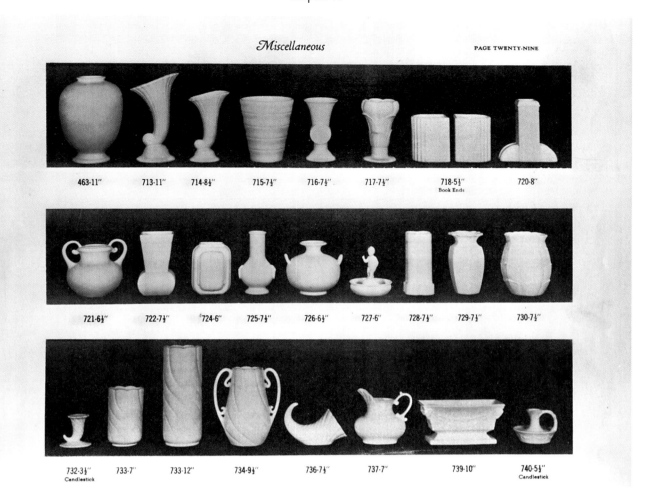

Miscellaneous

463-11″   713-11″   714-8½″   715-7½″   716-7½″   717-7½″   718-5½″ Book Ends   720-8″

721-6½″   722-7½″   724-6″   725-7½″   726-6½″   727-6″   728-7½″   729-7½″   730-7½″

732-3½″ Candlestick   733-7″   733-12″   734-9½″   736-7½″   737-7″   739-10″   740-5½″ Candlestick

Hostess Group

PAGE THIRTEEN

470-13½″   471-10″   472-7½″   473-10″ and 12″

475 Jug-8½″
476 Plate-9½″   511-13″   512-15″

464-10″   467-12″   468-11″   469-13″

1938

RED WING ART Pottery

RED WING POTTERIES, INC.

RED WING ... MINNESOTA

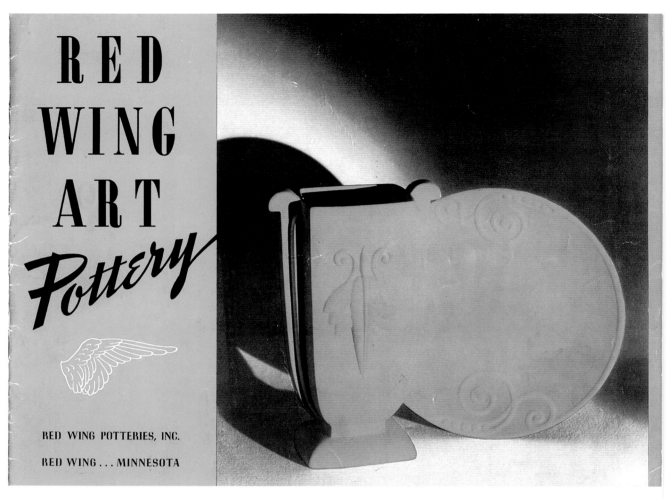

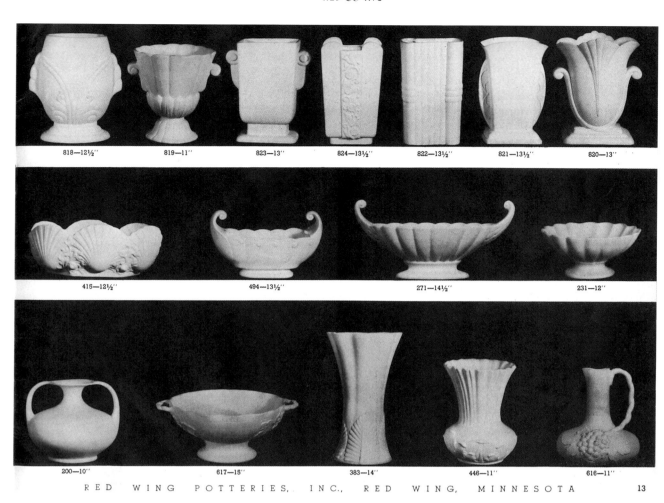

818—12½''   819—11''   823—13''   824—13½''   822—13½''   821—13½''   820—13''

415—12½''   494—13½''   271—14½''   231—12''

200—10''   617—15''   383—14''   446—11''   616—11''

RED WING POTTERIES, INC., RED WING, MINNESOTA   13

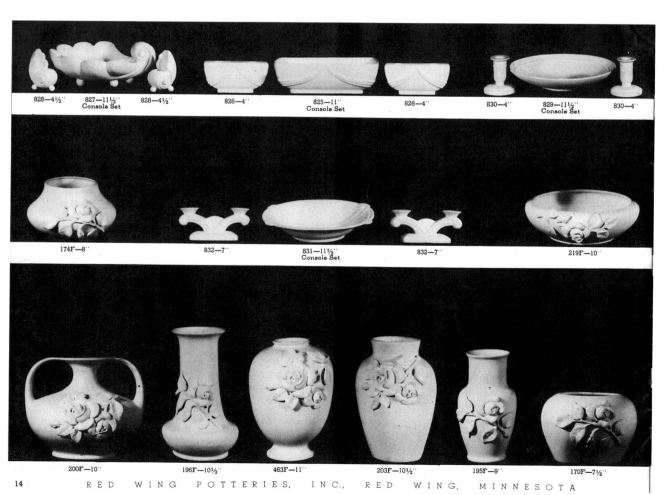

828—4½''   827—11½''   828—4½''   826—4''   825—11''   826—4''   830—4''   829—11½''   830—4''
Console Set   Console Set   Console Set

174F—8''   832—7''   831—11½''   832—7''   219F—10''
                       Console Set

200F—10''   196F—10½''   463F—11''   203F—10½''   195F—9''   170F—7½''

14   RED WING POTTERIES, INC., RED WING, MINNESOTA

CANDLESTICKS

554—3¾"   622—5½"   673—4"   732—3½"   740—5"   357—2½"   409—3"   417—3¾"   546—4½"   433—3½"
Candlestick

231C—7"   397—5¼"   495—7½"   529—6"   563—10"   564—9"   576—9½"   408—6½"   454—4½"

832—7"   826—4"   848—5"   539—14½"   849—5"   847—3½"   830—4"   828—4½"

WHATNOTS — ASH TRAYS

651—4"   558—3"   653—2½"   650—3"   327—3"   557—3"   741—4"   323—4"   652—4"   549—4"   54—4"

RED WING POTTERIES, INC., RED WING, MINNESOTA   15

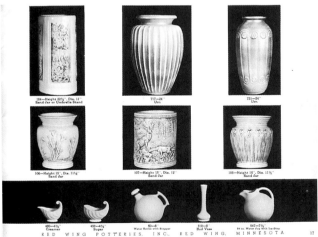

Red Wing Art Pottery

We take pleasure in presenting to the trade this catalog of Red Wing Art Pottery. This line has been carefully planned to meet the requirements of both large and small dealers. Adequate groups at each retail price level have been created. Those groups where there is the largest retail demand are naturally larger and more varied but the demand for higher priced pieces has also been adequately met.

Design has been paramount. Over one hundred new and original shapes have been added. These are the creation of Belle Kogan —widely known contemporary industrial designer of New York City. Increased plant facilities, modern methods, new and attractive finishes, careful workmanship and professional designing all combine in making Red Wing Art Pottery the most profitable line the trade has been offered for years.

RED WING POTTERIES, INC.
RED WING, MINNESOTA

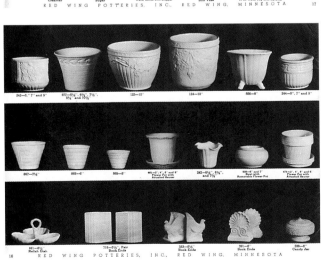

1942

Gypsy Trail Ware

MARMALADE JARS WITH ATTACHED SAUCERS

MISCELLANEOUS

For Prices and Colors See Pages Seven and Eight

RED WING POTTERIES, INC.
Red Wing, Minnesota

CASSEROLES — MARMITES

COOKIE JARS

KATRINA "The Dutch Girl" Height 10½" — PIERRE "Chef" Height 11" — FRIAR TUCK "THOU SHALT NOT STEAL" Height 10½"

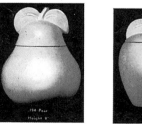  

MIXING BOWLS

 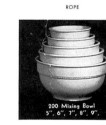

BRIDES—Two-toned 195 Mixing Bowl — ROPE 200 Mixing Bowl — REED Reed Mixing Bowls

TEA POTS — COFFEE SERVERS

19 42

Pitchers ⟶ Jugs ⟶ Batter Sets ⟶ Watering Pots

REED DINNER WARE

Salad Bowl Sets

6"—8" and 10" Bowls

MUGS ⟶ CHOP PLATE ⟶ COVERED BUTTER

RED WING POTTERIES, INC.
RED WING, MINN.

Gypsy Trail Ware **List Prices** *June 15th, 1942*

	Standard Colors	Orange	Colors
BATTER PITCHER TRAY			
F131 Fondoso	$14.40 doz.	$19.20 doz.	2
BATTER SET—FONDOSO			
Consisting of			
1—F129 32-oz. Covered Batter Pitcher			
1—F130 12-oz. Covered Syrup Pitcher	34.80	46.40	2
1—F131 Tray			
BUTTER BOATS			
206	4.50	6.00	2
BUTTER DISHES—COVERED			
207—¼ lb.	7.80	10.40	2
CASSEROLES WITH COVERS			
103—8½" Reed	13.20	17.60	1
F127—8½" Fondoso	15.00	20.00	2
248—Fish	18.00		4
249—Chicken	24.00		4
COFFEE SERVERS WITH COVERS			
124—Plain—Wooden Handles	18.00	24.00	2
F111—Fondoso—Wooden Handles	18.00	24.00	2
COOKIE JARS			
193—Apple	18.00		4
194—Pear	18.00		4
205—Pineapple	18.00		4
231—Banana	18.00		4
232—Grape	18.00		4
243—Katrina	24.00		7
244—Pierre	24.00		7
245—Friar Tuck	24.00		7
CUPS and SAUCERS			
112—Reed Tea Cups	3.60	4.20	1
112—Reed Tea Saucers	1.80	2.40	1
CUSTARDS			
107—Reed	1.80	2.40	1
DESSERTS			
104—Reed—Footed	3.60	4.80	1
MARMALADES WITH ATTACHED SAUCERS			
227—Apple	7.20	9.60	2
228—Pear	7.20	9.60	2
229—Pineapple	7.20	9.60	2
MARMITES—LOW			
110—4½"	4.50	6.00	1
247—Fish	7.80		4
250—Chicken	9.00		4
MIXING BOWLS			
127— 5" Reed	3.00 doz.	4.00 doz.	1
127— 6" Reed	3.60	4.80	1
127— 7" Reed	5.40	7.20	1
127— 8" Reed	6.00	8.00	1
127— 9" Reed	7.20	9.60	1
127—10" Reed	10.20	13.60	3

	No. 1 Colors	5" Orange	All Orange
127 sets 5"-6"-7"-8"-9"-10"	$2.95 each	$3.03 each	$3.93 each
127 sets 5"-6"-7"-8"-9"	2.10	2.18	2.80
127 sets 5"-6"-7"-8"	1.50	1.58	2.00
127 sets 6"-7"-8"-9"	1.85		2.47
127 sets 6"-7"-9"	1.30	1.38	1.73
195— 5" Shower		$ 4.50 doz.	5
195— 6" Shower		5.25	5
195— 7" Shower		8.25	5
195— 8" Shower		9.00	5
195— 9" Shower		10.50	5
195—10" Shower		15.00	5
Nest 5"-9"		3.15 each	
Nest 5"-10"		4.40	

	Standard Colors	Orange	Colors
200—5" Rope	3.00 doz.		6
200—6" Rope	3.60		6
200—7" Rope	5.40		6
200—8" Rope	6.00		6
200—9" Rope	7.20		6
Nest 5"-6"-7"-8"-9"	2.10 each		
MUGS			
101—10 oz. Reed	3.60	4.80	1
115— 7 oz. Fluted	3.00	4.00	1
116—10 oz. Fluted	3.60	4.80	1
NAPPIES			
188—7"	5.40	7.20	1
188—8"	6.00	7.80	1
PITCHERS			
122—14 oz. Plain Syrup	5.40	7.20	1
122—14 oz. Plain Syrup with Cover	7.20	9.60	1
125—19 oz. Reed	5.40	7.20	1
179—64 oz. Swirl	13.20	17.60	2
189—64 oz. Modern	14.40	19.20	2
547—64 oz. Tilt	13.20	17.60	2
F129—32-oz. Fondoso Covered Batter Pitcher	13.20	17.60	2
F130—12 oz. Fondoso Covered Syrup Pitcher	7.20	9.60	2
251—64 oz.	18.00		4
PLATES			
134—8" Reed	3.00	3.60	1
134—8½" Reed	4.20	5.40	1
134—9½" Reed	4.80	6.60	1
130—15" Plain Chop	16.50	21.60	1
PLATTERS			
129—12" Reed Oval	13.20 doz.	17.60 doz.	1
RELISH DISHES			
175—Reed—Individual	3.60	4.80	1
461—Compartment with Handle	14.40	19.20	2
SALAD BOWLS			
979— 8"	3.60	4.80	2
979— 8"	6.00	8.00	2
979—10"	10.20	13.60	2
Set of 4-6" Bowls, 1 each O-B-Y-T	1.30 each		
Same with 1-8" Bowl	1.80		
Same with 1-10" Bowl	2.15		
SALTS and PEPPERS			
118—Plain	8.40 doz. pr.	11.20 doz. pr.	1
239—Double	5.60 each	9.00 each	2
240—Double	6.60 each	9.00 each	2
SAUCE DISHES			
172—Reed	2.40	3.00	1
SHIRRED EGG DISHES			
145—8½" Reed	4.20 doz.	5.40 doz.	1
SOUPS			
106—Reed	3.60	4.80	1
SUGARS and CREAMERS			
102—Reed Sugars	3.60	4.80	1
102—Reed Sugars with Covers	5.40	7.20	1
111—Creamers	3.60	4.80	1
184—Snack Sugars	3.60	4.80	2
185—Snack Creamers	3.60	4.80	2
TEA POTS			
121—6 cup Reed	14.40	18.00	1
234—6 cup	14.40	18.00	2
235—6 cup	14.40	18.00	2
236—8 cup	14.40	18.00	2
238—8 cup	18.00	24.00	2
VEGETABLE DISHES			
123—8" Reed—Open	5.40	7.20	1
WATERING POT			
242	18.00		4

COLORS:

(1) Orange, Royal Blue, Yellow, Turquoise, Cream Ivory.
(2) Orange, Royal Blue, Yellow, Turquoise, Cream Ivory, Green, Pink.
(3) Orange, Royal Blue, Yellow, Turquoise, Cream Ivory, Pink.
(4) Royal Blue, Yellow, Turquoise, Cream Ivory, Green, Pink.
(5) Ivory Pink Lined, Ivory Green Lined.
(6) 5" Lavender, 6" Green, 7" Pink, 8" Blue, 9" Yellow (All Pastel)
(7) Blue, Yellow, Tan with Underglaze Decoration.

1942

RED WING ART POTTERY

CATALOG No. 42
RED WING POTTERIES, INC.   RED WING, MINNESOTA

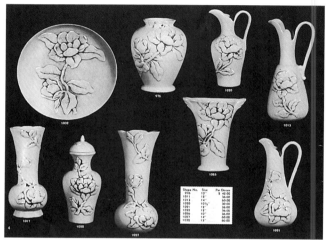

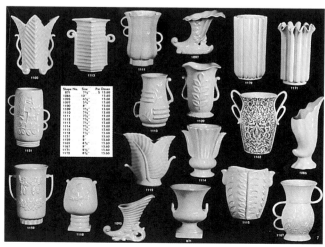

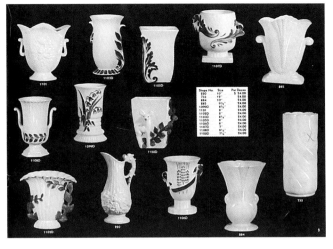

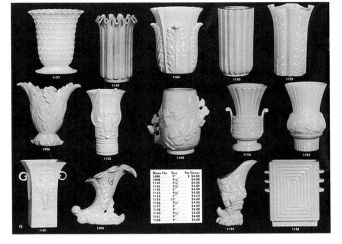

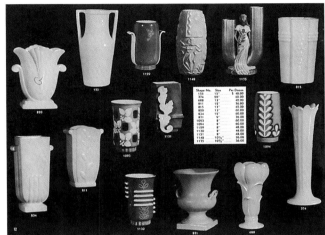

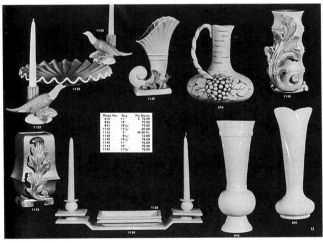

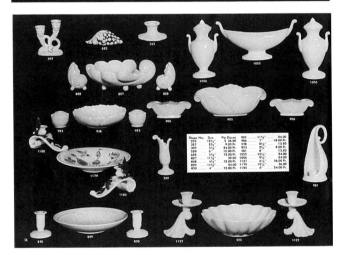

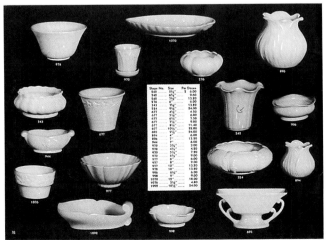

Red Wing Art Ware

CATALOGUE NO. 47

Red Wing Potteries, Inc.   *Red Wing, Minn.*

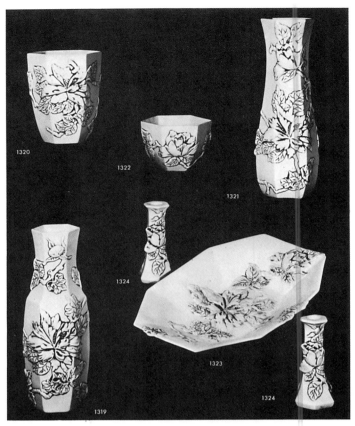

| 1319-12" | $48.00 Doz. | 1321-14" | 60.00 Doz. | 1323-14½" | 48.00 Doz. |
| 1320-7" | 24.00 Doz. | 1322-5½" | 15.60 Doz. | 1324-6", prs. | 26.40 Doz. |

FOR COLORS, SEE COLOR CHART ENCLOSED.

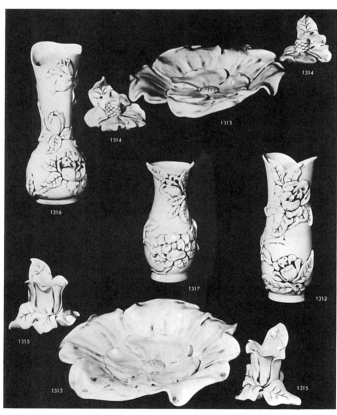

| 1312-12" | $48.00 Doz. | 1314-5", prs. | 36.00 Doz. | 1316-14" | 60.00 Doz. |
| 1313-14½" | 90.00 Doz. | 1315-5½" prs. | 36.00 Doz. | 1317-10" | 36.00 Doz. |

FOR COLORS, SEE COLOR CHART ENCLOSED.

| 975-6" | $15.60 Doz. | 1216-8" | 18.00 Doz. | 1227-3", prs. | 18.00 Doz. | 1232-7½" | 13.20 Doz. |
| 1012-7" | 15.60 Doz. | 1223-12" | 36.00 Doz. | 1228-4½", prs. | 24.00 Doz. | 1234-14" | 48.00 Doz. |

FOR COLORS, SEE COLOR CHART ENCLOSED.

1947

505-7½" $15.60 Doz.   892-7½"   15.60 Doz.   1112-7½"   15.60 Doz.
871-6"   15.60 Doz.   1097-5½"   15.60 Doz.   1169-7"   15.60 Doz.
886-7½"   15.60 Doz.   1105-7"   15.60 Doz.   1263-6"   15.60 Doz.

FOR COLORS, SEE COLOR CHART ENCLOSED.

278-9" $21.00 Doz.   1120-7½"   24.00 Doz.   1171-8½"   18.00 Doz.   1242-5"   18.00 Doz.   1265-10"   24.00 Doz.
871-7½"   18.00 Doz.   1165-8"   18.00 Doz.   1171S-8½"   30.00 Doz.   1259-9"   24.00 Doz.   1268-12"   18.00 Doz.

FOR COLORS, SEE COLOR CHART ENCLOSED.

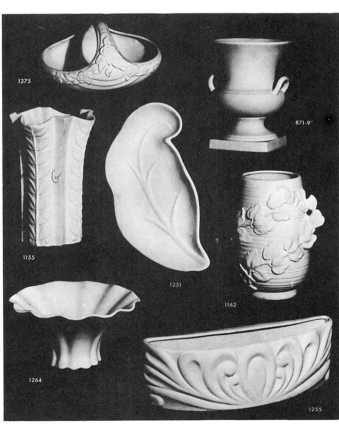

871-9" $42.00 Doz.   1162-9"   30.00 Doz.   1255-14"   42.00 Doz.   1275-9½"   36.00 Doz.
1155-10"   30.00 Doz.   1251-13"   24.00 Doz.   1264-9"   24.00 Doz.

FOR COLORS, SEE COLOR CHART ENCLOSED.

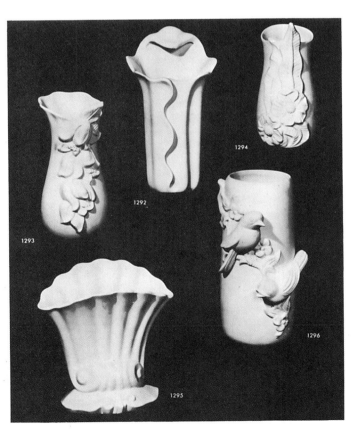

1292-11" $24.00 Doz.   1294-8"   18.00 Doz.   1296-10"   48.00 Doz.
1293-9"   24.00 Doz.   1295-8"   24.00 Doz.

FOR COLORS, SEE COLOR CHART ENCLOSED.

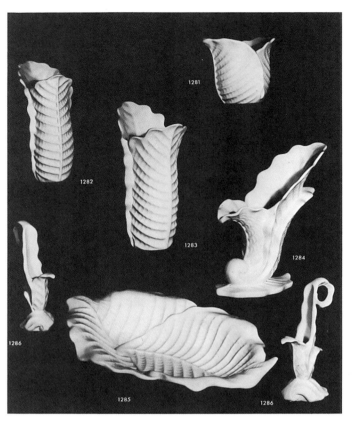

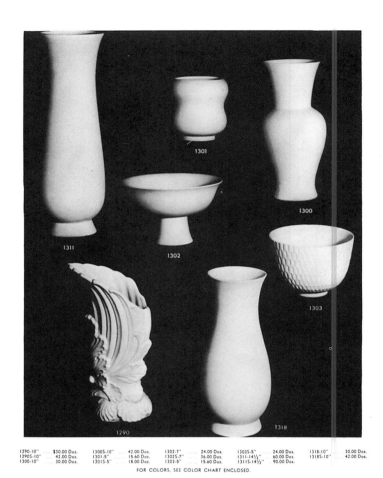

1281-5" $15.60 Doz.   1282S-8"   30.00 Doz.   1284-11"   30.00 Doz.   1285S-8"   72.00 Doz.
1281S-5"   24.00 Doz.   1283-10"   24.00 Doz.   1284S-11"   42.00 Doz.   1286-8", prs.   18.00 Doz.
1282-8"   18.00 Doz.   1283S-10"   36.00 Doz.   1285-8"   48.00 Doz.   1286S-8", prs. 24.00 Doz.

FOR COLORS, SEE COLOR CHART ENCLOSED.

1290-10" $30.00 Doz.   1300S-10"   42.00 Doz.   1302-7"   24.00 Doz.   1303S-5"   24.00 Doz.   1318-10"   30.00 Doz.
1290S-10"   42.00 Doz.   1301-5"   15.60 Doz.   1302S-7"   36.00 Doz.   1311-14½"   60.00 Doz.   1318S-10"   42.00 Doz.
1300-10"   30.00 Doz.   1301S-5"   18.00 Doz.   1303-5"   15.60 Doz.   1311S-14½"   90.00 Doz.

FOR COLORS, SEE COLOR CHART ENCLOSED.

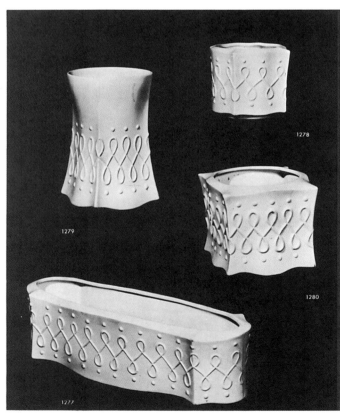

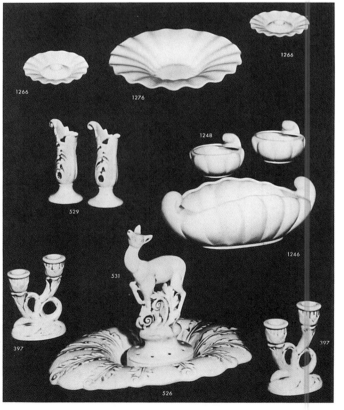

1277-14" $48.00 Doz.   1278-4"   15.60 Doz.   1279-8"   18.00 Doz.   1280-6"   18.00 Doz.
1277S-14"   72.00 Doz.   1278S-4"   24.00 Doz.   1279S-8"   30.00 Doz.   1280S-6"   30.00 Doz.

FOR COLORS, SEE COLOR CHART ENCLOSED.

397-5", prs. $30.00 Doz.   526-12"   36.00 Doz.   1246-12"   30.00 Doz.   1266-5", prs.   18.00 Doz.
529-6", prs.   13.20 Doz.   531-10"   18.00 Doz.   1248-4", prs. 18.00 Doz.   1276-11"   30.00 Doz.

FOR COLORS, SEE COLOR CHART ENCLOSED.

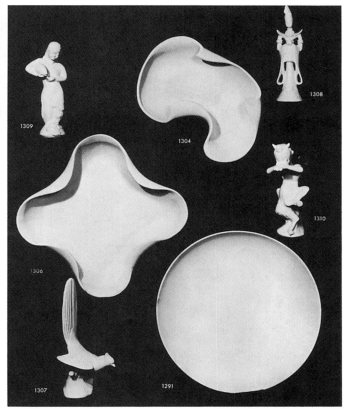

1291-14''	$48.00 Doz.	1304S-13''	72.00 Doz.	1307-9½''	18.00 Doz.	1308S-10'''	30.00 Doz.	1310-9''	24.00 Doz.
1291S-14''	72.00 Doz.	1306-12''	48.00 Doz.	1307S-9½''	30.00 Doz.	1309-9''	24.00 Doz.	1310S-9''	42.00 Doz.
1304-13''	48.00 Doz.	1306S-12''	72.00 Doz.	1308-10''	18.00 Doz.	1309S-9''	42.00 Doz.		

FOR COLORS, SEE COLOR CHART ENCLOSED.

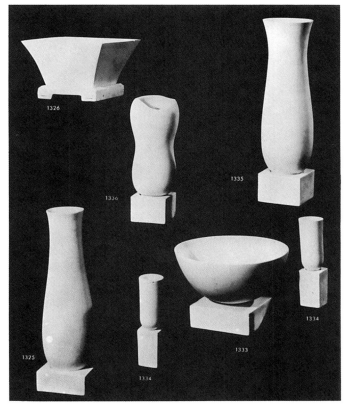

1325-12''	$90.00 Doz.	1333-8''	90.00 Doz.	1335-14''	120.00 Doz.
1326-7''	90.00 Doz.	1334-6'', prs.	36.00 Doz.	1336-9''	72.00 Doz.

FOR COLORS, SEE COLOR CHART ENCLOSED.

1327-7½''	$90.00 Doz.	1329-18½''	120.00 Doz.	1331-6½'' x5''	60.00 Doz.
1328-10''	72.00 Doz.	1330-5''	15.00 Doz.	1332-4''	15.00 Doz.

FOR COLORS, SEE COLOR CHART ENCLOSED.

677-4½''	$ 4.95 Doz.	677-7½''	10.20 Doz.	1287 for 4'' Pot	9.00 Doz.
677-5½''	6.60 Doz.	677-8½''	12.60 Doz.	1288 for 5'' Pot	18.00 Doz.
677-6½''	8.40 Doz.	677-10½''	30.00 Doz.	1289 for 6'' Pot	24.00 Doz.

FOR COLORS, SEE COLOR CHART ENCLOSED.

19
54

RED
WING

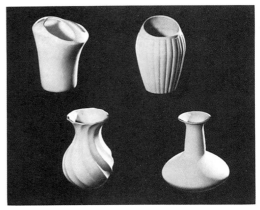

Vases

Upper, from left
B-1429 — 8½"
B-1430 — 8½"

Lower, from left
B-1431 — 8½"
B-1426 — 8½"

Vases

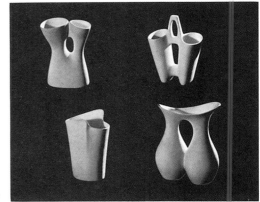

Upper, from left
B-1427 — 8¼"
B-1428 — 8½"

Lower, from left
B-1425 — 8"
B-1433 — 10"

See Price List for Color Chart
and Prices

Red Wing Potteries, Inc.

Vases

Upper, from left
892 — 7½"
1356 — 7½"

Lower, from left
1359 — Discontinued
1357 — Discontinued

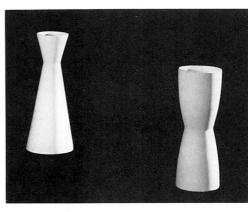

Vases

Charcoal Black
Stippled White

Upper left
M-2318 — 12"

Lower right
M-2319 — 12"

Vases
Cache Pots
Window Box

Top, from left
B-1404 — 5½"
B-1403 — 4" Violet Pot

Lower, from left
B-1392 — 7½"
B-1391 — 7½"
B-1399 — 5"

See Price List for Color Chart
and Prices

Red Wing Potteries, Inc.

Vases

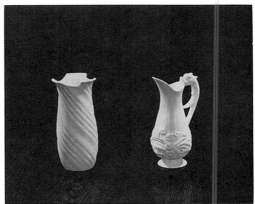

Left
M-1449 — 10¼"

Right
220 — 10½"

See Price List for Color Chart
and Prices

Red Wing Potteries, Inc.

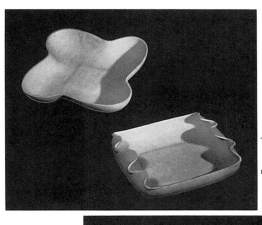

Bowls

Top
B-1405 — 9" x 9"

Lower
B-1406 — 8½" x 13"

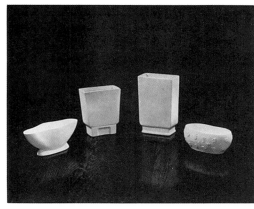

**Planters
Vases**

Left to Right

2016 — 10³₁ x 3¾"
2001 — 8"
2003 — 10"
M-1448 — 8" x 4½"

Bowls

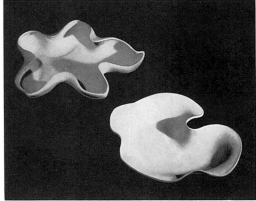

Top
B-1407 — 10" x 13"

Lower
B-1408 — 10" x 13"

See Price List for Color Chart and Prices

Red Wing Potteries, Inc.

Bowls

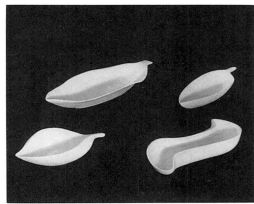

Top
Left
M-1453 — 18³₁ x 8"
Right
M-1445 — 12¼" x 5"

Lower
Left
M-1446 — 11" x 7"
Right
M-1447 — 12" x 5"

See Price List for Color Chart and Prices

Red Wing Potteries, Inc.

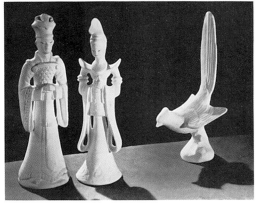

Figurines

From left

B-1389 — 10"
1308 — 10"
1307 — 9½"

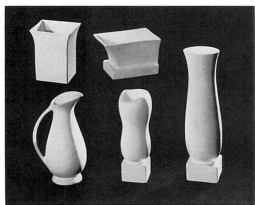

**Planter
Vases**

Charcoal Black
Stippled White

Upper
2309 — 6½" x 5"
2308 — 6" x 4"

Lower, from left
2313 — 9¼"
2306 — 9"
2305 — 14"

Vases

Left to Right

M-1452 — 14"
M-1438 — 14"
M-1438 — 10"
M-1450 — 9½"
M-1451 — 14"

See Price List for Color Chart and Prices

Red Wing Potteries, Inc.

**Bowls
Vases**

Charcoal Black
Stippled White

Upper, from left
2301 — 4½" x 7"
2304 — 8" x 4"

Lower, from left
B-2316 — Discontinued
B-2316 — Discontinued
2310 — 13" x 7"

See Price List for Color Chart and Prices

Red Wing Potteries, Inc.

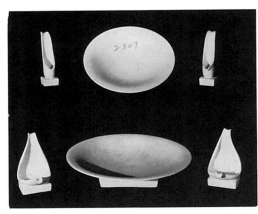

Console Bowls
Candlesticks

Charcoal Black
Stippled White

Upper

Candlestick
2311 — 8½"

Bowl
2307 — 14"

Lower

Candlestick
2312 — 7½" x 5"

Bowl
2307 — Discontinued

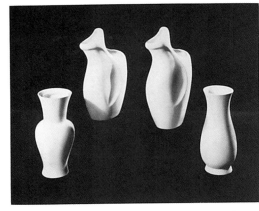

Vases

Charcoal Black
Stippled White

Upper, from left
B-2317 — Discontinued
B-2317 — Discontinued

Lower, from left
2300 — 10¼"
2302 — 10¼"

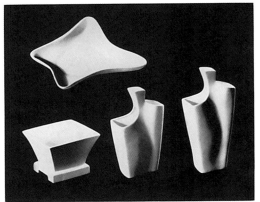

Bowl
Planter
Vases

Charcoal Black
Stippled White

Upper
2314 — 14¼" x 13"

Lower, from left
2303 — 5" x 7"
2315 — 10¼"
2315 — Discontinued

See Price List for Color Chart
and Prices

Red Wing Potteries, Inc.

Console Units

Charcoal Black
Stippled White

Left
2308 — 6" x 4"
2309 — 6½" x 5"
No. 2309 is the center section of
each unit. Side units are 2308

Vase

Right
413 — 14"

See Price List for Color Chart
and Prices

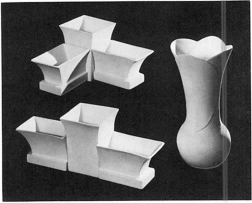

Red Wing Potteries, Inc.

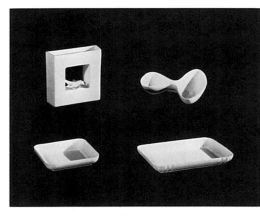

Vase
Bowls

Upper, from left
430 — 10½" x 10"
B-1434 — Discontinued

Lower, from left
421 — 8" x 8"
422 — 12½" x 8"

Bowls

Upper
425 — Discontinued

Lower, from left
B-1435 — 14" x 13"
426 — 10½"

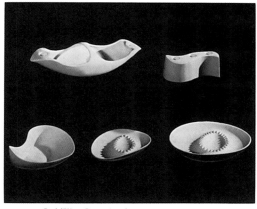

Bowls
Candlesticks
Ash Trays

Upper, from left
Gondola Bowl with
Sticks
B-1420 — 15" x 5½"
Candlestick *
B-1422 — 8"
Lower, from left
Bowl
B-1421 — 8" x 7"
Ash Trays
B-1436 — 8" x 6"
B-1437 — 11" x 8½"

* To be used with two B-1421
for ensemble

See Price List for Color Chart
and Prices

Red Wing Potteries, Inc.

Urn
Vase
Planters

Top
871 — 7½"

Lower, from left
1265 — 10"
1259 — 9¼"
1378 — 5" x 5¼" high

See Price List for Color Chart
and Prices

Red Wing Potteries, Inc.

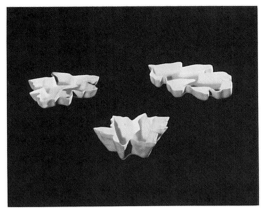

Bowls

Upper, from left

427 — 10½" x 9"

428 — 14" x 7½"

Lower

429 — 10" x 10"

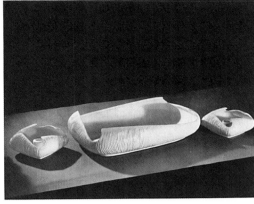

Bowl Candlesticks

Textured

Bowl
B-2110 — 14½"

Candlesticks
B-2111 — 5" x 5"

Window Box Bowl Candlesticks

Upper

1255 — 14"

Lower

1384 — Candlesticks
4½" x 1¼"

1383 — Discontinued

See Price List for Color Chart and Prices

Red Wing Potteries, Inc.

Candlesticks Bowl

Shell Candlesticks
B-2502 — 4½"

Shell Bowl
B-2501 — 13"

See Price List for Color Chart and Prices

Red Wing Potteries, Inc.

Tropicana

BOWL
CANDELABRA

Tropicana Candelabra
B-2019 — 6" long

Bird of Paradise Bowl
B-2014 — 14"

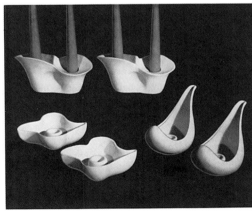

Candlesticks

Top
B-1410 — Discontinued

Left
B-1411 — 4" x 4"

Right
B-1409 — 5"

Vases Window Box

Top

406 — 9½"

Lower, from left

412 — 9½"

407 — 12"

410 — Discontinued

See Price List for Color Chart and Prices

Red Wing Potteries, Inc.

Garden Club Bowls

Top, from left

414 Plain Bowl — 8"

415 — Discontinued

278 Scallop Bowl — 8"

Lower, from left

417 — Discontinued

418 — Discontinued

See Price List for Color Chart and Prices

Red Wing Potteries, Inc.

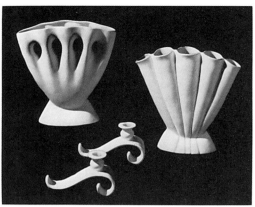

Gladiolus Vases
Candlesticks

Upper, left
B-1419 Gladiolus Vase
12"

Middle, right
416 — Gladiolus Vase
12"

Lower
419 — Discontinued

Vases
Bowl
Planters

Left to Right
M-1440 — 5½"
242 — 5½" Diam.
348 — 7½" x 3¼"
276 — 6"
207 — 6"
M-1439 — 6"

Vases

From left
1377 — Discontinued
1379 — Discontinued
1376 — 11"

See Price List for Color Chart
and Prices

Red Wing Potteries, Inc.

Vases

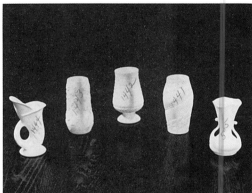

Left to Right
M-1444 — 8½"
M-1443 — 8½"
M-1442 — 8½"
M-1441 — 8½"
505 — 7½"

See Price List for Color Chart
and Prices

Red Wing Potteries, Inc.

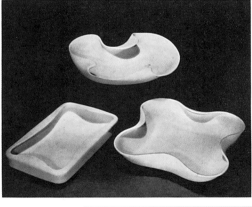

Garden Club
Bowls

Top
1304 — 13"

Lower, from left
1348 — 12"
1306 — Discontinued

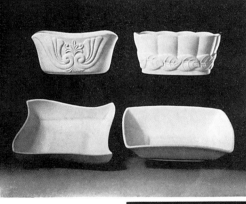

Planters
Bowls

Top, from left
B-1401 — Discontinued
B-1402 — 7"

Lower, from left
B-1396 — 7" x 7"
B-1393 — 5½" x 9"

Vases

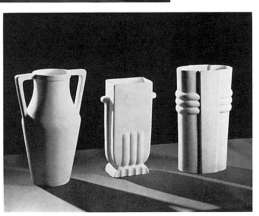

From left
403 — Discontinued
405 — 10½"
404 — 12"

See Price List for Color Chart
and Prices

Red Wing Potteries, Inc.

Jardinieres

677 — 4½"
677 — 5½"
677 — 6½"
677 — 7½"
677 — 8½"
677 — 10½"

See Price List for Color Chart
and Prices

Red Wing Potteries, Inc.

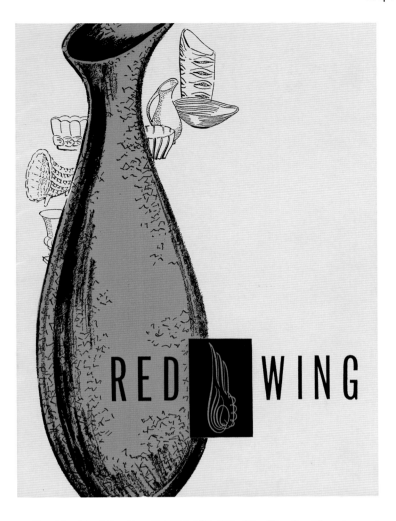

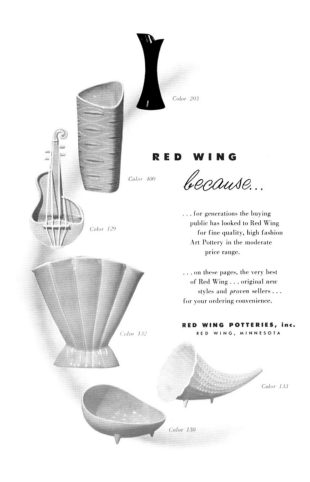

1956

RED WING
because...

... for generations the buying
public has looked to Red Wing
for fine quality, high fashion
Art Pottery in the moderate
price range.

... on these pages, the very best
of Red Wing ... original *new*
styles and *proven* sellers ...
for your ordering convenience.

RED WING POTTERIES, inc.
RED WING, MINNESOTA

Color 203
Color 400
Color 129
Color 132
Color 133
Color 130

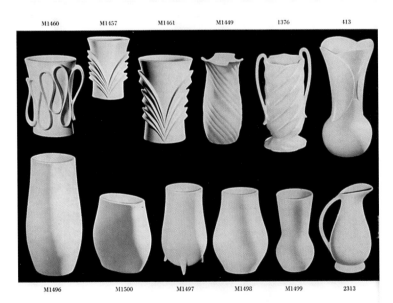

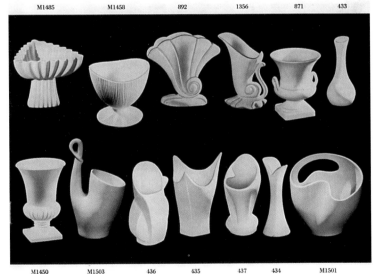

LARGE VASES

TOP ROW, *left to right*
M1460 — 9″ vase, 1.25
M1457 — 8″ vase, 1.00
M1461 — 10½″ vase, 1.50
M1449 — 10¼″ vase, 1.25
1376 — 11″ vase with handles, 1.50
413 — 14″ vase, 2.50

BOTTOM ROW, *left to right*
M1496 — 14″ vase, 2.50
M1500 — 9″ vase, 1.25
M1497 — 10″ footed vase, 1.25
M1498 — 10¼″ vase, 1.25
M1499 — 9″ vase, 1.00
2313 — 9¼″ pitcher vase, 1.25

Order colors by number from Color Chart on inside back cover

SMALL VASES, BOWL

TOP ROW, *left to right*
M1485 — bowl, 8″ x 6½″ high, 1.25
M1458 — 6″ compote-vase, 1.00
892 — 7½″ fan vase, .80
1356 — 7½″ vase, .80
871 — 7½″ trophy vase, 1.25
433 — 7½″ slender vase, .65

BOTTOM ROW, *left to right*
M1450 — 9½″ trophy vase, 1.25
M1503 — pipe vase, 6″ x 10¼″, 1.25
436 — 8″ vase, 1.00
435 — 8″ vase, 1.00
437 — 7¾″ vase, 1.00
434 — 8″ slender vase, .65
M1501 — cut out vase, 7½″ x 7¾″, 1.50

Order colors by number from Color Chart on inside back cover

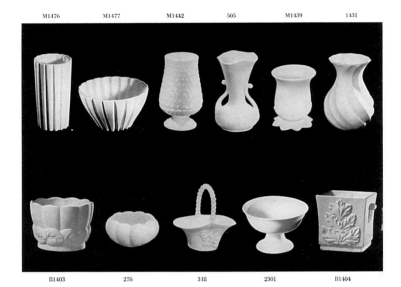

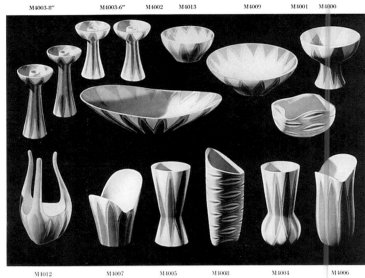

SMALL
VASES,
BOWLS,
PLANTERS

TOP ROW, *left to right*

M1476 — 6″ vase, .80
M1477 — 6″ bowl, .80
M1442 — 8½″ snifter vase, 1.00
505 — 7½″ vase, 1.00
M1439 — 6″ footed vase, .80
M1431 — 8½″ vase, 1.00

BOTTOM ROW, *left to right*

B1403* — 4″ violet pot with common red flower pot, .80
276 — 6″ bowl, .80
348 — May Basket vase, 7½″ x 3¼″, 1.00
2301 — compote, 4½″ x 7″, 1.25
B1404 — 5½″ planter, 1.00
* solid color outside only

Order colors by number from Color Chart on inside back cover

TOP ROW, *left to right*

M4003-8″ — candleholders, 4.00 pr.
M4003-6″ — candleholders, 3.50 pr.
M4002 — oval bowl, 18″ x 8″, 3.50
M4013 — small bowl, 7″ x 3¼″ high, 1.50
M4009 — round bowl, 12″ x 4″ high, 2.50
M4001 — bowl, 7″ x 4″ high, 2.00
M4000 — 6½″ compote-bowl, 2.25

BOTTOM ROW, *left to right*

M4012 — planter, 12″ x 7½″ high, 2.50
M4007 — 9″ vase, 2.00
M4005 — 10″ vase, 2.00
M4008 — 10″ vase, 2.50
M4004 — 10″ vase, 2.50
M4006 — 10″ vase, 2.00

SGRAFFITO

Order colors by number from Sgraffito Color Chart on inside back cover

Vases,
Bowls,
Candleholders

TOP ROW, *left to right*

M1483* — bowl, 18″ x 8″, 3.00
M1490 — bowl, 7″ x 3½″, 1.00
446 — 5 compartment nut bowl, 12½″, 1.50

BOTTOM ROW, *left to right*

M1481* — 11″ vase, 1.50
M1480* — 9″ vase, 1.25
M1482* — 12″ vase, 2.00
M1505 — console candleholders, 2″ x 4″, 1.75 pr.
M1504 — console bowl with legs, 5″ x 8″, 1.50
* solid color outside only

Order colors by number from Color Chart on inside back cover

TOP ROW, *left to right*

441 — wall planter, 7½″ x 4¼″, .80
443 — cornucopia, 10″ x 7″, 1.50
442 — cornucopia, 15″ x 9″, 2.00
531 — 10″ deer insert, 1.00
526* — bowl, 15½″ x 10¼″, 1.50

BOTTOM ROW, *left to right*

416 — 12″ gladiolus vase, 2.50
M1464 — 12¼″ chessman vase (king), 2.00
M1465 — 12¼″ chessman vase (queen), 2.00
444 — swan bowl, 9″ x 6″, 1.50
M1454-L* — wall planter-sconce, 11¼″ x 6″, 1.25
M1454-R* — wall planter-sconce, 11¼″ x 6″, 1.25
* solid color outside only

Planters,
Cornucopias,
Vases, Bowl
and Insert

Order colors by number from Color Chart on inside back cover

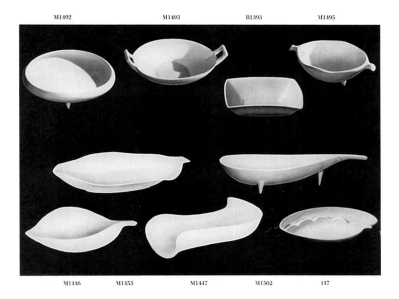

M1492   M1493   B1393   M1495

M1446   M1453   M1447   M1502   447

BOWLS

TOP ROW, *left to right*

M1492* — 10½" round bowl, 1.25

M1493* — bowl with handles, 11¼" x 6¾", 1.00

B1393* — bowl, 5½" x 9", .80

M1495* — footed bowl, 11" x 6½", 1.00

BOTTOM ROW, *left to right*

M1446* — leaf bowl, 11" x 7", 1.00

M1453* — long leaf bowl, 18¾" x 8", 2.00

M1447* — bowl, 12" x 5", 1.00

M1502 — footed leaf bowl, 3" x 6" x 16¼", 1.75

447 — ash tray, 8½" x 10½", 1.25

* solid color outside only

Order colors by number from Color Chart on inside back cover

Page 8

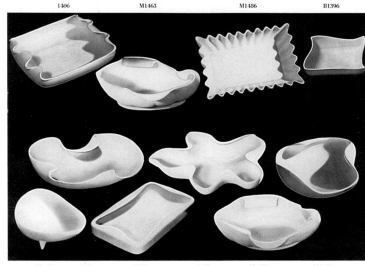

1406   M1463   M1486   B1396

M1494   1304   1348   1407   M1468   M1491

BOWLS

TOP ROW, *left to right*

1406* — bowl, 8½" x 13", 1.25

M1463* — bowl, 12½" x 6", 1.50

M1486* — bowl, 12" x 8", 1.25

B1396* — bowl, 7" x 7", 1.00

BOTTOM ROW, *left to right*

M1494* — footed bowl, 9½" x 9", 1.50

1304* — 13" bowl, 1.75

1348* — 12" oblong bowl, 1.25

1407* — leaf bowl, 10" x 13", 1.50

M1468* — bowl, 15" x 9½", 2.50

M1491* — bowl, 11½" x 11¾", 1.75

* solid color outside only

Order colors by number from Color Chart on inside back cover

Page 9

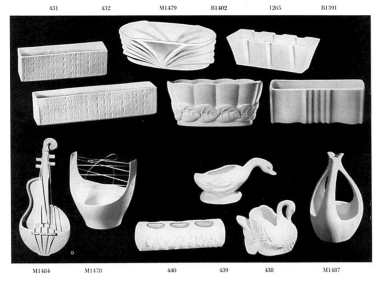

431   432   M1479   B1402   1265   B1391

M1484   M1478   440   439   438   M1487

PLANTERS, BOWLS

TOP ROW, *left to right*

431 — planter, 9½" x 2¾", 1.00

432 — planter, 13" x 2¾", 1.25

M1479 — planter, 10¼" x 4¼", 1.25

B1402 — 7" planter, .80

1265 — 10" bowl, 1.00

B1391 — 7¼" bowl, .80

BOTTOM ROW, *left to right*

M1484* — planter, 13½" x 6", 1.25

M1478* — planter, 8" x 6½", 1.00

440* — planter, 10" x 3¾", 1.25

439* — planter, 9½" x 3½", .80

438* — bowl, 6" x 3¾", .80

M1487* — 10" vase-bowl, 1.50

* solid color outside only

Order colors by number from Color Chart on inside back cover

Page 10

B2111   B1411   B2110   M1462   B1409   M1471

M4011   M4010   M1473   M1472

Candleholders, BOWLS, ASH TRAYS

TOP ROW, *left to right*

B2111* — 5" candleholders, 1.75 pr.

B1411* — candleholders, 4" x 4", 1.50 pr.

B2110* — 14½" bowl, 2.50

M1462* — bowl, 16" x 4½", 1.50

B1409* — 5" candleholders, 1.75 pr.

M1471* — 4¾" candleholders, 1.50 pr.

BOTTOM ROW, *left to right*

M4011 — Sgraffito ash tray, 13" x 5", 2.00

M4010 — Sgraffito ash tray, 12" x 5", 1.75

M1473 — bird ash tray, 9½" x 8¾", 1.50 (1.25 in doz. lots)

M1472 — horse head ash tray, 8¾" x 8½", 1.50 (1.25 in doz. lots)

* solid color outside only

Order colors by number from Color Chart on inside back cover

Page 11

JARDINIERES, CAKE PLATE

677 — 4½" jardiniere, .40
677 — 5½" jardiniere, .50
677 — 6½" jardiniere, .60
677 — 7½" jardiniere, .75

677 — 8½" jardiniere, 1.00
677 — 10½" jardiniere, 1.50
Cake Plate* — 11¼" diameter, 1.50
445 — 12½" jardiniere, 2.50
solid color outside only

Order colors by number from Color Chart on inside back cover

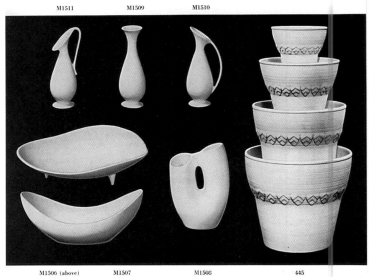

TOP ROW, *left to right*

M1511 — 7" short handled bud vase, .65
M1509 — 7" plain bud vase, .65
M1510 — 7" long handled bud vase, .65

BOTTOM ROW, *left to right*

M1506 — bowl with legs, 11"x11", 1.75
M1507 — gondola bowl, 12½"x 5" high, 1.50
M1508 — tree vase, 6½"x9" high, 1.25
445 — 6" jardiniere, .60
445 — 8" jardiniere, 1.00
445 — 10" jardiniere, 1.50
445 — 12" jardiniere, 2.50

Vases, Bowls, Jardinieres

Order colors by number from Color Chart on inside back cover of catalog

Hanging Planter, Jardiniere Stand

M1487 — 10" hanging planter with bracket and chain (plant not included), 2.00

Jardiniere Stand
3 legs, brass
(jardiniere 445 not included)
6" — 1.25
8" — 1.50
10" — 1.75
12" — 2.00

Order colors by number from Color Chart on inside back cover of catalog

Order Art Pottery Colors by Number

COLOR CHART

(for all Red Wing Art Pottery except Sgraffito)

NO.	OUTSIDE	INSIDE
105	Matt White	Matt Green
129	Fleck Zephyr Pink	Light Gray
130	Fleck Nile Blue	Colonial Buff
132	Fleck Green	Colonial Buff
133	Fleck Yellow	Light Celadon
203	Luster Black	Luster Black

SGRAFFITO COLOR CHART

(for Sgraffito Art Pottery only)

400 .... Hand painted with tan speckle overglaze
401 .... Hand painted with green speckle overglaze

We will decline to accept any goods returned to us unless the customer first secures our permission and agrees to pay the cost of packing, transportation and a 10% handling charge.
All shipments F.O.B. Red Wing, Minnesota.
No allowance for transportation, drayage or storage.
These are your net cost prices.
Package charge only on orders under $10.00.
Orders under $50.00 plus 10%.
Absolutely no allowance for breakage in transit. The carriers assume this responsibility and collection can be made from them.
All claims for shortage must be made within 5 days after receipt of merchandise.

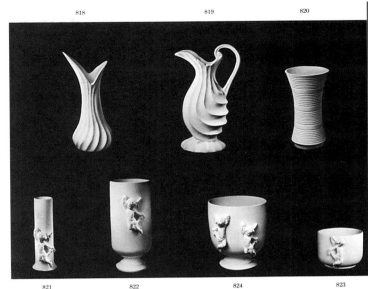

818   819   820

**19
63**

TOP ROW, left to right
818 — 12" vase, 2.75
819 — 12" handled vase, 3.25
820 — 8½" vase, 2.50

BOTTOM ROW, left to right
*821 — 8" cherub vase, 2.75
*822 — 10" footed cherub vase, 3.75
*824 — 8" footed cherub compote, 5.50
*823 — 4½" cherub planter, 2.75

821   822   824   823

NEW ITEMS FOR 1963

Available in the following colors only:
36 — Cypress Green
40 — Cocoa Brown
41 — Blue
105 — Mat White
*Available in color No. 105 only

See color chart Page 2

Page A

Cookie Jars

Drum, 5.95   Pumpkin, large, 5.95   Pumpkin, small, 5.95

Round Up, 4.50   Bob White, 4.50   Happy, 4.50

Relishes—Chip 'N Dips

800, 3.00   804, 3.50

801, 2.50   802, 3.00   803, 2.25

Page 1   Available in Lemon Yellow, Celadon, and Tahitian Gold

ARTWARE COLOR CHART
Prismatique Line
Pictured on pages 3 and 4

16 — Lemon Yellow   17 — Persian Blue
18 — Celadon (Orange Lining)   19 — Orange (White Lining)
19 — Orange (Celadon Lining)   20 — White (Orange Lining)

Regular Line
Pictured on pages A, 5, 6, 7, 8, 9, 10, 11, 12, 13, 14

36 — Cypress Green   40 — Cocoa Brown   41 — Blue   105 — Mat White
Jardinieres also available in Black

Ash Tray Line
Pictured on pages 15, 16, 17, 18

Birch Bark Line
Pictured on page 17

91 — Silver Green   92 — Burnt Orange

14 — Ice Green

Also available in Color No. 40, Cocoa Brown, pictured above.

Page 2   *Order Art Pottery Colors by Number*

Prismatique Line
designed by Belle Kogan

SMARTLY STYLED PIECES OF ART POTTERY WITH A COLOR TREATMENT THAT'S BOTH BEAUTIFUL AND UNIQUE

All pieces can be obtained in an outside color of Lemon Yellow or Persian Blue with White linings. In addition, the vases are finished in an outside color of Mandarin Orange with White lining and Celadon with Mandarin Orange lining. The colors are reversed on the bowls, planters, and compotes, i.e.: Outside color of White with Mandarin Orange lining . . . Outside color of Mandarin Orange with Celadon lining.

Vases

Left to right

795 — 8" vase, 2.50
794 — 11" vase, 3.75
799 — 14" vase, 5.00
797 — 11" vase, 3.75
798 — 8" vase, 2.50

Available in following colors only:

Color No.	Outside	Lining
16	Lemon Yellow	White
17	Persian Blue	White
18	Celadon	Mandarin Orange
19	Mandarin Orange	White

Bowls—Planters—Compotes

TOP ROW, left to right

791 — small bowl, 6½" across, 2.00
787 — compote, 6½" high, 3.50
790 — medium bowl, 8¾" across, 2.75
796 — compote, 8½" high, 5.50
789 — large bowl, 10½" across, 3.50
785 — planter, 5½" high, 2.50

BOTTOM ROW, left to right

786 — planter, 5½" high, 2.25
793 — planter, 5½" high, 2.50
788 — compote, 5½" high, 4.00
792 — bowl, 7" wide, 2.50

Available in following colors only:

Color No.	Outside	Lining
16	Lemon Yellow	White
17	Persian Blue	White
19	Mandarin Orange	Celadon
20	White	Mandarin Orange

See color chart Page 2

Prismatique Line
Vases

795   794   799   797   798

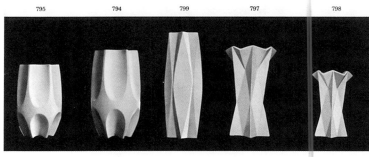

See opposite page for Color, Description and Price

Bowls—Planters—Compotes

791 (below)   787   790 (below)   796   789 (below)   785

786   793   788   792

See opposite page for Color, Description and Price

777   1625   1557   778   892

767   776   768   416 — 12"

Large Vases

TOP ROW, left to right

777 — 7" vase, 2.50
1625 — 10" vase, 2.75
1557 — bulbous vase, 10" tall, 2.50
778 — 7" vase, 2.50
892 — 7½" fan vase, 2.00

BOTTOM ROW, left to right

767 — 14" vase, 5.50
776 — 12" vase, 4.00
768 — 14" vase, 5.50
416 — 12" gladiolus vase, 5.50

Available in the following colors only:

36 — Cypress Green
40 — Cocoa Brown
41 — Blue
105 — Mat White

See color chart

1621   1510   1509   755   756   752

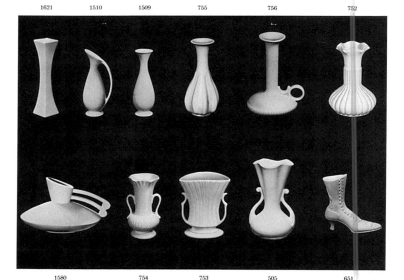

1580   754   753   505   651

TOP ROW, left to right

1621 — square bud vase, 8", 1.60
1510 — long-handled bud vase, 1.60
1509 — plain bud vase, 7" tall, 1.60
755 — 7½" bud vase, 1.80
756 — 7½" bud vase, 2.00
752 — 7½" vase, 2.25

BOTTOM ROW, left to right

1580 — pitcher vase, 5" high, 3.00
754 — 8" vase with handles, 2.25
753 — 8½" vase with handles, 2.50
505 — vase with handles, 7½" tall, 2.25
651 — shoe vase, 6" high, 2.50

Small Vases

Available in the following colors only:

36 — Cypress Green
40 — Cocoa Brown
41 — Blue
105 — Mat White

See color chart

764 762 763

815 806 807 813

TOP ROW, left to right

764 — compote, 13" across, 4.50
762 — 10½" urn vase, 4.00
763 — 8" urn vase, 3.50

BOTTOM ROW, left to right

815 — bowl, 9" square, 3.00
806 — 6" planter, 2.50
807 — 8" vase, 2.25
813 — 10" vase, 3.00

Vases
Planters

Available in the following colors only:

36 — Cypress Green
40 — Cocoa Brown
41 — Blue
105 — Mat White

Page 7

See color chart

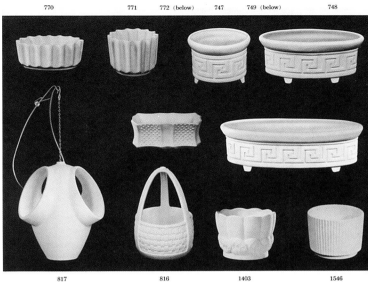

770 771 772 (below) 747 749 (below) 748

817 816 1403 1546

TOP ROW, left to right

770 — planter, 7¾" across, 2.00
771 — planter, 5" across, 1.80
772 — planter, 7¾" across, 2.25
747 — round footed planter,
    5" across, 2.00
749 — oval footed planter,
    13" across, 3.00
748 — oval footed planter,
    9" across, 2.50

BOTTOM ROW, left to right

817 — 9" hanging planter with bracket
    and chain, 5.00
816 — 8" hanging planter with bracket
    and chain, 4.50
1403 — violet pot with common
    red clay insert, 2.00
1546 — ribbed, round planter,
    5" across, 1.60

Planters

Available in the following colors only:

36 — Cypress Green
40 — Cocoa Brown
41 — Blue
105 — Mat White

See color chart

Page 8

104 108 110 112

512 510 508

TOP ROW, left to right

104 — 5½" pedestal jardiniere, 2.25
108 — 8" pedestal jardiniere, 3.50
110 — 10" pedestal jardiniere, 5.00
112 — 12" pedestal jardiniere, 7.00

BOTTOM ROW, left to right

512 — 12" jardiniere, 6.50
510 — 10" jardiniere, 5.00
508 — 8" jardiniere, 3.50

Jardinieres

Available in the following colors only:

36 — Cypress Green
40 — Cocoa Brown
41 — Blue
60 — Black
105 — Mat White

Page 9

See color chart

445 445 Low Stand 445 Tall Stand

445 — jardiniere,
    6" size, 1.60
    8" size, 2.50
    10" size, 4.00
    12" size, 5.50
brass stands, low
    6" stand, 2.00
    8" stand, 2.50
    10" stand, 3.00
    12" stand, 3.50
brass stands, tall
    10" stand, 3.00
    12" stand, 3.50

Jardinieres

Available in the following colors only:

36 — Cypress Green
40 — Cocoa Brown
41 — Blue
60 — Black
105 — Mat White

See color chart

Page 10

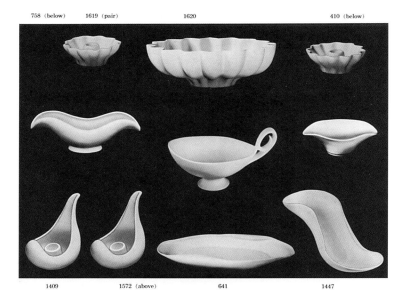

758 (below)   1619 (pair)   1620   410 (below)
1409   1572 (above)   641   1447

TOP ROW, left to right
758 — compote, 11½″ across, 2.50
1619 — scallop-edged console
candleholders, 4½″, 3.50 pair
1620 — scallop-edged console bowl,
10″, 3.00
410 — bowl, 8¾″ across, 2.00

BOTTOM ROW, left to right
1409 — candleholders, 5″ tall,
4.00 pair
1572 — novelty bowl with handle,
10″ x 7″, 3.00
641 — bowl, 7″ x 15″, 3.50
1447 — contoured bowl, 12″ x 5″, 2.75

Bowls
Candleholders

Available in the following colors only:
36 — Cypress Green
40 — Cocoa Brown
41 — Blue
105 — Mat White

Page 11   *See color chart*

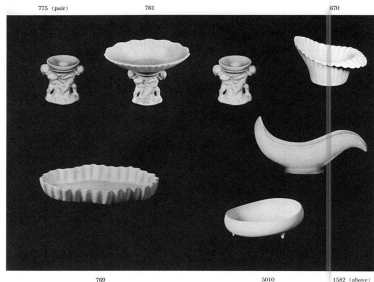

775 (pair)   761   670
769   5010   1582 (above)

TOP ROW, left to right
775 — candleholders, 4.00 pair
761 — compote, 6″ tall, 3.50
670 — bowl, 6″ wide, 2.50

BOTTOM ROW, left to right
769 — 11″ bowl, 2.50
5010 — footed bowl, 8″ across, 2.75
1582 — oval planter or bowl, 10″ x 4″, 2.75

Bowls

Available in the following colors only:
36 — Cypress Green
40 — Cocoa Brown
41 — Blue
105 — Mat White

See color chart   Page 12

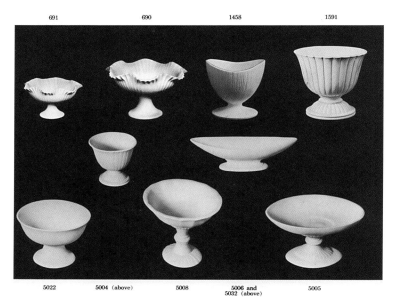

691   690   1458   1591
5022   5004 (above)   5008   5006 and
5032 (above)   5005

TOP ROW, left to right
691 — compote, 7½″ across, 3.50
690 — compote, 9″ across, 5.00
1458 — 6″ compote vase, 2.75
1591 — fluted compote, 6½″, 3.25

BOTTOM ROW, left to right
5022 — modern compote, 4½″ x 7″, 2.75
5004 — round, hour-glass compote,
4½″ tall, 2.25
5008 — round compote, 6″ tall, 3.25
5006 — contemporary low, oval compote,
11″ long, 2.25
5032 — contemporary low, oval compote,
14″ long, 3.25
5005 — graceful, tall, oval compote, 3.25

Bowls
Compotes

Available in the following colors only:
36 — Cypress Green
40 — Cocoa Brown
41 — Blue
105 — Mat White

Page 13   *See color chart*

44*   43*   47*   1574*
773   48 Bowl   46*

TOP ROW, left to right
44* — cowboy figurine, 22″, 20.00
43* — cowboy figurine, 22″, 15.00
47* — figurine, 3.00
1574* — madonna figurine, 10″ tall, 2.00

BOTTOM ROW, left to right
773 — planter, 8″ across, 2.50
48 — bowl, 12½″ across, 2.50
46* — figurine, 3.00

*Available in color No. 105 only

Bowls
Miscellaneous

Available in the following colors only:
36 — Cypress Green
40 — Cocoa Brown
41 — Blue
105 — Mat White

See color chart   Page 14

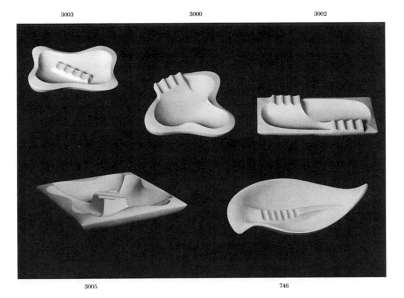

3003   3000   3002

3005   746

TOP ROW, left to right
3003 – ash tray, 9½" x 6", 3.00
3000 – ash tray, 9" x 10½", 4.00
3002 – ash tray, 5¼" x 12", 4.00

BOTTOM ROW, left to right
3005 – ash tray, 11" x 11", 5.00
746 – ash tray, 11" across, 2.00

Ash Tray Line

Available in the following colors only:
14 — Ice Green
40 — Cocoa Brown
91 — Silver Green
92 — Burnt Orange

Page 15   *See color chart*

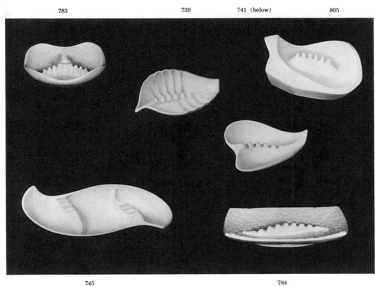

783   739   741 (below)   805

745   784

TOP ROW, left to right
783 – ash tray, 7¼" across, 2.50
739 – leaf ash tray, 7" across, 1.25
741 – ash tray, 6½" across, 1.50
805 – ash tray, 7½" across, 2.50

BOTTOM ROW, left to right
745 – ash tray, 11½" across, 2.00
784 – ash tray, 11" long, 2.50

Ash Tray Line

Available in the following colors only:
14 — Ice Green
40 — Cocoa Brown
91 — Silver Green
92 — Burnt Orange

See color chart   Page 16

781 (below) 693 774 (below)   734   735   733

782   766 (above)   780   732   731 (above)   730

Ash Tray Line   ## Birch Bark Line

TOP ROW, left to right
781 – ash tray, 8¼" across, 1.80
693 – ash tray, 9" each side, 3.00
774 – ash tray, 8½" across, 2.00

BOTTOM ROW, left to right
782 – ash tray, 7" across, 1.80
766 – ash tray, 5" across, 1.50
780 – ash tray, 7½" across, 2.00

Available in the following colors only:
14 — Ice Green
40 — Cocoa Brown
91 — Silver Green
92 — Burnt Orange

TOP ROW, left to right
734 – canoe, 10" long, 2.00
735 – canoe, 12" long, 3.00
733 – canoe, 17" long, 5.00

BOTTOM ROW, left to right
732 – vase, 7½" high, 2.00
731 – planter, 4" high, 3.00
730 – planter, 11" long, 4.00

Available in Birch Bark Finish only

Page 17   *See color chart*

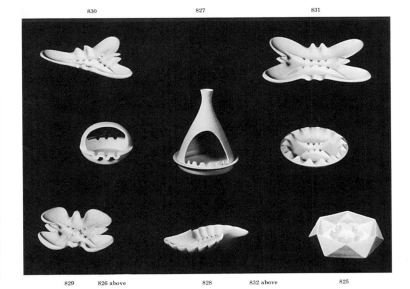

830   827   831

829   826 above   828   832 above   825

TOP ROW, left to right
830 – ash tray, 10" across, 2.00
827 – ash tray, 9½" high, 4.75
831 – ash tray, 11" across, 3.00

BOTTOM ROW, left to right
829 – ash tray, 8¼" across, 2.00
826 – ash tray, 6" across, 2.50
828 – ash tray, 9½" long, 1.80
832 – ash tray, 8" across, 2.50
825 – ash tray, 9½" across, 3.00

Available in the following colors only:
14 — Ice Green
40 — Cocoa Brown
91 — Silver Green
92 — Burnt Orange

See Color Chart

Ash Tray Line

Page 18

RED WING ART POTTERY AND GIFT CATALOG 1965

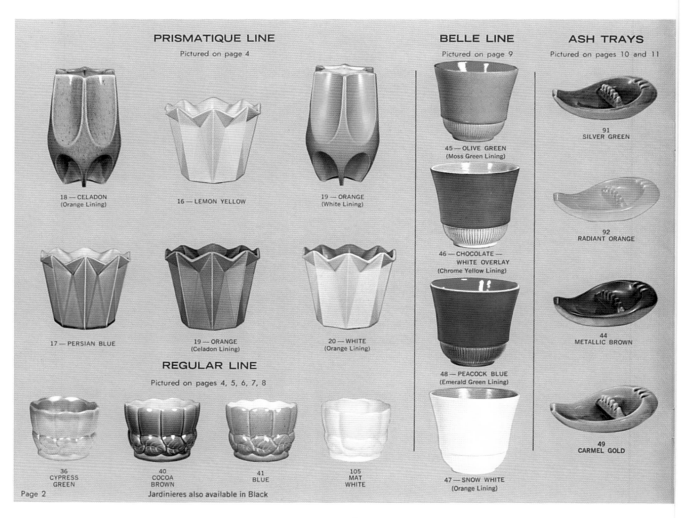

PRISMATIQUE LINE
Pictured on page 4

BELLE LINE
Pictured on page 9

ASH TRAYS
Pictured on pages 10 and 11

18 — CELADON
(Orange Lining)

16 — LEMON YELLOW

19 — ORANGE
(White Lining)

17 — PERSIAN BLUE

19 — ORANGE
(Celadon Lining)

20 — WHITE
(Orange Lining)

45 — OLIVE GREEN
(Moss Green Lining)

46 — CHOCOLATE —
WHITE OVERLAY
(Chrome Yellow Lining)

48 — PEACOCK BLUE
(Emerald Green Lining)

47 — SNOW WHITE
(Orange Lining)

91
SILVER GREEN

92
RADIANT ORANGE

44
METALLIC BROWN

49
CARMEL GOLD

REGULAR LINE
Pictured on pages 4, 5, 6, 7, 8

36
CYPRESS
GREEN

40
COCOA
BROWN

41
BLUE

105
MAT
WHITE

Page 2   Jardinieres also available in Black

BRONZE LINE

1409 — candleholders, 5" high, 5.95 pair

5006 — compote, 11" long, 2.95

911 — wine pitcher, 10" high, 6.95

819 — 12" pitcher vase, 4.95

505 — 7½" vase, 3.00

850 — round urn, 7½" high, 4.95

912 — 9" vase, 2.95

1510 — 7" bud vase, 2.25

763 — 8" urn vase, 5.25

762 — 10½" urn vase, 6.95

913 — 9" candleholder (candle not included), 4.95

818 — 12" vase, 4.25

Page 3

19 65

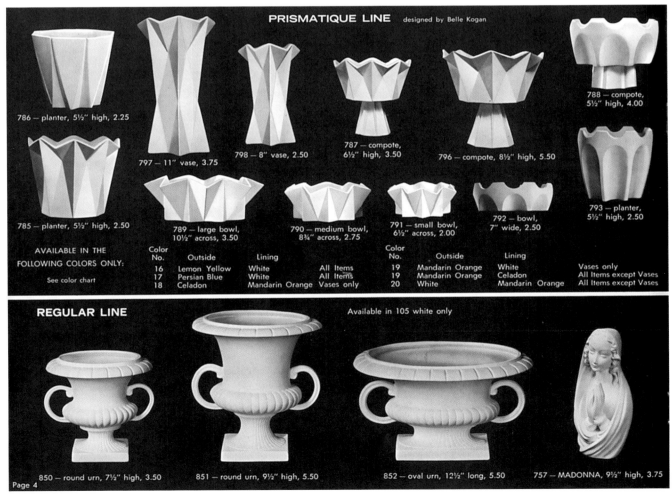

PRISMATIQUE LINE designed by Belle Kogan

786 — planter, 5½" high, 2.25

797 — 11" vase, 3.75

798 — 8" vase, 2.50

787 — compote, 6½" high, 3.50

796 — compote, 8½" high, 5.50

788 — compote, 5½" high, 4.00

785 — planter, 5½" high, 2.50

789 — large bowl, 10½" across, 3.50

790 — medium bowl, 8¾" across, 2.75

791 — small bowl, 6½" across, 2.00

792 — bowl, 7" wide, 2.50

793 — planter, 5½" high, 2.50

AVAILABLE IN THE FOLLOWING COLORS ONLY:

See color chart

Color No.	Outside	Lining	
16	Lemon Yellow	White	All Items
17	Persian Blue	White	All Items
18	Celadon	Mandarin Orange	Vases only

Color No.	Outside	Lining	
19	Mandarin Orange	White	Vases only
19	Mandarin Orange	Celadon	All Items except Vases
20	White	Mandarin Orange	All Items except Vases

REGULAR LINE   Available in 105 white only

850 — round urn, 7½" high, 3.50

851 — round urn, 9½" high, 5.50

852 — oval urn, 12½" long, 5.50

757 — MADONNA, 9½" high, 3.75

Page 4

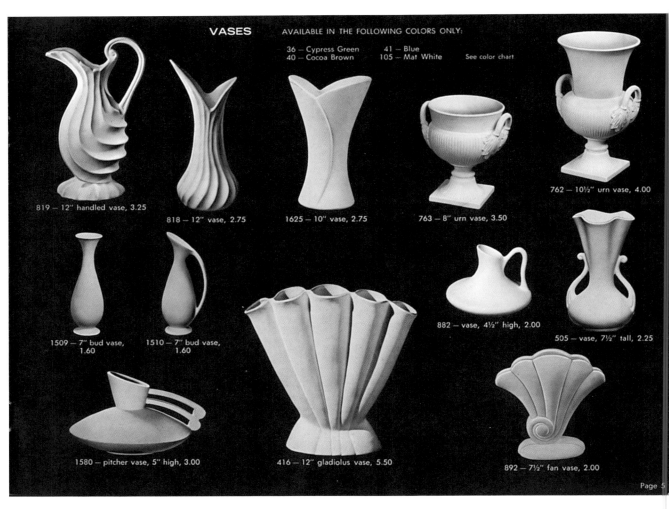

VASES AVAILABLE IN THE FOLLOWING COLORS ONLY:

36 — Cypress Green 41 — Blue
40 — Cocoa Brown 105 — Mat White See color chart.

819 — 12" handled vase, 3.25

818 — 12" vase, 2.75

1625 — 10" vase, 2.75

763 — 8" urn vase, 3.50

762 — 10½" urn vase, 4.00

1509 — 7" bud vase, 1.60

1510 — 7" bud vase, 1.60

882 — vase, 4½" high, 2.00

505 — vase, 7½" tall, 2.25

1580 — pitcher vase, 5" high, 3.00

416 — 12" gladiolus vase, 5.50

892 — 7½" fan vase, 2.00

Page 5

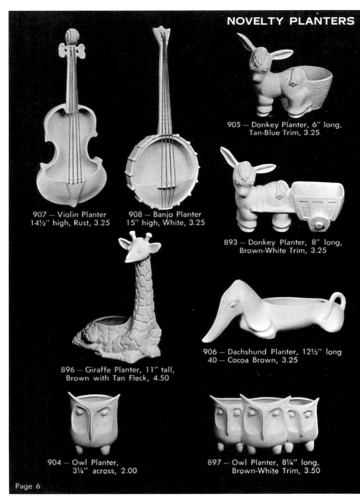

NOVELTY PLANTERS

907 — Violin Planter 14½" high, Rust, 3.25

908 — Banjo Planter 15" high, White, 3.25

905 — Donkey Planter, 6" long, Tan-Blue Trim, 3.25

893 — Donkey Planter, 8" long, Brown-White Trim, 3.25

896 — Giraffe Planter, 11" tall, Brown with Tan Fleck, 4.50

906 — Dachshund Planter, 12½" long 40 — Cocoa Brown, 3.25

904 — Owl Planter, 3¼" across, 2.00

897 — Owl Planter, 8¼" long, Brown-White Trim, 3.50

Page 6

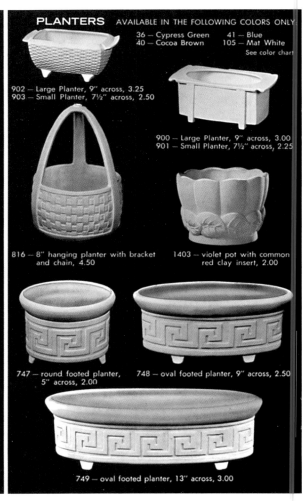

PLANTERS AVAILABLE IN THE FOLLOWING COLORS ONLY

36 — Cypress Green 41 — Blue
40 — Cocoa Brown 105 — Mat White
See color chart

902 — Large Planter, 9" across, 3.25
903 — Small Planter, 7½" across, 2.50

900 — Large Planter, 9" across, 3.00
901 — Small Planter, 7½" across, 2.25

816 — 8" hanging planter with bracket and chain, 4.50

1403 — violet pot with common red clay insert, 2.00

747 — round footed planter, 5" across, 2.00

748 — oval footed planter, 9" across, 2.50

749 — oval footed planter, 13" across, 3.00

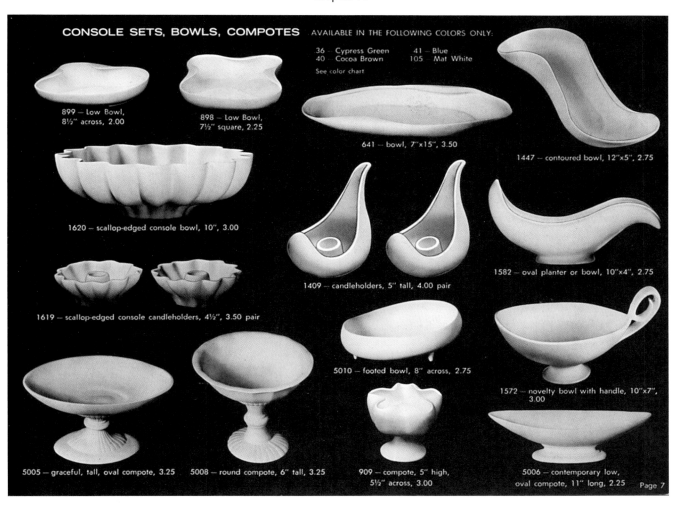

CONSOLE SETS, BOWLS, COMPOTES AVAILABLE IN THE FOLLOWING COLORS ONLY:

36 — Cypress Green   41 — Blue
40 — Cocoa Brown   105 — Mat White
See color chart

899 — Low Bowl, 8½″ across, 2.00

898 — Low Bowl, 7½″ square, 2.25

641 — bowl, 7″x15″, 3.50

1447 — contoured bowl, 12″x5″, 2.75

1620 — scallop-edged console bowl, 10″, 3.00

1409 — candleholders, 5″ tall, 4.00 pair

1582 — oval planter or bowl, 10″x4″, 2.75

1619 — scallop-edged console candleholders, 4½″, 3.50 pair

5010 — footed bowl, 8″ across, 2.75

1572 — novelty bowl with handle, 10″x7″, 3.00

5005 — graceful, tall, oval compote, 3.25

5008 — round compote, 6″ tall, 3.25

909 — compote, 5″ high, 5½″ across, 3.00

5006 — contemporary low, oval compote, 11″ long, 2.25

Page 7

JARDINIERES AVAILABLE IN THE FOLLOWING COLORS ONLY:

36 — Cypress Green   41 — Blue   105 — Mat White
40 — Cocoa Brown   60 — Black   See color chart

512 — 12″ jardiniere, 6.50
510 — 10″ jardiniere, 5.00
508 — 8″ jardiniere, 3.50

104 — 5½″ pedestal jardiniere, 2.25
108 — 8″ pedestal jardiniere, 3.50
110 — 10″ pedestal jardiniere, 5.00
112 — 12″ pedestal jardiniere, 7.00

BRASS STANDS, TALL,
445 — 10″ stand, 3.00
12″ stand, 3.50

445 — 6″ size, 1.60   8″ size, 2.50
10″ size, 4.00   12″ size, 5.50

BRASS STANDS, LOW

445 — 6″ stand, 2.00   8″ stand, 2.50
10″ stand, 3.00   12″ stand, 3.50

BELLE LINE JARDINIERES
AVAILABLE IN THE FOLLOWING COLORS ONLY:
45 — Olive Green   47 — Snow White
46 — Chocolate with White Overlay   48 — Peacock Blue
See color chart

612 — 12″ jardiniere, 7.50
610 — 10″ jardiniere, 5.50
608 — 8″ jardiniere, 4.00

Page 8

173

RedWing

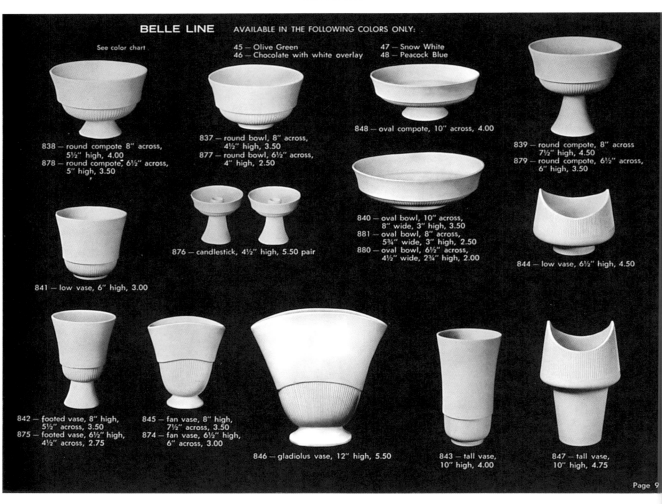

BELLE LINE AVAILABLE IN THE FOLLOWING COLORS ONLY:

See color chart

45 — Olive Green
46 — Chocolate with white overlay
47 — Snow White
48 — Peacock Blue

838 — round compote 8" across,
5½" high, 4.00
878 — round compote, 6½" across,
5" high, 3.50

837 — round bowl, 8" across,
4½" high, 3.50
877 — round bowl, 6½" across,
4" high, 2.50

848 — oval compote, 10" across, 4.00

839 — round compote, 8" across
7½" high, 4.50
879 — round compote, 6½" across,
6" high, 3.50

876 — candlestick, 4½" high, 5.50 pair

840 — oval bowl, 10" across,
8" wide, 3" high, 3.50
881 — oval bowl, 8" across,
5¾" wide, 3" high, 2.50
880 — oval bowl, 6½" across,
4½" wide, 2¾" high, 2.00

844 — low vase, 6½" high, 4.50

841 — low vase, 6" high, 3.00

842 — footed vase, 8" high,
5½" across, 3.50
875 — footed vase, 6½" high,
4½" across, 2.75

845 — fan vase, 8" high,
7½" across, 3.50
874 — fan vase, 6½" high,
6" across, 3.00

846 — gladiolus vase, 12" high, 5.50

843 — tall vase,
10" high, 4.00

847 — tall vase,
10" high, 4.75

Page 9

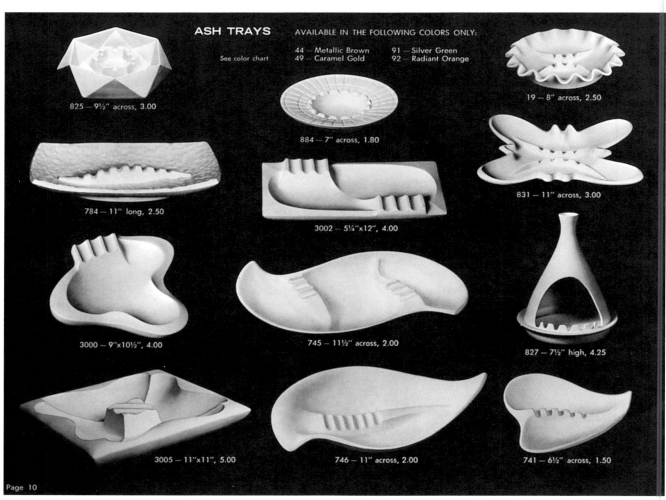

ASH TRAYS AVAILABLE IN THE FOLLOWING COLORS ONLY:

See color chart

44 — Metallic Brown
49 — Caramel Gold
91 — Silver Green
92 — Radiant Orange

825 — 9½" across, 3.00

884 — 7" across, 1.80

19 — 8" across, 2.50

784 — 11" long, 2.50

3002 — 5¼"x12", 4.00

831 — 11" across, 3.00

3000 — 9"x10½", 4.00

745 — 11½" across, 2.00

827 — 7½" high, 4.25

3005 — 11"x11", 5.00

746 — 11" across, 2.00

741 — 6½" across, 1.50

Page 10

174

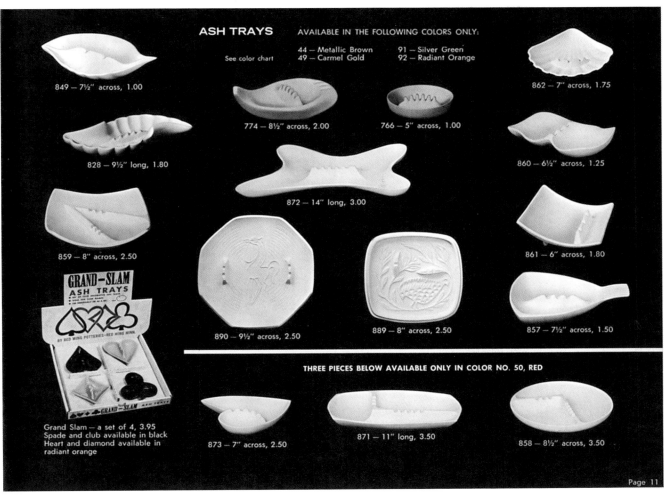

ASH TRAYS

AVAILABLE IN THE FOLLOWING COLORS ONLY:

See color chart

44 — Metallic Brown
49 — Carmel Gold
91 — Silver Green
92 — Radiant Orange

849 — 7½" across, 1.00

774 — 8½" across, 2.00

766 — 5" across, 1.00

862 — 7" across, 1.75

828 — 9½" long, 1.80

860 — 6½" across, 1.25

872 — 14" long, 3.00

859 — 8" across, 2.50

890 — 9½" across, 2.50

889 — 8" across, 2.50

861 — 6" across, 1.80

857 — 7½" across, 1.50

GRAND-SLAM ASH TRAYS

Grand Slam — a set of 4, 3.95
Spade and club available in black
Heart and diamond available in
radiant orange

THREE PIECES BELOW AVAILABLE ONLY IN COLOR NO. 50, RED

873 — 7" across, 2.50

871 — 11" long, 3.50

858 — 8½" across, 3.50

Page 11

ARTWARE SPECIALS

SPECIAL NET PRICES
No Freight Allowance on these Items

AVAILABLE AS FOLLOWS:
Packed 2 dozen to a carton.
Each carton contains one color.
Available in #43 White or #42 Green

869 — planter, 8" across, .40 net

867 — planter, 5" across, .50 net

868 — low bowl, 9" across, .50 net

836 — oblong planter, 8½" across, .50 net

835 — low bowl, 10" across, .50 net

834 — compote planter, 6" high, .70 net

833 — round planter, 4" high, .50 net

Page 12

GIFT ITEMS

No Freight Allowance on these Items

COOKIE JARS

ROUND UP, 4.50

BOB WHITE, 4.50

HAPPY, 4.50

COLONIAL DEEP-DISH PIE PLATE

Handsome in glowing brown earthenware, this 9 inch, deep-dish pie plate is a unique gift item. The original recipe for famous Hiawatha Valley Apple Custard Pie is on the label. Pie boxed. 1.50

SINGLE-TIERED PLATE
ASSORTED PATTERNS, 2.20

FONDUE CASSEROLE & WARMER STAND

This 2½ quart Fondue is a lustrous brown with Village Green interior, the warmer stand in matching brown. Genuine Swiss Fondue recipe and rules for the Fondue Fun Game are on the label. Individually boxed, with warmer stand and candle. 7.95

TWO-TIERED PLATE
ASSORTED PATTERNS, 4.00

Set of 4 Ind.
Salad Bowls
Tan Fleck
4.00 Set

SALAD SET — TAN FLECK
2.70

#446 NUT OR RELISH TRAY
TAN FLECK
2.00

175

Fig. 1. Two early cattail motif lamp bases, both unmarked (12½" and 7¾"). (Courtesy of Goodhue County Historical Society, Red Wing, Minnesota)

Fig. 2. *(Above)* All of these appear in the 1931 catalog (except the vase in the right rear). All are marked with the RED WING UNION STONEWARE COMPANY stamp except the bottom right piece, which has a RED WING ART POTTERY stamp. The shape numbers are not marked on these, but the shape numbers according to the catalog are: back row #133–10¾" and 9¾"; front row #105–4¾", #120–8½"D and #115–6"D.

Fig. 3. *(Right)* This planter was sold in many shapes. This exact shape was also made by several other potteries. Although unmarked it is listed as #108–7¼" x 8" (saucer 7¼"D).

Fig. 4. *(Below, left)* Three early planters all with a speckled effect. From the left: 5" x 7¼", hanging planter 4⅜" x 7¼" and 3⅛".

Fig. 5. Spongeware, named after the method of applying glaze colors. A variety of bowls, pitchers, and even umbrella stands were glazed in this manner. 4¼" x 7⅛" bowl marked RED WING OVEN WARE and larger bowl 5¼" x 10¼".

Fig. 6. Cattail motif vases 10" and 7½".

CHAPTER 19

$\mathscr{P}$HOTOS AND MORE PHOTOS

The photographs in this chapter have been arranged in chronological order, although we did take artistic license in some of the groupings. The measurement is always the height of the piece unless indicated with a "D," in which case the longest diameter of the piece was measured. When two measurements are given the height is first and the diameter is second. Piece descriptions are always given from left to right and front to back unless otherwise noted. In a few rare cases the catalogs list a letter after the shape number such as "S" (for small). They will be listed in the captions although they almost never appear on the pottery itself.

Fig. 7. Shape #132 was offered both glazed and unglazed in three sizes: 7", 9" and 11". The 7" vase above is in *Dark Blue*.

Fig. 8. (Above) #183–8" *Dark Blue.* **Fig. 9. (Right)** #177–8½" *Dark Blue.*

Fig. 10. (Below) #213–6¾" This glaze was named *Dark Blue* or *Blue Black*, and commonly referred to as cobalt. **(Left)** The rich blue color shows up best under direct sunlight.

Fig. 11. *(Left)* A pair of candleholders #231C–7" and #226–11" in *Dark Blue*. **Fig. 12.** *(Above)* Pair of candleholders #232C–4½" and #254–8" in *Dark Blue* unmarked.

Fig. 13. #195–9".

Fig. 14. *Nokomis* bowl #231–12"D.

Fig. 16. #50–6" pitcher.

Fig. 15. *Nokomis* #206–7¼" and #212–9½".

Fig. 17. #198–3⅝" x 7½".

Fig. 19. *(Above)* The smallest piece offered in the *Nokomis* glaze #A53–2⅜".

Fig. 18. *(Left)* Nokomis #205–7¼" and #208–10¼".
Fig. 20. *(Right)* Nokomis #204–9½" and #231C–7".

Fig. 21. *Light Green #173–6¾"* and *Mulberry #173–6⅞".*

Fig. 22. *Yellow #249–11".*

Fig. 23. *Yellow #166–8⅝"* and *#166–12".*

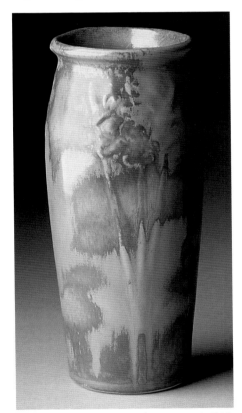

Fig. 24. (Above) *Nokomis #166–8½"* on a shape not part of the officially offered line (as with elephant figurine below). **Fig. 27. (Below)** *Nokomis* elephant *#236B–4⅛"* and *Yellow* elephant *#236A–3⅝".*

Fig. 25. *#249–11" Light Green.*

Fig. 26. (Above) *Yellow #187–7½".* **Fig. 28. (Below)** *7½" Mulberry* piece with two shape numbers on bottom: #267 and #935.

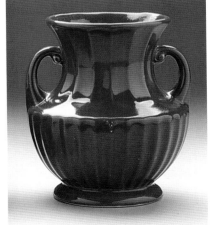

Fig. 29. *Yellow #215S–6", the smaller of the two versions offered.*

Fig. 32. *Yellow #175–4½".*

Fig. 30. *Yellow #186–12¼" and #186–9½".*

Fig. 31. *Yellow #184–6¾".*

Fig. 33. *Yellow #214–5⅝".*

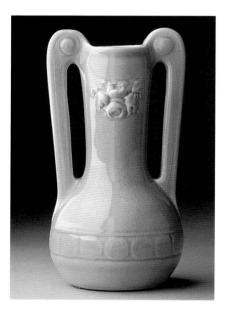

Fig. 34. *Yellow #211–10½".*

Fig. 35. *Light Green #261–7½".*

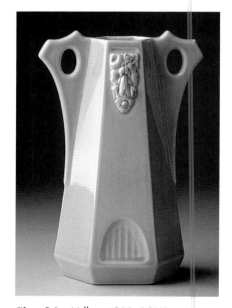

Fig. 36. *Yellow #211–10½".*

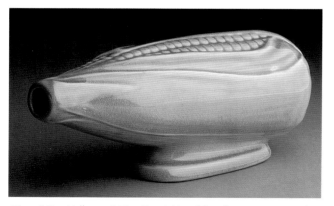

Fig. 37. *Yellow #A51–4" x 10" sold with a ceramic and cork stopper (missing from this photo).*

Fig. 38. *Yellow #256–6".*

Fig. 39. *Light Green #176–6¾" and Yellow #176–8¼".*

Fig. 40. *Light Green* window box #237S–3½" x 10" **(detail below).**

Fig. 41. **(Above and above right)** *Light Green* jewel box #238–3" x 6½".

Fig. 42. *Light Green* #223–10".

Fig. 43. *Yellow* #224–10¼".

Fig. 44. *Light Green* #174–4½", #183–8⅛" and #182–6⅞".

Fig. 45. *Light Green* #179W–8½" (the letter "W" actually on the bottom), a variation that never showed up in any catalog and on right #179–9⅞".

Fig. 46. *Light Green* #250–9".

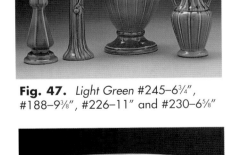

Fig. 47. *Light Green* #245–6¾", #188–9⅜", #226–11" and #230–6⅝"

Fig. 49. *Light Green* #234–6", #255–8⅛" and #189–5⅞".

Fig. 48. *Light Green* #239–11"D.

Fig. 50. *Light Green* #181S–5⅝".

Fig. 51. *Light Blue #155–9"* The floral decoration was applied over the glaze. Red Wing reportedly hired decorators at one time to hand paint pieces for its seconds shop, but owners occasionally painted on decorations themselves.

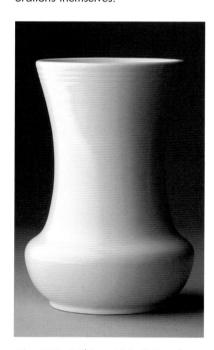

Fig. 54. White #609–9¾" with Red Wing Potteries blue star mark. Based on the sequential ordering of the shape numbers, this came out about 1936, although there are no company records of this piece. It was not sold as RumRill pottery being made at the same time.

Fig. 57. *(Right)* In the center #228 in *Dark Blue* and #230–6½" in *Mulberry, Light Green,* a pink stipple (see Fig. 5–14) and another *Mulberry.*

Fig. 52. *(Above)* *Combination Green and Mulberry #163–9¾"* and *Combination Green and Tan 9½"* The vase on the left is an example of a nice even glaze. Both are marked RED WING UNION STONEWARE CO.

Fig. 55. *(Above)* *Dark Blue #154–12⅛"* which has 12" marked in the clay body on its base. The other a rich blue that was not listed in any company literature #154–9½".

Fig. 53. *(Above)* *Dark Green #155–12⅜", Luster Gray—Luster Coral #403–12⅜", and Chartreuse—Luster Gray #403–12⅜".* Although there is a slight difference between the two, shape #155 was reintroduced in 1952 as shape #403.

Fig. 56. *(Below)* *Combination Green and White #158–9⅜", #157–15¼", #158–12⅛" and #157–9⅜".*

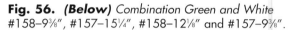

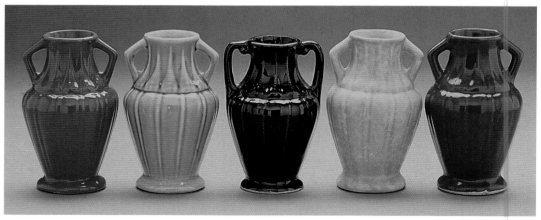

Fig. 58. #200–8⅝" in a light green color used after 1931. Marked with only a shape number, but also has a Red Wing Art Pottery sticker.

Fig. 59. *Yellow* #220–10¼" marked RED WING ART POTTERY with a blue ink stamp; *Antiqued White* #220–10⅜" and *Travertine* #220–10¼" marked RED WING U.S.A., as is the *Black* example below.

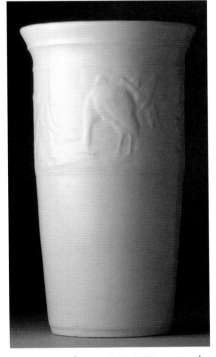

Fig. 60. White #144–10" previously a *Brushed Ware* piece. Marked only with Red Wing Potteries blue star mark.

Fig. 61. #227–10⅞" in a white glaze used after 1931. Marked RED WING ART POTTERY with a blue ink stamp.

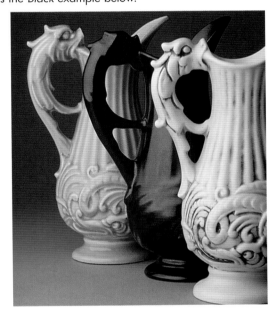

Fig. 62. *Dark Blue* #155–15⅛", #155–12⅛" and #155–9".

Fig. 63. A dark green #166–8⅝" and a pastel blue #166–12⅜".

Fig. 64. *(Above) Mermaid Green—Semi-matt Green, Brown Stippled #514–6" and #353–7⅛". Both marked* RumRill.

Fig. 65. *Suntan—Green Lined #509–3" x 5¼" and Seafoam—Ivory, Green Lined #509–3¾" x 6⅞". Both marked with only a shape number.*

Fig. 66. *Suntan—Green Lined #532–7⅜" marked* RumRill.

Fig. 67. *Suntan—Green Lined #599–8⅞" marked* RumRill.

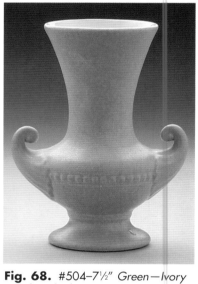

Fig. 68. *#504–7½" Green—Ivory Lined marked* RumRill.

Fig. 69. *Nile Green—Antiqued. #232–4¾" x 8¾" marked with only a shape number and #329–6⅝" marked* RumRill.

Fig. 70. *Suntan—Green Lined #510–8" and #587–7". Both marked with only a shape number.*

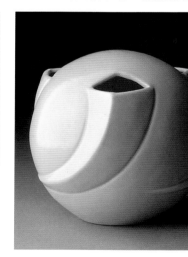

Fig. 72. *#600–6" in Suntan marked* Red Wing.

Fig. 73. *#589–4¾" Eggshell—Ivory, Semi-Matt marked* RumRill.

Fig. 71. *Suntan—Seal Brown Lined. A pair of candleholders #529–6⅛", both marked with only a shape number and a #297–5⅜" marked* RumRill.

Fig. 74. *Seafoam—Ivory, Green Lined #708—7⅝"* and *Ivory, Black Lined #501—4¾".* Both marked RUMRILL.

Fig. 75. *Ivory, Black Lined #314—5¼"* marked RUMRILL and *Riviera —Ivory, Semi-matt, Matt Blue Lined #310—4⅝",* mark unreadable.

Fig. 76. *Snowdrop–Ivory and Green #297–5¼"* marked RUMRILL.

Fig. 78. *Riviera—Ivory, Semi-matt, Matt Blue Lined #636–6"* marked RUMRILL.

Fig. 80. *Seafoam—Ivory, Green Lined #500–5¾"* marked RUMRILL.

Fig. 79. *Seafoam—Ivory, Green Lined #628–7⅝"* marked RUMRILL.

Fig. 77. A glossy black #318–5¾", a semi-gloss black #320–5¾" and *Charcoal—Matt Black #320–5⅝".* All three marked RUMRILL.

Fig. 81. *Riviera—Ivory, Semi-matt, Matt Blue Lined #311–5¼"* and *#638–5⅜".* Both marked RUMRILL.

Fig. 82. *(Above)* *Seafoam— Ivory, Green Lined #542–7⅛"* marked RUMRILL.

Fig. 83. *(Right)* *Riviera— Ivory, Semi-matt, Matt Blue Lined #311–7"* and *#638–7¾".* Both marked RUMRILL.

Fig. 84. Detail shot of #352–11" (from Fig. 87).

Fig. 85. *Turquoise* #441–5" marked RUMRILL.

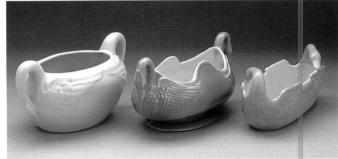

Fig. 86. *Matt Pink* #283–5⅛" marked with shape number only. *Turquoise* #441–5" and *Saffron* #440–4⅛" both marked RUMRILL.

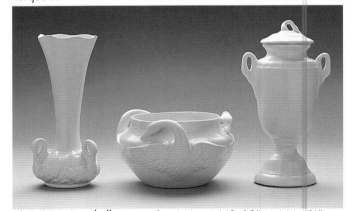

Fig. 87. *Eggshell—Ivory, Semi Matt* #442–10", #444–4¾" and #352–11". All marked RUMRILL.

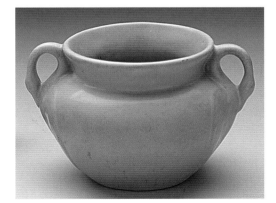

Fig. 88. #279–4½" *Apple Blossom—Green over Rose* marked with only a shape number.

Fig. 89. *Seafoam—Ivory, Green Lined* #537–5¼" marked with only a shape number, #331–10¾"D marked RUMRILL and #700–5½" marked with only a shape number.

Fig. 90. *Jade—Green Matt #312–8⅞"* and #297–5⅜". Both marked RUMRILL.

Fig. 91. *Jade—Green Matt #321–4⅞", #389–6¾" and #274–4⅜".* All three marked RUMRILL.

Fig. 92. A blend with matt green at the top with a dark blue at the bottom. #306–4½", #406–8½" and #305–6". All three marked RUMRILL.

Fig. 93. *(Above left)* #714–8¼" *Ocean Green—Green Lined.* Marked with only a shape number.

Fig. 94. *(Above right) Jade—Green Matt #348–6½".* Marked with only a shape number.

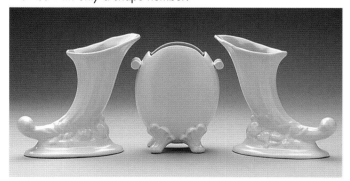

Fig. 95. A pair of cornucopias #413–7¼" and a #711–6⅞" in *Seafoam—Ivory, Green Lined.* All marked RUMRILL.

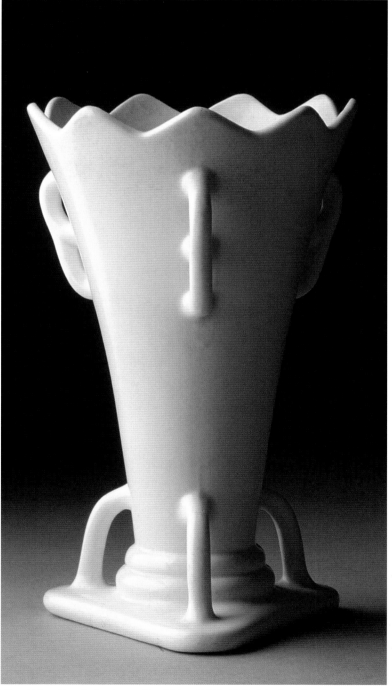

Fig. 96. *Eggshell—Ivory, Semi-Matt #691–9⅝".* Marked RUMRILL.

Fig. 97. *(Left)* In *Dutch Blue,* a pair of candleholders #357–2⅛" marked with only a shape number and a #242–4¼" marked only Red Wing.

Fig. 98. *(Right)* While this *Orange—White Lined* piece is marked "601 RumRill 8", the actual size is 7¼". The other is *Suntan—Lined in Green* #601–5⅝" marked RumRill.

Fig. 99. *Eggshell—Ivory, Semi-Matt* #601–6" and another in *Dutch Blue—Blue, White Stipple.* Both marked RumRill.

Fig. 100. *(Above)* The rare *Gypsy Trail* sticker on this *Dutch Blue—Blue, White Stipple* #897–4½" depicts the kettle-like piece on the right, #653–2½". This is the only *Gypsy Trail* sticker the author has ever seen.

Fig. 101. #369–7½" *Luster Yellow* marked with only a shape number.

Fig. 102. *(Above),* Two unusual RumRill pieces #293–5⅝" and #329–6⅝" in a cobalt although no dark blue glaze was ever listed. Both marked RumRill.

Fig. 103. *(Above)* *Dutch Blue—Blue, White Stippled* #342–9"D marked with only a shape number.

Fig. 105. *Dutch Blue* #347–7¼" marked with only a shape number and #296–8" marked RumRill.

Fig. 104. *Dutch Blue—Blue, White Stipple* #297–5⅜" and #636–6⅛". Both marked RumRill.

Fig. 106. *Dutch Blue—Blue, White Stipple #300–5" and #272–6¼" marked* RUMRILL. *#341–4½" marked with only a shape number.*

Fig. 107. (Above) *Dutch Blue—Blue, White Stipple #510–7¼" and #516–10¼" marked* RUMRILL. *#356–7" marked with only a shape number.*

Fig. 108. (Right) *Dutch Blue—Blue, White Stipple #635–7¼" marked with only a shape number.*

Fig. 109. (Below) *Dutch Blue—Blue, White Stipple #207–5½" and a "pink stipple" #207–5½". Both marked with only a shape number.*

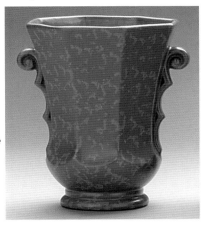

Fig. 110. *Luster Yellow #290–9¼" marked* RUMRILL *and #510–7⅞" marked with only a shape number.*

Fig. 111. *Dutch Blue—Blue, White Stipple #215S–6¼" marked with only a shape number and #302–5½" marked* RUMRILL.

Fig. 112. *Dutch Blue—Blue, White Stipple #367–5⅞". Marked with only a shape number.*

Fig. 113. *Goldenrod—Green over Orange #318–5⅞"* and *#304–4"* marked RumRill. *#351–7¼"* marked with only a shape number.

Fig. 114. This RumRill glaze is called *Red Wing—Scarlet and Bay #427–6⅝"*.

Fig. 115. *Goldenrod—Green over Orange #52–8¼"* water pitcher. The catalog shows a lid for this, although the author has never seen one.

Fig. 116. (Above) *Goldenrod—Green over Orange #361–4"* marked with only a shape number.

Fig. 117. (Left) *Red Wing—Scarlet and Bay* candleholder *#454–4⅝"* marked RumRill.

Fig. 119. In the rear *Seal Brown—Suntan #332–8½"*. In front, *Red Wing—Scarlet and Bay #332–8⅜"*, a glaze that varied over the years with the offsetting brown or yellow tones that were used with the base scarlet or orange. Both marked RumRill.

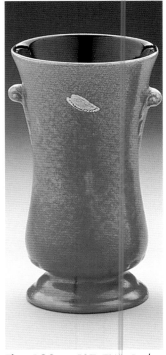

Fig. 120. *#507–7½"*, *Red Wing—Scarlet and Bay*. Marked RumRill, it has a Red Wing Art Pottery sticker.

Fig. 118. *Egg Shell—Cream Matt #594–8"* and *#306–4⅝"*. Both marked RumRill.

Fig. 121. *Egg Shell—Cream Matt #414–5⅞"* marked RumRill.

Fig. 122. *Seal Brown—Suntan Lined #562–3⅝" x 12½"* marked with only a shape number.

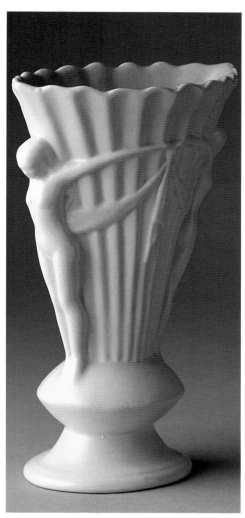

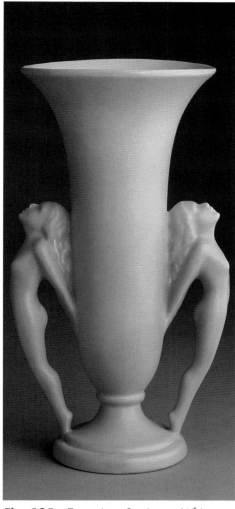

Fig. 123. From the *Athenian Group, Eggshell—Ivory, Semi-matt #564–9″* marked with only a shape number.

Fig. 124. *Suntan—Green Lined #595–9″.* The piece has a Red Wing Art Pottery sticker, but is marked RumRill.

Fig. 125. *Turquoise—Semi-matt, White Lined #568–11¼″* from the *Athenian Group,* marked RumRill.

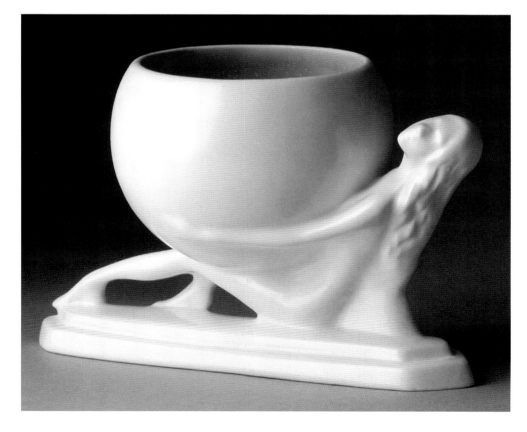

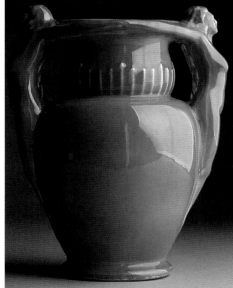

Fig. 127. *(Above)* Marked RED WING ART POTTERY, this #249–11″ Red Wing piece is assumed to be the basis for the RumRill *Athenian Group* nude series, in *Light Green.*
Fig. 126. *(Left)* From the *Athenian Group, Seafoam—Ivory, Green Lining #567–5⅜″* marked RumRill.

Fig. 128. *(Above)* #592–7⅛″ *Alpine Blue* marked RUMRILL.

Fig. 130. *(Above)* *Lilac—Green over Lavender* #320–5⅝″ marked RUMRILL. #294–5⅝″ marked with only a shape number.

Fig. 129. *(Above, center)* *Seafoam—Ivory, Green Lined* #637–7⅝″ marked RUMRILL; *Lotus— Ivory, Yellow Lined* #635–7⅛″ marked with only a shape number and *Ivory, Black Lined* #507–7½″ marked RUMRILL.

Fig. 131. *Sherwood Green—Blue Green, Semi-matt* #639–7½″ marked with only a shape number.

Fig. 132. *Horizon—Blended Blue and Tan* #276–2⅝″ marked with only a shape number.

Fig. 133. *Seafoam—Ivory, Nile Green Lined* #274–4⅜″ marked RUMRILL.

Fig. 134. *Seafoam—Ivory, Green Lined* #664–9″.

Fig. 135. *Turquoise—Semi-Matt, White Lined* #385–5½″ unmarked.

Fig. 136. *Seafoam—Ivory, Green Lined,* #1055–6½″ x 12⅛″ marked RED WING.

Fig. 137. *Seafoam—Ivory, Green Lined* #697–7½″ and #670–8⅝″. Both marked RUMRILL.

Fig. 138. Sold with a lid. #350–6″ in *London Fog* marked with only a shape number.

Fig. 139. *Ripe Wheat*—described in one trade magazine as "brown bottom, light at top." #455–8"D marked RUMRILL. #287–6"and #509–7"D both marked with only a shape number.

Fig. 140. *Ripe Wheat* #436–5⅞" x 9½", #528–7⅝" and #355–6⅛". All three marked with only a shape number.

Fig. 142. The piece on the left is *Ocean Green* **(Detail above)** and is marked #174 (listed as #174F in catalog). On the right, *Eggshell Ivory—Semi Matt* #418–12⅜"D first made in 1952, marked RED WING U.S.A.

Fig. 147. (Above) *Ripe Wheat* #448 –10", and *Luster Rachelle—Luster Cream Lined* #449– 9⅛" (sold with a lid). Both marked RUMRILL.
Fig. 148. (Left) *Shell Pink—Ivory Lined* #514– 5½" marked with only a shape number.

Fig. 143. *Marigold—Yellow Semi-Matt* #296–8¼" marked RUMRILL.

Fig. 149. *Luster Cream—Luster Rachelle Lined* #271–7½" x 15⅛" marked with only a shape number.

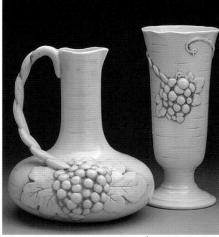

Fig. 141. #616L–11" and #620–11⅞" in *Pompeian—Brown Antiqued Ivory*, this type of glaze was used later on the *Magnolia Group*. Both marked RUMRILL.

Fig. 144. *Pompeian—Brown Antiqued Ivory* #622–5½"D candleholders and #618–12½"D marked RUMRILL.

Fig. 145. (Above) *Pompeian—Brown Antiqued Ivory* #520–4⅞" x 7¾" marked RUMRILL. **Fig. 146. (Below)** *Apple Blossom—Green over Rose* #287–6" marked RUMRILL.

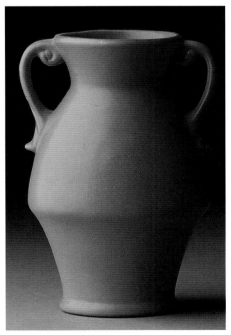

Fig. 150. Copper #859–7″, #746–7⅞″ and #855–6¼″.

Fig. 151. Copper #856–8″, #774–8¼″ and #947–6½″.

Fig. 152. Copper #276–3¼″ x 6″ and #499–5″.

Fig. 153. Copper #757–7¾″ and #803–10⅜″.

Fig. 154. Copper #771–7⅞″, #753–6″ and #737–6¾″.

Fig. 156. Copper—Cream Lined #763–7¾″ and #748–7½″.

Fig. 155. Copper #944–2⅞″ x 7¼″ and #808–11½″.

Fig. 157. Copper—Cream Lined #929–10″ and #925–7½″.

Fig. 158. Copper #765–7⅝″.

Fig. 159. Copper—Cream Lined #773–7¼″.

Fig. 160. (Above) *Adobe—Apricot Lined #958–5" x 11¾"* from the *Terra-Craft* line.

Fig. 161. (Right) *Green Luster, Cream Ivory Lined #967–4⅞" and #957–8⅝"* also from the *Terra-Craft* line.

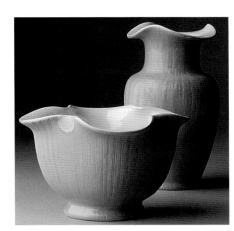

Fig. 162. (Right) *Terra Cotta—Luster Cream Ivory #1003–9⅛" and #961–12⅛"* from the *Terra-Craft* line.

Fig. 163. *Eggshell-Ivory, Semi Matt #856–7⅜".*

Fig. 164. *Eggshell Ivory—Semi Matt #951–6¼".*

Fig. 165. *Lotus—Ivory, Yellow Lined #762–7⅝".*

Fig. 166. *Green—Luster Green Lined #965–8¼" and Adobe—Apricot Lined #963–10⅜".*

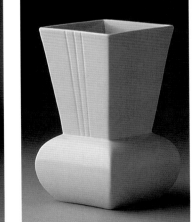

Fig. 167. *Lotus—Ivory, Yellow Lined #722–7½".*

Fig. 168. *Copper—Cream Lined #764–8½".*

Fig. 169. (Right) *Seafoam—Ivory, Green Lined* pair of bookend planters *#760–7"* and a *#775–7½".*

Fig. 170. These are both marked #1033. Notice the subtle difference between the bases of these 6" pieces. Left, *Ocean Green* (1940-41) and *Luster Green* (1942).

Fig. 171. *(Above)* Duck #1034–8"D *Ocean Green* and pelican #1035–7" *Matt Lily Green.*

Fig. 172. *(Above, center)* Wren #1036–6" *Matt Green*, owl #650–9" *Cypress Green* (made only in 1959) and duck #914–7"D in *Luster Green.* A 4½" version (#972) of this duck was also made.

Fig. 174. *(Left)* Snail #920-7" in *Luster Mazarin Blue.*

Fig. 173. *(Far Left)* Eagle #1163–9" in *Matt Lily Green.*

Fig. 175. *(Left)* Llama #916–5½"D *Luster Green* unmarked, turtle #1006–6"D *Luster Yellow* and teddy bear #989-4½"D *Luster Ivory* also unmarked.

Fig. 176. Frog #992–5"D, pig #990–4"D and rabbit #988–4½"D, all in *Luster Green.*

Fig. 177. #1133-5" *Luster Pink* candle-holder (also sold with handpainted under-glaze) and #1141–5" *Matt White.*

Fig. 178. Pair of geese #910–6" *Luster Ivory* and #918–3½" *Luster Pink.*

Fig. 179. This #941–6½" *Luster Green* seal is similar to a #330 depicted in a RumRill catalog balancing a bowl. Fish #386–7"D *Luster Ivory* (also offered earlier in a RumRill catalog) and deer #911–6½"D *Luster Green.*

Fig. 180. #1061–4½" in *Matt Yellow*, #1060–3" *Luster Pink* and #1059–2¾" *Matt Yellow.*

Fig. 181. *(Above)* #909–4½"D *Rachelle.*

Fig. 182. *(Right)*
Luster Rachelle shell #987–5½"D, *Matt Green* shell #986–6½"D and cornucopia #736–7½"D *Luster Cream—Luster Rachelle Lined.* This cornucopia was offered in three sizes: 6½", 7½" and 10½".

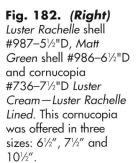

Fig. 183. *(Right)* #899–4½" a mat maroon, #907–4" *Matt Lily Green,* #872–4¾" a glossy brown and #873–4½" *Yellow—Semi-Matt.*

Fig. 184. *Luster Blue* #766–6¾" and *Blue—Semi-Matt* #908–3½".

Fig. 185. *Suntan* #653–2½", *Light Green* #323–4⅛", a dark green #325–4" and *Apricot* #327–3". All marked with only a shape number.

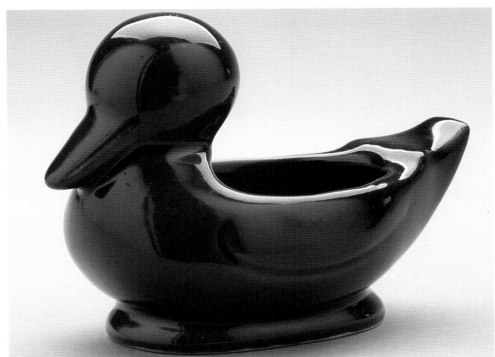

Fig. 186. #972–4½"D *Luster Mazarin Blue.*

Fig. 187. *Eggshell Ivory—Semi Matt* #946–6" and *Ocean Green—Semi Matt-Green Lined* #950–6".

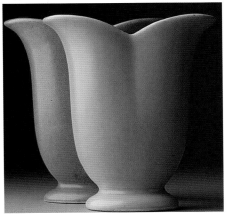

Fig. 188. Front, *Matt Lily Green* #999–6" and rear *Rattan.*

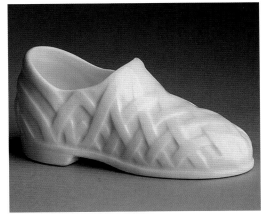

Fig. 189. *Mexican shoe* #991–2¼" x 5½" in *Matt Ivory.*

Fig. 190. *(Left)* *Dutch Blue—Blue, White Stippled* #860–7" and #776 –8", both marked RED WING. This glaze was used up through 1940.

Fig. 191. *(Right)* #1000–8" This polka-dot variation of *Dutch Blue* has been found in a few pieces. Two more examples are in Fig. 192.

Fig. 192. *(Left)* #943–2¾" x 5⅞" and #827–5" x 11".

Fig. 193. *(Below)* *Seafoam—Ivory, Green Lined* #870–3⅞" x 8".

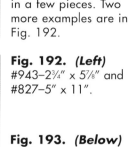

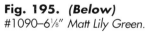

Fig. 194. *Dutch Blue* #841–8½".

Fig. 195. *(Below)* #1090–6⅛" Matt Lily Green.

Fig. 197. *(Right)* Matt Turquoise, Eggshell Ivory Lined #537–5⅛" x 11⅝".

Fig. 198. *(Bottom right)* Crocus—Green Gray Outside, Pink Lined #537–5⅛" x 11⅝".

Fig. 196. *(Below)* Eggshell Ivory—Semi Matt #950–6", #504–7½" and #948–6".

Fig. 199. In *Luster Yellow*, a pair of vase bookends #718–5½" and #369–7½".

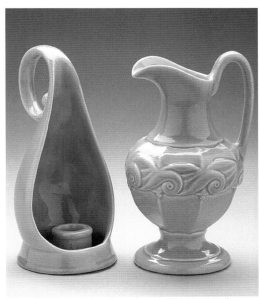

Fig. 200. *Luster Tan—Luster Green Lined* #981–8½" and #1081–8⅜".

Fig. 201. *Luster Cream—Luster Rachelle Lined* #888–7¼" and #883–10".

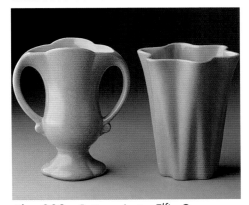

Fig. 202. *Rattan—Luster Elfin Green Lined* #1054–8" and #887–7⅜". This glaze was offered only in 1942.

Fig. 203. #814–10½" *Ocean Green.*

Fig. 204. *(Above)* #1114– 7¼" *Luster Tan—Luster Green Lined.* **Fig. 205.** *(Below)* Two green vases from the Belle Kogan 100. The #755-7⅜" on the left has a darker, mottled quality. The larger vase is a #785–10⅜".

Fig. 206. *Copper* #861–7¼", a mottled green #864–7⅞" and *Matt Yellow* #861–7¼".

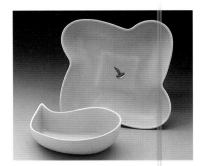

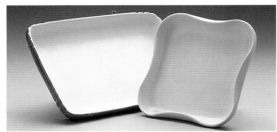

Fig. 210. (Above) *Autumn Glory—Eggshell Ivory Lined* #1040–12¼" and *Peach Glow—Eggshell Ivory Lined* #1037F–8" **(Detail below)**.

Fig. 207. (Top left) Two bowls in *Matt Ivory—Luster Green Lined* #1164-9½"D and #1037–8"D. This shape was listed in the catalog as #1037P. Also listed was a #1037F (Fig. 210), identical except for the fluted edge.

Fig. 208. (Top center) *Eggshell Ivory— Luster Elfin Green* #1251–13¾".

Fig. 209. (Top right) From the 1950s: *Matt White— Matt Green* #B1421–8⅜" and in rear #B1405–9".

Fig. 211. (Right) #1360–7½" *Eggshell Ivory* with an underglaze decoration.

Fig. 212. (Left) *Luster Gray—Yellow Lined* with underglaze decoration, #1120D–7⅛".

Fig. 213. (Below left) *Luster Tan— Green Lined* underglaze decorated #1102D–8", #1162D–9" and #1103D–8¼".

Fig. 214. (Bottom right) Three hand painted *Magnolia Group* pieces, one in the middle signed ALS (possibly a handpainter's signature, or from the Wednesday night art class). #1028–6", #1023–10½" and #1014–12½"D.

Fig. 215. *(Above left)* #1121 and #1122: a pair of school children, front and back view, all 8¾".

Fig. 216. *(Above center)* #1145–11½" *Bronze Tan Engobe with Turquoise Decoration* and #1143–10" *Gray Engobe with Solid Turquoise.*

Fig. 217. *(Above right)* *Luster Gray* #1044–8⅜" and *Eggshell Ivory—Semi-Matt* #1045–8¾".

Fig. 218. *(Left)* *Gray Engobe with Solid* Turquoise #1175–10½".

Fig. 219. *(Above Left)* #1043–8½" *Ocean Green.*

Fig. 220. *(Above)* #463–10½" *Luster Rose—Grey Lined.*

Fig. 221. *(Left)* Three plates designed by Charles Murphy, and offered for only a short time around 1942: #1128 A, C and B, offered in both a tan and blue background 14¼".

Fig. 222. *(Below)* *Bronze— Tan Engobe with Turquoise Decoration* #1142–11".

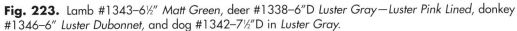

Fig. 223. Lamb #1343–6½" *Matt Green,* deer #1338–6"D *Luster Gray—Luster Pink Lined,* donkey #1346–6" *Luster Dubonnet,* and dog #1342–7½"D in *Luster Gray.*

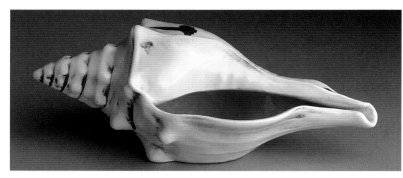

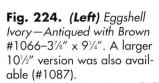

Fig. 224. (Left) Eggshell Ivory—Antiqued with Brown #1066–3⅞" x 9¼". A larger 10½" version was also available (#1087).

Fig. 225. (Right) Eggshell Ivory—Antiqued with Brown cornucopia #1098–8⅜".

Fig. 226. (Below center) This deer console was sold from 1936–1950 (and was on the front cover of both the RumRill and Red Wing 1938 catalogs). It was reintroduced briefly in 1955. In Eggshell Ivory—Antiqued with Brown; bowl #526–2⅛" x 16" and deer #531–9⅞".

Fig. 227. (Right) Three deer inserts from front: Eggshell Ivory—Antiqued with Brown, Fleck Green, and Eggshell Ivory—antiqued with a black.

Fig. 228. (Right below) Three glazed deer console bowls from top to bottom: Eggshell Ivory—antiqued with a black, Luster Burnt Orange, and Fleck Green.

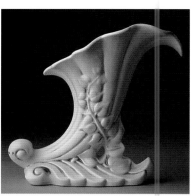

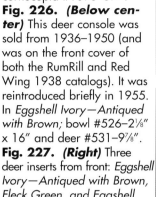

Fig. 229. (Above) Magnolia Group #1228–4⅝", Eggshell Ivory—Antiqued with Brown #397–5½" and Magnolia Group #1314–4⅝".

Fig. 230. (Below left) Magnolia Group #1321–14⅛".

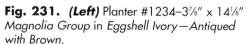

Fig. 231. (Left) Planter #1234–3⅞" x 14⅛" Magnolia Group in Eggshell Ivory—Antiqued with Brown.

Fig. 233. (Below left) Magnolia Group in Eggshell Ivory—Antiqued with Brown; large bowl #1313–13½"D and candle holders #1314–4⅝".

Fig. 234. (Below center) #1229–4⅛"D ashtray, #1233–2½" x 4⅞" box (with lid) and #1019–4¾"D all part of the Magnolia Group.

Fig. 235. (Right, below) #1323–2½" x 14½" Magnolia Group in Eggshell Ivory—Antiqued with Brown.

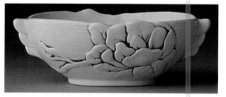

Fig. 232. #1017–2¾" x 8" Magnolia Group.

Fig. 236. *(Above)* Magnolia Group, #1320–7″ and #1322–4″.

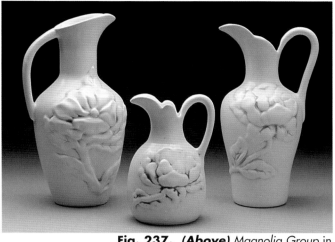

Fig. 237. *(Above)* Magnolia Group in Eggshell Ivory—Antiqued with Brown. #1220–11¼″, #1012–7″ and #1020–10½″.

Fig. 238. *(Below)* Part of the Magnolia Group glazed with the more scarce Ivory Antiqued with Green #1022–9¾″ (sold with a lid) and #1010–8⅜″.

Fig. 239. *(Below)* Magnolia Group #1216–8″ and #1216–10⅛″.

Fig. 240. *(Below)* #1218–9″ Magnolia Group in Eggshell Ivory—Antiqued with Brown.

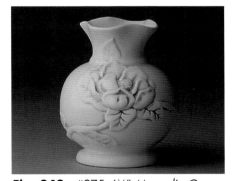

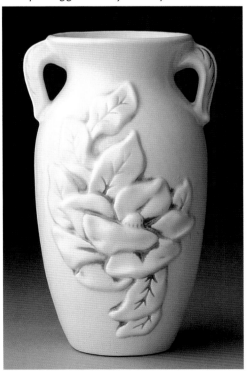

Fig. 241. Luster Yellow Green #1010–8¼″, a scarce Magnolia Group glaze.

Fig. 242. #975–6⅛″ Magnolia Group in Eggshell Ivory—Antiqued with Brown.

Fig. 243. *(Left)* Magnolia Group in Eggshell Ivory—Antiqued with Brown #1030–10″.
Fig. 244. *(Right)* Magnolia Group in Eggshell Ivory—Antiqued with Brown #1215–8″ (also made in 10″) and #1317–10½″.

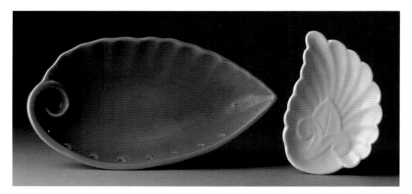

Fig. 245. *(Above left)* Matt Blue #1070–12⅛"D and *Peach Glow* #850–7" ashtray.
Fig. 246. *(Above right)* Luster Columbia Blue—Luster Coral Pink Lined #1242–5" and #1172–8½".
Fig. 247. *(Left)* Salmon—White Lined #1246–12"D.
Fig. 248. *(Right)* Salmon—White Lined #1242–5⅛" and #410–8⅛".

Fig. 249. *(Above)* These groupings show the variety of glazes Red Wing could use on a single piece, including "lunch hour" pieces (such as the personalized boy above). Top row #1344 boy, and #1345 girl and a series of swans with a little chick #1337–5". The bottom row is #259–6", produced from around 1932 until 1946. A renumbered version, #444, was offered only during 1956.

Fig. 250. *(Left)* Chartreuse—Travertine Lined #1255–4½" x 14½".
Fig. 251. *(Below left)* Chartreuse—Luster Gray Lined #1353–7¾" and #1357–7¾"
Fig. 252. *(Below middle)* Two #1279–8" in Chartreuse—Luster Burgundy Lined and Como Blue—Yellow Lined, and a #1278–4" Matt White—Matt Green Lined.
Fig. 253. *(Below right)* Chartreuse—Luster Burgundy Lined #1105–8" and #1362–7⅝".

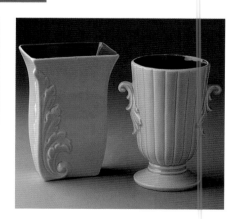

Fig. 254. *(Left)* Pair of #1056–8" in *Matt Ivory—Luster Green Lined* (sold with lid), and in the center #1051–8" *Matt Lily Green—Eggshell Ivory Lined.*

Fig. 255. *(Right)* *Ocean Green—Semi-Matt-Green Lined* #952–6", *Matt Lily Green—Ivory Lined* #1111–7½" and *Ocean Green—Semi-Matt-Green Lined* #947–6½".

Fig. 256. *Matt Lily Green— Eggshell Ivory Lined* #1160–9".

Fig. 257. *Como Blue—Yellow Lined* #1362–7⅝" and #1347–2⅛" x 11⅞".

Fig. 258. *Matt Lily Green— Eggshell Ivory Lined* #1167–8⅛".

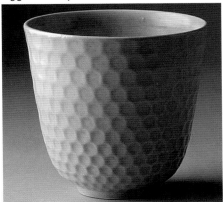

Fig. 259. *(Left)* #1287–5¼" in *Matt Green.* Smallest of three sizes with a lip inside designed to hold a flower pot , in this case a 4" pot.

Fig. 260. Two #1096 vases. *Eggshell Ivory Antiqued with Brown* 9" and *Luster Chartreuse—Eggshell Ivory Lined* 8¾".

Fig. 261. #1302–4⅜" *Como Blue—Yellow Lined.*

Fig. 262. *(Far left)* *Matt Lily Green—Eggshell Ivory Lined* #693–4¾" x 9⅝", marked only with a shape number on bottom.

Fig. 263. *(Far left below)* *Eggshell Ivory Antiqued with Brown.* #1188–5¼", on left, was part of a series made briefly around 1943. #1165–8½", on right, came out in July 1942 and was made until 1949.

Fig. 264. *(Below)* *Eggshell Ivory Antiqued with Brown* #1186–7" and #1183–6".

Fig. 265. First produced in 1938, *Ocean Green—Green Lined* #756–7½.

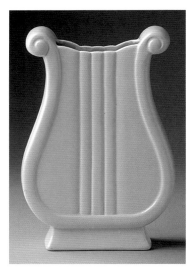

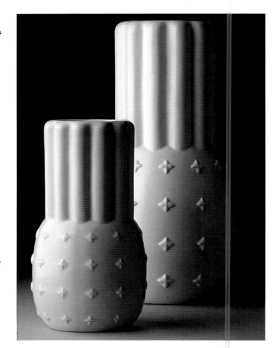

Fig. 266. (Far left) Matt Ivory—Luster Green Lined #724–6".

Fig. 267. (Left) Matt Ivory—Luster Green Lined #1049–8¼".

Fig. 268. (Right) #1197–9⅛" Peach Glow—Eggshell Ivory Lined and #1200–14", Eggshell Ivory—Luster Elfin Green Lined.

Fig. 270. (Right) Eggshell Ivory—Semi Matt #1169–7".

Fig. 269. (Left) Matt Turquoise—Eggshell Ivory Lined. In front; #1174–7" and #1095–6½". In rear; #1157–8¾", #1155–10" and #1100–8½".

Fig. 272. Eggshell Ivory—Luster Elfin Green Lined #1172–8½" and #820–8½" in Mat White from 1963.

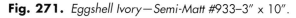

Fig. 271. Eggshell Ivory—Semi-Matt #933–3" x 10".

Fig. 273. (Left) Matt White—Matt Green Lined #1105–8" and Matt White #1112–7⅛".

Fig. 274. (Right) #721–6¾" Eggshell—Ivory, Semi Matt glaze from around 1938 and #770–7⅞" Matt Ivory—Luster Green Lined glaze introduced in 1939.

Fig. 275. *(Above left)* One of the crackle glazes made in 1947 to 1949, *Crackled Turquoise—Bronze Lined* #1307–9½".

Fig. 276. *(Above right)* *Crackled Turquoise* #1300–10".

Fig. 277. (Right) *Matt Green* #1309–9" and #1310–8¾" in *Luster Columbia Blue.*

Fig. 278. (Left) *Coronation Purple— Eggshell Ivory Lined* #1156–9½".

Fig. 279. *Coronation Purple—Eggshell Ivory Lined* #693–4⅞" x 9½".

Fig. 280. A group of *Crackled Turquoise—Bronze Lined* pieces. From left rear: #1310–9", #1369–7¼" and #1304–13"D low bowl. In front, ashtray #1374–9⅛"D and #1301–4¾".

Fig. 281. Two from the *Tropicana* line in *Dubonnet—Luster Gray Lined* #B2006–12¼″ and #B2003–10″.

Fig. 282. *Luster Burgundy—Luster Gray Lined* #B1404–5½″ square planter and #1381–7″ *Luster Dubonnet—Luster White Lined,* the centerpiece of a five-part set.

Fig. 283. *Tropicana* #B2016–4″ in *Dubonnet—Luster Gray Lined* and a #B1398–7½″ in *Luster Burgundy—Luster Gray Lined.* These similar glazes were offered simultaneously, with the *Dubonnet* sold only on the *Tropicana* line (1950–1952).

Fig. 284. *(Above left)* Bright Dubonnet, #1308–9¼″ one of four figurines offered in 1947. Fig. 285. *(Above) and* Fig. 286. *(Right)* Roosters #M1438–9½″ in *Luster Burgundy—Gray Lined* and *Fleck Zephyr Pink.*

Fig. 288. *(Above)* Luster Burgundy #B2015–4⅜″ x 12″.
Fig. 289. *(Below)* Two candleholders from the *Magnolia Group:* #1228–4¾″ *Eggshell Ivory—Antiqued with Brown* and *Luster Ox Blood.*

Fig. 287. *(Above)* #M1438–13″ *Matt White—Matt Green Lined,* larger version of the two sizes offered.
Fig. 290. *(Below)* Luster Burgundy—Luster Gray Lined #B1395–7¾″, #1054–8″ and #1117–7¾″.

Fig. 291. (Above) *Crackled White—Bronze Footed and Lined.* Bowl #1333–5⅛" x 7¾" and a pair of candleholders marked #1334–6". **Fig. 292. (Right)** *Crackled White* #1364–12¼" deer figurine.

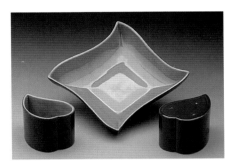

Fig. 293. *Crackled White—Bronze Footed and Lined* square vase #1368–6⅜" and candleholders #1334–5¼". Notice the difference in size from the candleholders in Fig. 291, also marked #1334.

Fig. 294. (Right) *Gypsy Brown—Yellow Ochre Lined* bowl #B1396–10¾"D and candleholders #B1412A–2¾". This glaze was offered for only one year.

Fig. 295. (Right) *Copper Lined with Champagne* #1356–7½".

Fig. 297. (Below) *Chartreuse and Luster Gray* combinations: #278–8⅜"D and #276–6"D.

Fig. 296. *Eggshell Ivory—Luster Elfin Green Lined* #1151–8".

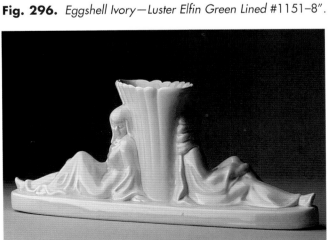

Fig. 298. "The Nymphs" in *Chartreuse* #B2500–6⅝" x 16½".

Fig. 299. *Chartreuse—Luster Gray Lined* bowl #1393–9⅛"D and *Chartreuse* candleholder #1266–5"D.

Fig. 300. (Below) *Copper—Light Green Lined* #404–12⅜" and #429–2⅞" x 9½".

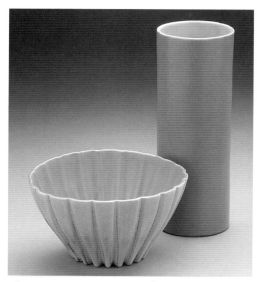

Fig. 301. #1587–10″ *Salmon—Colonial Buff Lined* vase with the opposite colors on the bowl #M1477–6″D.

Fig. 302. *Colonial Buff—Salmon Lined* #M1442–8½″, #M1460–9¼″ and #M1497–9⅞″.

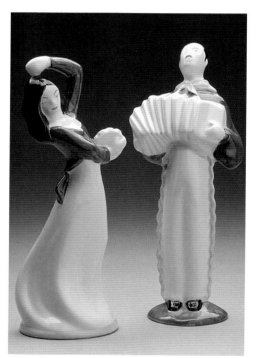

Fig. 303. *(Above)* Matt White cowboy #B1415–10¾″ and a cowgirl #B1414–10¾″ in a reddish-brown.

Fig. 306. *(Below left)* Luster Cream #995–3⅛″ x 8¾″.

Fig. 307. *(Below center)* Part of a series of hand painted designs from dinnerware lines. These two 10″ vases in the *Lotus* pattern were also available in the dinnerware patterns *Blossom Time* and *Magnolia*: #H503–10½″ and #H504–10″.

Fig. 304. Dancer #B1416–10¼″ and accordionist #B1417–10¼″, both marked HANDPAINTED with a red ink stamp.

Fig. 305. Two hand painted figurines in unusual colors, #1308–10″ and #B1398–10″ marked HANDPAINTED in a red ink stamp.

Fig. 308. *(Below)* #H508–4½″ Matt White—Matt Green Lined. This shape was usually used for the *Handpainted* (with dinnerware patterns) Series.

Fig. 309. *(Left)* Matt White—Matt Green Lined #435–8".

Fig. 310. *(Right)* Matt White—Matt Green #B1430–8⅛".

Fig. 311. *(Far right)* Matt White—Matt Green #401–7¾" and #B2000–8" with Bird of Paradise design.

Fig. 312. *Matt Ivory—Luster Green #1107–7", #1379–11⅛" and #1106–7⅞".*

Fig. 313. *(Right)* From 1960, Mat White #690–6⅛".

Fig. 314. *(Below)* Matt White—Matt Green #412–9⅜", #M1500–8⅜" and #1555–9¾" all introduced in the 1950s.

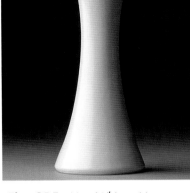

Fig. 315. *Matt White—Matt Green Lined #434–8¼".*

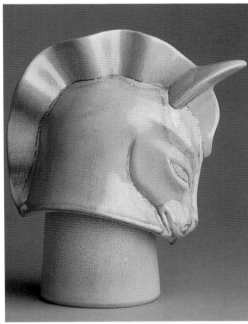

Fig. 316. This piece was sold as a cigarette box with cover #M1474–7" in *Colonial Buff.*

Fig. 317. *(Below)* Matt White—Matt Green Lined #M1458–6", #M5005–4⅞" and #5022–4½". The piece on the right was listed in the 1956 catalog as #2301, one of only two #2300 shape numbers used for something other than one of the special anniversary glazes. It reappeared as #5022 in 1957 as part of the *Garden Club Pottery* line.

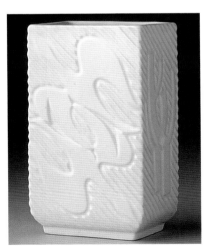

Fig. 318. *Matt White—Matt Green Lined #M1456–7⅝",* a Murphy design with bird motif.

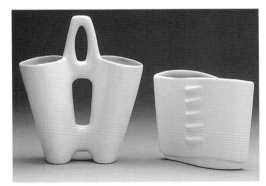

Fig. 319. *Matt White—Matt green Lined #B1428–8¼" and #B1400–5". The #B1428 shape was used a lot by hobby shops.*

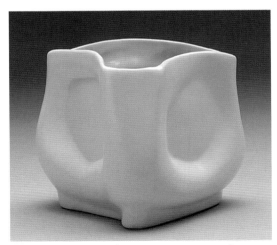

Fig. 320. *Matt White—Matt Green Lined #M1488–4¾",* a three-sided piece; any two sides form the appearance of an owl's face.

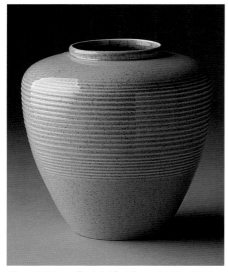

Fig. 321. *Fleck Nile Blue #1583–7¼".*

Fig. 322. *Fleck Zephyr Pink—Light Gray Lined #M1512–4", Fleck Green—Colonial Buff Lined #M1476–7½" and Fleck Nile Blue #M1477–4".*

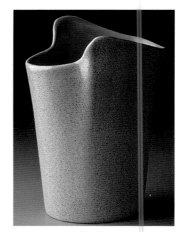

Fig. 323. *Fleck Zephyr Pink— Light Gray Lined #B1425–8".*

Fig. 324. (Above) Two ring bowls in *Fleck Zephyr Pink,* left #448–1¾" x 8⅝" and right #M1523–2" x 7", both made for less than two years. In between them is a *Fleck Nile Blue* #M1605–5".

Fig. 325. (Below) Shoe in *Fleck Zephyr Pink* #651–6¼". A larger 9" version of the shoe was also made. Cornucopia in *Fleck Nile Blue* #1562–5¾" and a *Fleck Zephyr Pink* bowl #M1463–4".

Fig. 326. *Fleck Green— Colonial Buff Lined #M1449– 10½" and #437–7½".*

Fig. 328. (Above) *Fleck Yellow #M1509–7⅛", Fleck Zephyr Pink #1554–11⅞" and Fleck Nile Blue #M1510–7".*
Fig. 329. (Left middle) *Fleck Zephyr Pink* bowl #B1406–2⅜" x 9½".
Fig. 330. (Below left) Large bowl in *Fleck Zephyr Pink* #5020–2⅜" x 12½"; smaller bowls stacked #5019–2¼" x 9⅝".

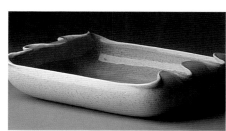

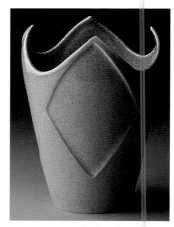

Fig. 327. *Fleck Nile Blue #1613–7¾".*

Fig. 331. (Left) *Fleck Yellow* compotes: #M1601–7⅝", in front bird bath compote #1548–4" and #M5008–6¼".

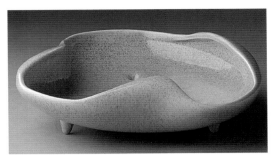

Fig. 335. A series of *Fleck Zephyr Pink.* Center piece #M1477–4" has a *Travertine* lining. Left rear #M5014–2½" x 10⅝", front, #M1502–3½" x 16¼" and right rear #1582–5⅜".

Fig. 332. (Above left) *Fleck Yellow* series. Pair of #M1505–1⅞" console candleholders and a #416–9".

Fig. 333. (Above middle) #M1491–3½" x 12".

Fig. 334. (Top right) Scallop top jardinieres #M1610–5½" with brass handles in *Fleck Zephyr Pink* and *Fleck Nile Blue.* 6½" version without handles in *Matt White—Matt Green Lined.* These jardinieres have the diameter size written as part of the shape number.

Fig. 336. (Right) *Fleck Green* and *Matt White* series: Pair of #M1485–6⅜" and a #M1528–9".

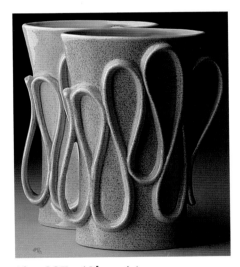

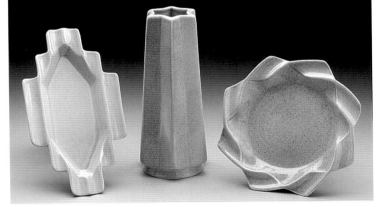

Fig. 338. Three flecks: *Yellow* #1544–10⅛"D, *Zephyr Pink* #656–9½" and *Nile Blue* #1543–8⅛"D. This #1543 shape was also used for the Hiawatha Bridge commemorative ashtray.

Fig. 339. *Fleck Yellow* #871–7⅛". Also came in 6" and 9".

Fig. 337. (Above) A pair of #M1460–9⅛". Front is *Fleck Zephyr Pink—Light Gray Lined* and in rear *Fleck Nile Blue—Colonial Buff Lined.*

Fig. 340. (Right) English vase in *Fleck Nile Blue* marked #1563–14", *Fleck Yellow* #M1598–8" and *Fleck Nile Blue— Colonial Buff Lined* trophy vase #M1450–9⅝".

Fig. 342. (Above) The larger of two sizes available, #M1468–14¾"D *Fleck Yellow.* **Fig. 341. (Above left)** *Fleck Nile Blue* #M1504–5", was available with matching candleholders.

Fig. 344. (Below) Hobnail bowl *Fleck Nile Blue* #1578–7"D. **(Detail left)**

Fig. 343. (Left) In front a *Fleck Nile Blue* #1547–3½"; middle row #431–3" and #1552–4¼" both in *Fleck Yellow—Light Celadon Lined;* rear, *Fleck Nile Blue— Colonial Buff Lined* #1553–6½".

Fig. 345. *(Above)* #2307–11"D in the two different *Over-lay* glazes.

Fig. 347. *(Below)* Oxford Line, Charcoal Black Stippled White—Matt Black #2315–10⅛". This shape was available in two sizes.

Fig. 346. A pair of #652–10" that came out in 1960 in a glossy blue and *Mat White*, and in the center, an *Over-lay* glaze in *Luster Black-White* #2300–10⅛".

Fig. 348. *(Left)* Over-lay glazes: *Luster Burgundy-Gray* #2302–10⅛" and *Luster Black-White* #2305–14".

Fig. 349. *(Above left)* Oxford Line #2306–9".

Fig. 350. *(Above right)* Over-lay glaze in *Luster Burgundy-Gray* #2306–9".

Fig. 353. *(Below)* Over-lay glaze in *Luster Burgundy-Gray* bowls: #2301–4½" x 6⅞" and square-based #2304–4½" x 7¾".

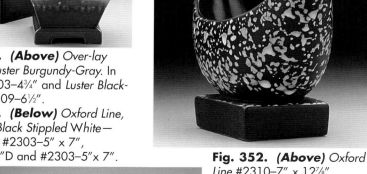

Fig. 351. *(Above)* Over-lay glaze in *Luster Burgundy-Gray*. In front, #2303–4¾" and *Luster Black-White* #2309–6½".

Fig. 354. *(Below)* Oxford Line, Charcoal Black Stippled White—Matt Black #2303–5" x 7", #2314–14"D and #2303–5"x 7".

Fig. 352. *(Above)* Oxford Line #2310–7" x 12⅞".

Fig. 355. *(Right)* Over-lay glaze *Luster Burgundy-Gray* #2310–7" x 13" and *Luster Black-White* candleholders #2312–8".

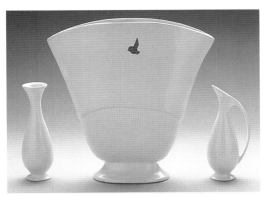

Fig. 356. (Left) Mat White—Mat Green #M1509–7¼", #846–12⅛" from the 1960s *Belle Line* and #1510–7¼".

Fig. 357. (Right) *Black* #B1405–2" x 11⅞" and #M1476–7½".

Fig. 358. *Black* #649–9⅛" compote vase.

Fig. 359. #M1609–10¼" *Mat White* with what the catalog called brass handles.

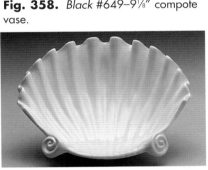

Fig. 361. (Above) #1567–9¼"D.
Fig. 362. (Right) These two #1580–5" in *Mat White* and *Black* with distinct Art Deco styling premiered in 1958.

Fig. 360. *Matt White—Matt Green Lined* #B1390–7⅝" and *Eggshell Ivory, Semi Matt* #1241–8½".

Fig. 363. *Mat White* #M1501–7¾" cut out vase.

Fig. 364. *Black and Mat White:* #1558–6¼", #M5001–6" and #1556–6" cloverleaf vase.

Fig. 365. *Black* compotes #M5005–5" and #M5007–4½".

Fig. 366. *Mat White* #1581–8¼"D and *Black* #M5012–6¾"D.

Fig. 367. *(Left)* Luster Gray—Luster Coral #401–7⅝" with cattail motif and a gladiolus vase #B1419–12".

Fig. 368. *(Right)* Three bowls in *Luster Gray—Luster Coral* : leaf bowl #B1407–13¼", #425–10⅝" and #B2013–4½" x 13".

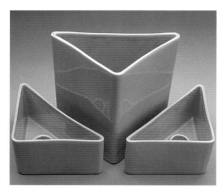

Fig. 370. *(Middle Left)* In Front, *Woodland Green—Luster Light Yellow* #400–7½" and in rear #407–4" x 12" *Gypsy Brown—Yellow Ochre.*

Fig. 371. *(Left)* *Luster Gray—Luster Coral.* In front #400–7½" and in rear #407–4" x 12".

Fig. 369. *Luster Gray—Luster Coral* #408–7" and a pair of candleholders #408A–2¾".

Fig. 374. *(Below)* #M2006–7¼"D *Hobnail* piece in a dark brown, not a standard color.

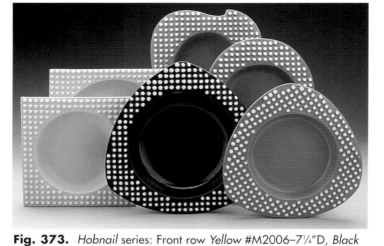

Fig. 373. *Hobnail* series: Front row *Yellow* #M2006–7¼"D, *Black* #M2002–10"D, *Brown* #M2005–8¾"D. Middle row *Yellow* #M2000–8⅝"D, *Green* (oval) #M2004–11"D and in the rear *Green* #M2001–12½".

Fig. 372. *(Above)* Oblong bowl #1348–12"D in *Luster Black* and #1384–4¼"D candle holders in *Luster Black* and *Luster Gray—Luster Coral.* **Fig. 375.** *(Left)* Black #637–11¼"D.

Fig. 377. *(Above)* *Luster Gray—Luster Coral* #B1401–3½".

Fig. 376. *(Above)* An oak leaf flat dish #1388–14"D in *Turquoise—White, Luster Gray—Luster Coral* and *Woodland Green—Luster Light Yellow.*

Fig. 378. *(Left)* Leaf bowl #689–11" in *Ice Green* and #740–4½" in *Cypress Green.*

Fig. 379. *(Right)* Two maple leaf bowls, #429–2¾" x 9¾" in *Travertine—Citron Yellow* and #1387–1" x 10" in *Chartreuse—Luster Gray.*

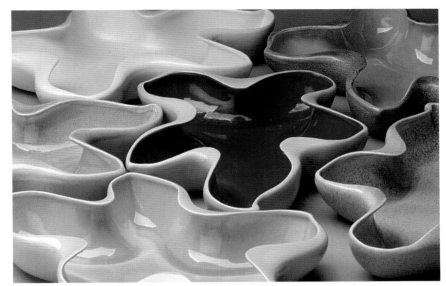

Fig. 381. (Right) #B1411 Candleholders clockwise from front: *Mat White—Mat Green, Luster Burgundy—Luster Gray, Gypsy Brown—Yellow Ochre and Woodland Green—Luster Light Yellow.*

Fig. 382. (Right) #1265–10" x 3⅝".

Fig. 380. (Left) Leaf bowls #B1407–13¼": Center, *Light Gray* (although it looks more like lavender)*—Luster Burgundy*. Clockwise from front: *Chartreuse—Luster Gray, Fleck Green, Mat White, Travertine—Citron Yellow* and *Fleck Nile Blue.*

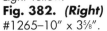

Fig. 383. (Left) #892–7½" introduced in 1939, this shape stayed in production through August 15, 1966—twenty-seven years! Maybe the decision to take this piece out of the catalog was the real reason the pottery closed a year later. *Fleck Zephyr Pink—Light Gray, Travertine—Citron Yellow, Mat White—Mat Green* and *Luster Burgundy—Light Gray.* One collector couple has this piece in thirty-three different color combinations!

Fig. 384. (Right) Nicknamed "stacked teacups", #1359–7¾" in *Luster Burgundy—Luster Blue Pine, Luster Gray—Luster Coral* and *Woodland Green—Luster Light Yellow.*

Fig. 385. Series of candleholders #B1409–5".

Fig. 386. (Right) This shape premiered in the fall 1951 catalog. In the six-month period from August 1951 through January 1952 (coincidently the only records that exist for sales), Red Wing sold 8,691 of this shape compared with other Art Pottery pieces which sold from a few hundred to a thousand or two. #B1402–3½" x 7½". From the front: *Salmon—Colonial Buff, Luster Gray—Luster Coral, Fleck Zephyr Pink—Light Gray, Light Gray—Luster Burgundy* and *Luster Light Yellow—Woodland Green.*

Fig. 387. Three #B2014–13¾"D bowls *Citron Yellow—Woodland Green, Mica Bronze—Citron Yellow* and *Dubonnet—Luster Gray.*

Fig. 388. (Right) This 9¼" pitcher first came out in 1953 as part of the "2300" series *Over-lay* glaze in *Luster Burgundy-Gray* #2313. It was carried until 1956 with various 50s glazes such as *Fleck Nile Blue.* In 1958 it became part of the *Garden Club Pottery* line and was renumbered #5023, of which the *Gray* and *Pink* pieces are examples.

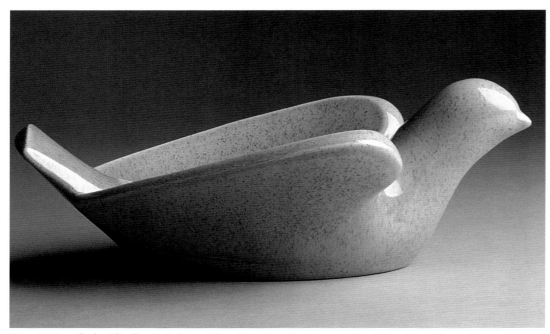

Fig. 389. *Fleck Nile Blue #M1467–4⅞″ x 13¼″.*

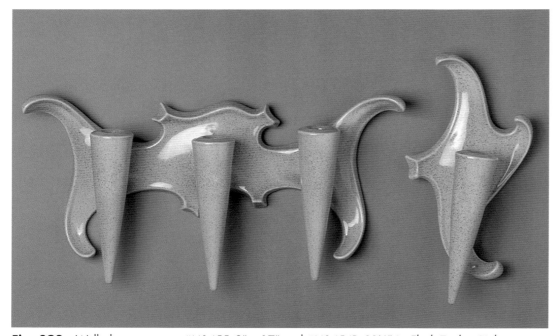

Fig. 392. Wall planter sconces #M1455–9″ x 17″ and #M1454R–11½″ in *Fleck Zephyr Pink.*

Fig. 390. *Gray Fleck—Light Gray #M1447–13″D and #B1433–10″.*

Fig. 391. This *Fleck Gray* was in the catalogs for only one year, *Light Gray—Fleck Gray #M1477–4″.*

Fig. 393. #M1439–6″ footed vase.

Fig. 394. **(left)** *Fleck Zephyr Pink #660–6¼″.*

Fig. 395. **(Right)** #M1448–3⅝″ *Light Gray—Gray Fleck* and #M1443–8⅝″ in *Travertine—Citron Yellow.*

Fig. 397. *(Above)* Garden Club Pottery #M5004–4¾" in *Green* and *White*.
Fig. 396. *(Left)* *Brown* #M5002–7" and #M5000–8".
Fig. 398. *(Right)* Garden Club Pottery in *Brown*: #M5010–2⅝" x 8½" and #M5001–6".

Fig. 399. *(Above)* From the *Sgraffito* line, Hand Painted with Green Speckle Overglaze #4001–4¼", Hand Painted with Tan Speckle Overglaze #M4000–6⅝" and Hand Painted with Green Speckle Overglaze #M4013–3½".

Fig. 400. *(Below)* Two from the *Garden Club Pottery* line from 1957 in *Gray*: modern vase #M5002–7" and classic urn #M5013–9½".

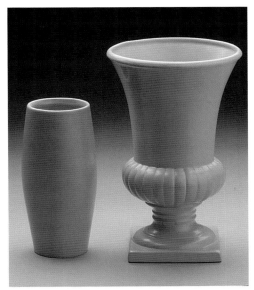

Fig. 401. Jardinieres from large to small: marked #445–12" (10⅝" x 12¼" actual size) in *Nile Blue Fleck* with jardiniere stand and #445–10" (9½" x 10½" actual size) in *Cypress Green*. The rest are unmarked, but are listed as shape #677, introduced in 1938 and made in a variety of sizes until 1960: *Luster Burgundy—Luster Blue Pine* 7" x 8⅝", *Woodland Green—Luster Light Yellow* 5" x 6½", *Fleck Zephyr Pink—Light Gray* 4⅛" x 5⅜" and *Luster Gray—Luster Coral* 3⅝" x 4½".

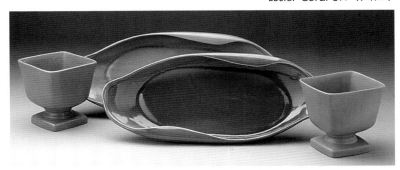

Fig. 402. Low bowls #641–15⅛"D and footed planters #M5009–4¾".

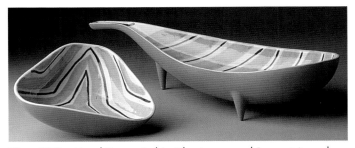

Fig. 403. Hand Decorated in *Chartreuse* and *Brown* triangular bowl #M1535D–6"D and footed leaf bowl #M1502D–16½"D.

Fig. 404. *Travertine—Citron Yellow* planter #1378–5⅜" and *Travertine* #1403–4" violet pot with an original retail sticker from Schuster's of Milwaukee.

Fig. 405. *(Left)* Series of *Tropicana* pieces in *Travertine—Citron Yellow*. Bird of Paradise #B2000–8", Shell Ginger #B2017–4" and *Desert Flower* #B2002–8" with 75th Anniversary sticker.
Fig. 406. *(Middle left)* Travertine—Citron Yellow #M1440–6¼" and #430–8½".
Fig. 409. *(Bottom left)* Two pieces in *Travertine—Citron Yellow*; bottom plate #415–9"D and planter #242– 4⅜".

Fig. 407. *(Above)* Chartreuse—Luster Gray and Travertine—Citron Yellow #B1431–8".
Fig. 410. *(Left)* Travertine—Citron Yellow #B1399–5".

Fig. 408. *Travertine—Citron Yellow* bowl #1304–13"D and candleholder #B1409–4⅞".

Fig. 411. *Travertine—Citron Yellow* #B1392–7½", #B1426–8" and #M1457–7¾".

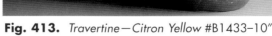

Fig. 413. *Travertine—Citron Yellow* #B1433–10"

Fig. 412. *(Above)* Travertine—Citron Yellow #1265–3⅜" x 10", #B2002–8⅛" and #1348–2" x 12".

Fig. 415. *(Below)* Pair of #B1426–8½".

Fig. 416. *(Above right)* Two #B1428–8¼" pieces. In *Chartreuse—Luster Gray* and *Travertine—Citron Yellow*.

Fig. 417. *(Left)* Two pieces Travertine—Citron Yellow #M1439–6" and bowl #414–8"D.

Fig. 418. *Travertine—Citron Yellow* #M1459–9¼".

Fig. 414. *(Above)* Travertine—Citron Yellow #M1451–14⅛".

Fig. 419. *(Left)* New shapes that Murphy designed when he returned to Red Wing in fall of 1953. These shapes were only carried for a couple of years: Travertine—Citron Yellow #M1452–14⅛" and #M1450–9½". Variations of this classic shape were made over the years with a variety of handles.

Fig. 420. Two cornucopias in *Woodland Green—Luster Light Yellow* #M1444–8⅝″ and #1097–5¾″.

Fig. 422. (Above) *Woodland Green—Luster Yellow* #B2316–10″, #B1427–8″ and #B2317–10⅛″.
Fig. 421. (Left) #M1440–6⅛″ *Chartreuse—Luster Gray* and *Black*.

Fig. 423. (Right) Two versions of hanging planters: #M1487-10¼″ in *Fleck Yellow, Fleck Green, White* and *Salmon*. These were sold also without the chain and hole at the top. The other planter, #M1606–5¾″, was able to hang in sets via a notch on the bottom to hold the chain for the planter below.

Fig. 424. (Left) Two #416 gladiolus vases: 10½″ in *White* and 12¼″ in *Chartreuse—Luster Gray*. The shorter one is also marked 10″.

Fig. 425. (Above) *Textura* piece in *Luster Woodland Green—Luster Light Yellow* #B2106–12¼″.

Fig. 426. (Above) This piece is marked (in pencil on the base) RED WING POTTERIES 1956, and was reported to have been made there. 9¾″ in height and 14¼″ from toe to finger.

Fig. 427. *Mica Bronze—Citron Yellow* #B2013–13″D and *Tropicana* #B2003–10″ *Bird of Paradise* design.

Fig. 428. #B1408–13″D bowl in *Woodland Green—Luster Light Yellow*.

Fig. 429. (Right) Two shadow box style vases with bird #430–8½″: *Chartreuse—Luster Gray* and *Copper—Champagne*.

Fig. 431. (Left) *Woodland Green—Luster Yellow* #M1457–7½″, #405–10⅝″ and #B1425–8″.

Fig. 432. More bird motifs from Charles Murphy: a pair of candlestick holders #M1470–5¼″ in *Colonial Buff* and in *Travertine* #M1473–10″D ashtray.

Fig. 430. Two colors not standard for *Textura* pieces: rear *Copper—Champagne* #B2104–10¼″ and *Chartreuse—Luster Gray* #B2103–8⅛″.

Fig. 433. Top view of #M1473 from Fig. 432.

Fig. 434. (Left) *Woodland Green—Luster Light Yellow* #1110–7¼″, #889–7⅝″ and #1355–7½″.

Fig. 435. A *Tropicana* #B2016-4″ with and without the *Desert Flower* motif, in *Ming Green* and *Citron Yellow*.

Fig. 436. *Chartreuse—Luster Gray* #423–6½″.

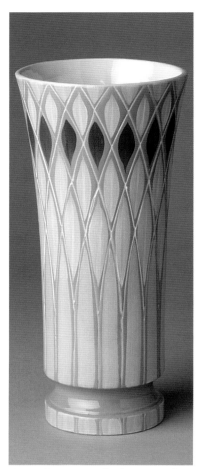

Fig. 437. Unmarked piece in the collection of the Goodhue County Historical Society, Red Wing, Minnesota. Probably was designed as part of the series #4000 *Sgraffito* line.

Fig. 439. *Bronze Line #850–7⅛"* and #948–7⅝".

Fig. 441. **(Left)** *Bronze Line* vase #818–12¼" and #819–11⅞" pitcher vase.

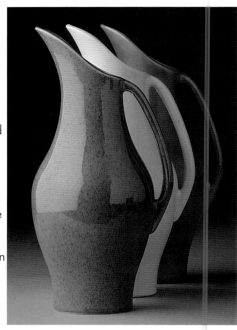

Fig. 438. (Left) *Bronze Line* vase #505–7¾", compote #5006–3⅛" x 11", and in rear a 6¼" planter marked RED WING USA, but having no shape number.

Fig. 440. (Right) Three pitcher vases #1559–9½", front one in an unusual dark green Fleck, *Matt White,* and *Cypress Green.*

Fig. 442. Basket weave bowl #647–12"D.

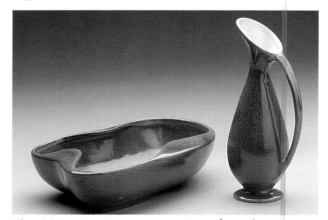

Fig. 445. Two pieces in *Cocoa Brown* from about 1965. Low bowl #899–9¼"D and #1510–7⅛".

Fig. 443. A group of string instrument planters: a *Fleck Zephyr Pink* violin #M1484–13½" was offered in the catalogs from 1955 through 1962, while the other two were listed from 1965 though closing (1967). *White* with blue trim Banjo #908–15¾" and a second version of a violin in *Rust* with black trim #907–14¾".

Fig. 444. *Bronze Line #913–9⅞".*

Fig. 446. #M1531–5" in *Butterscotch.*

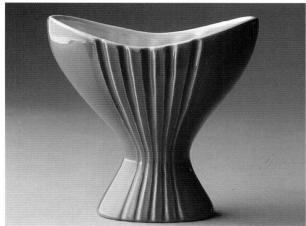

Fig. 449. *Mat White* #653–5⅛".

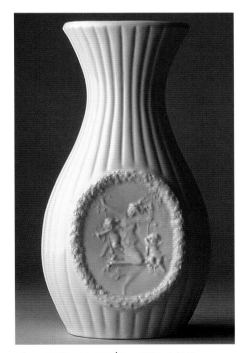

Fig. 450. Pair of *Cypress Green* candleholders #775–4⅛" and compote #761–6" in *Blue*.

Fig. 453. *Mat White* #776–12¼".

Fig. 451. #821–8" One of a series of four that were in the catalog for only one season.

Fig. 454. *Monarch Line* in *Contemporary Blue* #939–8½" x 3¾" and #938–6½" x 2⅜".

Fig. 447. *(Above Left)* Cocoa Brown #1510–7", #790–3¼" x 8¾" and #753–7½".

Fig. 448. *(Above Right)* #666–6⅛" Unusual color for a *Doric Ensemble* piece: A deep rust lined with a beige.

Fig. 452. This *Black* #856 was one of four in a set called Grand Slam Ash Trays. The spade and club were offered in *Black* and the heart and diamond in *Radiant Orange*.

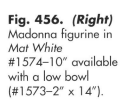

Fig. 455. *(Above)* Black #1631–8".

Fig. 456. *(Right)* Madonna figurine in *Mat White* #1574–10" available with a low bowl (#1573–2" x 14").

Fig. 457. *Cinnamon* toro bowl #659–8"D.

Fig. 458. Piano planter in *Yellow Fleck* #M1525–4½" x 11".

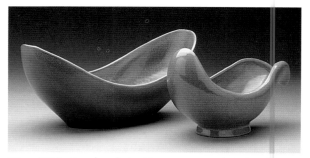

Fig. 459. Two bowls in *Cinnamon*: gondola bowl #M1507–12¾"D and oval bowl #1582–10"D.

Fig. 460. *Cinnamon* #M1566–8" and #1633–7¾".

Fig. 461. *Cinnamon—Light Celadon* #M1527–3½" x 8".

Fig. 462. (Right) *Cinnamon— Light Celadon* large cornu-copia #442– 8½" x 15" (this came in a smaller ver-sion also) and #348–6¾", a shape origi-nally used in the RumRill line in 1936.

Fig. 463. #439–3¾" x 10".

Fig. 464. Three from the *Belle Line;* gladiolus vase #846–12" in a white with green lining (not a standard color offering); two in *Olive Green—Moss Green Lining*, in front a #845–8" fan vase and #843–10".

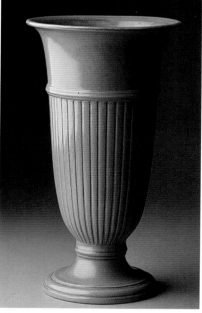

Fig. 465. *Cinnamon* #1563 marked 14" (14¼" actual size).

Fig. 466. #5033–6" colonial mug in *Cinnamon*.

Fig. 467. *Cinnamon* pair of #M1471–4¾" candleholders and #M1479–4¼" x 10¼" planter. A matching vase was sold in two different sizes: 8" and 10½".

Fig. 468. *Cinnamon* #M1565–12", #M1526–14" and #M1570–11⅜".

Fig. 469. *Cypress Green* stove planter #765–7⅞".

Fig. 470. From the 60's, #669–5".

Fig. 471. Two in *Meadow Green.* Square planter #1561–12"D (one also available in 18" length). Right, #M1600–7⅛" was sold in three sizes with handles and a series hand decorated with leaves.

Fig. 472. From 1961, the smallest in a series of pedestal jardinieres #104–5½".

Fig. 473. #777–7⅛" *Cocoa Brown.*

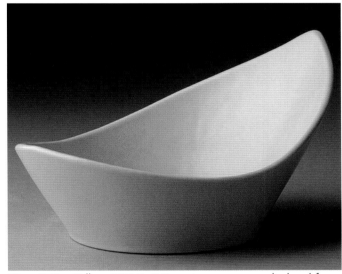

Fig. 474. *Yellow* #5017–4⅜" contemporary novelty bowl from the *Garden Club Pottery* line.

Fig. 475. Low bowl #835–10⅛"D and #M1627–4⅛" in *Cypress Green* and in the rear #643–4⅛".

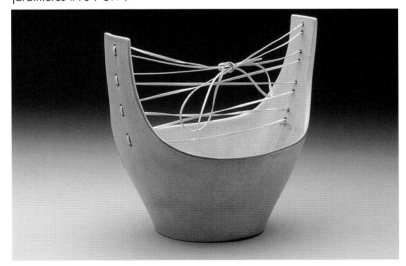

Fig. 476. #M1478–7⅞".

Fig. 477. #670–5".

Fig. 478. *Cypress Green* #510–8¾".

Fig. 479. *Decorator Line* in *Crystalline Blue,* a glaze that was predominately green with blue highlights. #M3017–4⅞" x 13¼", #M3014–12¼" and one of a series of planters not numbered in the #M3000 range like the other *Decorator Line* pieces, #808–7¼".

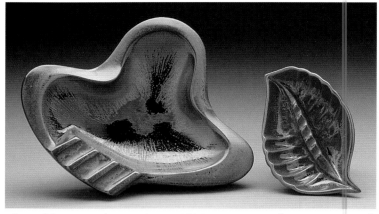

Fig. 480. Two ashtrays, the #M3000–8¾"D in a *Silver Green Crystalline Glaze* and a leaf ashtray #739–6½"D in a glaze that looks like a *Crystalline Glaze,* but is *Green with Orange Overlay.*

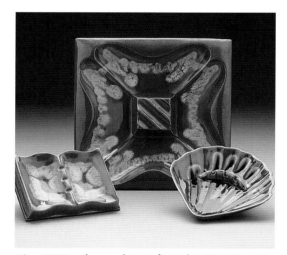

Fig. 481. Three ashtrays from the 60s, *Green with Orange Overlay:* book shape #863–6½"D, #M3005–11"D and shell shaped #862–6⅞"D.

Fig. 483. Series of *Burnt Orange Crystalline Glaze* ashtrays (although this glaze was simply called *Burnt Orange* in later years). Rear, #M3000–8¾"D, #M3002–12"D and #M3005–10⅝"D; Front, #774–8⅝"D and #M3003–10"D.

Fig. 482. #3012 in *Radiant Orange.*

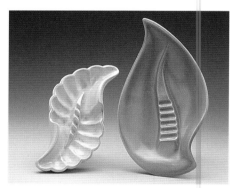

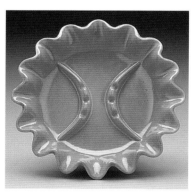

Fig. 485. *(Left)* This *Radiant Orange* ashtray, 7½" in diameter, has the lowest shape number Red Wing ever produced, #19. It was introduced in 1963. (There were some pieces in a separate catalog of *Decorator Planters* in 1965 that were numbered A10 and A11 and AA10 and AA11).

Fig. 484. (Right) Two ashtrays: #828–9½"D in *Butterscotch* and #746–11"D in *Sagebrush.*

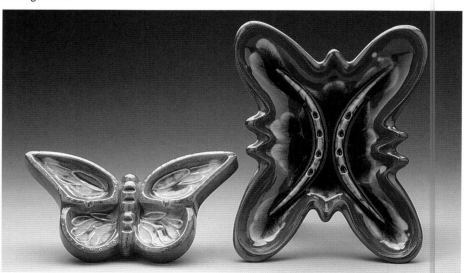

Fig. 486. Two butterfly ashtray in the 1965 glazes, #934–9½" *Green with Orange Overlay* and #831–11"D in *Brown with Red Overlay.*

Fig. 487. Two ashtrays in *Radiant Orange:* #890–9½"D and #889–8"D.

Fig. 488. *Radiant Orange* #827–7½".

Fig. 489. (Above) From the *Decorator Line:* #M3019–12" in *Burnt Orange Crystalline Glaze,* #M3016–20" in *Silver Green Crystalline Glaze* and #M3018–21" in *Burnt Orange Crystalline Glaze.*

Fig. 490. #M1453–18⅝" long leaf bowls in *Colonial Bluff* and *Luster Gray—Citron Yellow.*

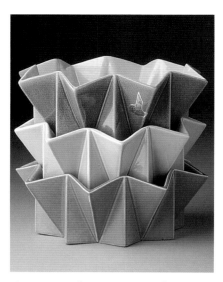

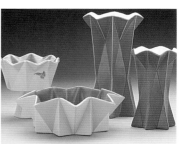
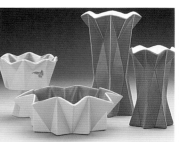

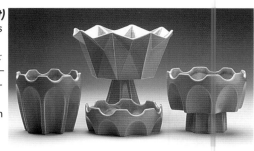

Fig. 493. (Right) Four *Prismatiques* in *Mandarin Orange-Celadon*; left, planter #793–5⅜", bowl #792–2½", compote #788–5½" and in rear large compote #796–8⅞".

Fig. 492. (Above) *Prismatiques* in *Mandarin Orange and White* combinations. Front; large bowl #789–3¾" x 10¼" and in the rear; compote #787–6¼", vase #797–11" and vase #798–7¾".

Fig. 494. (Left) Three *Prismatiques* in *Lemon Yellow—White*; compote #788–5½", vase #795–8⅛" and compote #787–6½".

Fig. 491. This *Prismatique* shape #790–3⅛" x 8¼", along with the #787, and the smaller bowl #791 continued to be made in 1966 and 1967 after the rest of the line was discontinued. From the top: *Cocoa Brown, Blue—Mat White* (not the regular Persian Blue from the *Prismatique* line that has flecks in it) and *Mandarin Orange—Celadon Lined*.

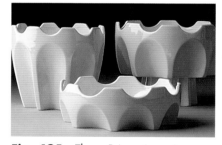

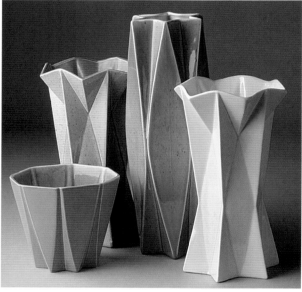

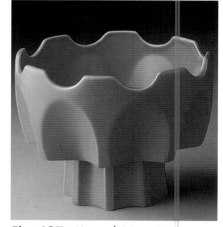

Fig. 497. Unusual *Prismatique* #788–5½" bowl with *Mandarin Orange* both inside and out.

Fig. 495. Three *Prismatiques* in *Lemon Yellow–White*, front bowl #792–2½", planter #793–5⅜" and compote #788–5½".

Fig. 496. *Mandarin Orange—Celadon* #786–5¼", *Celadon—Mandarin Orange* #797–11", *Persian Blue—White* #799–14" and *Lemon Yellow—White* #797–10¾".

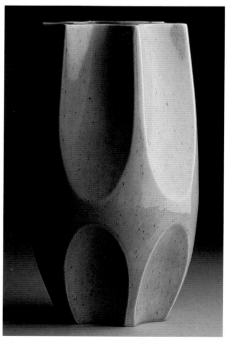

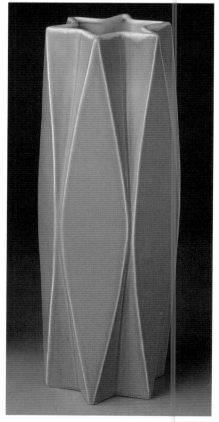

Fig. 498. *Prismatiques* in *Celadon and Mandarin Orange* combinations: front, compote #787–6½"; rear, vases #798–8", #794–10⅞" and #795–8⅛".

Fig. 499. #794–11" *Celadon.*

Fig. 500. #799–14" *Mandarin Orange.*

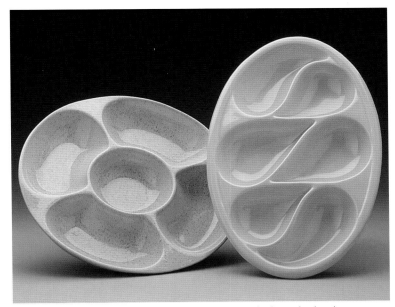

Fig. 501. A 12⅛"D nut or relish tray in *Tan Fleck* marked only RED WING USA (listed as shape #446 in the Art Pottery catalogs from 1964–1967). Right, from the Relishes—Chip 'n Dips category in the Art Pottery catalogs in 1962–64, #802–15"D in *Lemon Yellow* .

Fig. 502. This was listed as *Blue* in the 60s catalogs, with no mention of the "fleck" tones in it. In the 1951 catalog there were two "speckled" glazes offered—*Luster Blue (Speckled)* and *Luster Celadon (Speckled)*. These offer the fleck collectors more colors to acquire. Three compotes: left, #M5005–5¼" x 9⅞", middle, #5022–4½" x 7" and #M5008–6⅜" x 8".

Fig. 503. *Blue* #748–4" x 9½".

Fig. 504. An *Orchid* glaze was offered only in 1962, #M1572–5⅛" and bud vase #756–7⅛".

Fig. 505. 12½" *Blue* plate with an unusual two-digit shape #48, sold with #46 and #47 figurine.

Fig. 506. *Blue* #770–3¼" x 7¾" planter and scalloped edge console bowl #1620–3¼" x 10" in *Orchid*.

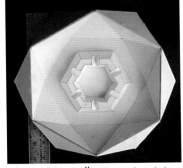

Fig. 508. Belle Kogan's original cardboard mock-up for ashtray below.

Fig. 509. *Orchid* #638–8", larger of the two sizes that was available.

Fig. 510. *(Left) Celadon* #801–12⅜"D Relishes-Chip 'n Dips and *Green with Orange Overlay* #825–10"D ashtray.

Fig. 507. Two in *Hyacinth* fluted compote #M1591–6⅜" and long bowl #697–17¼"D.

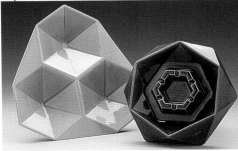

CARE and CLEANING

Common sense should be your guide for the care and cleaning of your pottery. Step-by-step recommendations are made for cleaning. Please be careful, and if it's a rare or valuable piece, seek the help of experts.

Cleaning

Plain dish detergent and water always work well as the first step to clean off much dirt and grime. If you are cleaning your pottery in a sink, line the sink with a towel to cushion the pottery and to deter accidental breakage. A note of caution: some glazes were prone to trap unseen air bubbles beneath the surface. At these places, the glaze wall will be extremely thin and vigorous scrubbing can easily break through, so go gently. If you are in doubt about your ability to proceed without damaging the glaze surface, consult an expert.

Take care not to disturb original stickers (either Red Wing's or a retailer's). Stickers are not waterproof and they add character (and value) to your pottery.

Resist the temptation to clean the bottom of pottery. Left intact, it is a reflection of the natural age of the pottery, and there are sometimes notations made by the original owner or retailer.

One museum recommends this gentler option: To remove large loose particles, rinse under running water. The entire surface should then be lightly rubbed with a cotton rag soaked in an Orvus solution. To make this solution, use one tablespoon Orvus Paste, a highly concentrated synthetic detergent (modified ammonium lauryl sulfate—available at conservation supply houses) to one gallon of distilled water. After a complete rinsing under running water, the exterior surface should be examined to see if additional spot cleaning is necessary. If so, use the same procedure on the selected area.

Pottery often will have "metal marks" that resemble pencil marks. These are said to be caused by the rings worn by people who handle the pottery. They can be removed, but great care must be taken to make sure that the glaze surface is not damaged in the process. Wet the affected area, apply a small quantity of liquid cleanser to it and gently scrub with a soft toothbrush.

If there are calcium (or lime) deposits inside the pottery, they can be dissolved by filling the pottery with plain white vinegar and letting it stand. Depending on the amount of calcium built up, the vinegar may dissolve the calcium in anywhere from a few hours to a

Fig. A-1. Pink #179–7½" pitcher (64 oz.). This "before" shot shows how badly stained this pitcher was.

couple of days.

Sometimes pottery is found that has been completely disguised with house paint. Most mild paint removers will remove the paint without damaging the pottery. Buyers beware, however—painting a piece of pottery does disguise certain serious flaws such as cracks.

Stains Under the Glaze

Treating stains under the glaze is a somewhat risky venture, please do so at your own risk. Such stains occur when the glaze surface integrity has been damaged in some way, due to severe crazing, chips or cracks. Dirt and other contaminates can then get under the glaze. Such stains can be bleached out. A small area can be bleached with a cotton ball soaked in hydrogen peroxide and a few drops of ammonia. This is then taped to the affected area. Seal the pottery in a plastic bag. Check and change the solution every day.

For larger areas simply fill or submerge the entire piece with household bleach, taking care not to soak off valuable labels. Check often, and when the stain has been bleached out, remove and rinse or soak for approximately the same amount of time as you bleached. Some pieces need less than an hour, while others may need several days.

One danger in this method of removing stains is that any pottery with surface damage that is submerged for extended periods of time is more prone to breakage due to clay deterioration that bleach can cause. Again, if you are not sure, consult an expert.

Fig. A-2. The "after" shot. An example of good results from bleaching. This piece required two days in bleach. Some pieces need only a few hours, while others need several days.

is most appropriate when a piece of pottery will undoubtedly continue to deteriorate unless it is fixed. Chips and cracks are repairable, but properly done the process can prove expensive. Whether or not non-threatening damage *should* be repaired is a highly subjective matter. Note that many museum conservators shy away from making any but the most necessary repairs.

In the collecting world, an unfortunate truth is that many repairs are made only to facilitate the resale of pottery. Spotting repairs is an acquired ability, and even the most experienced collectors can be deceived. Look closely at prospective purchases for irregularities in the texture of the glaze. Don't be ashamed to pull out a magnifying glass. Remember that it is easier to conceal a repair on highly decorated Art Pottery than it is on large areas of a single color.

Safely Displaying Your Pottery

Even the Midwest has earthquakes! And sometimes a heavy truck rumbling by outside can shake loose a shelf and send a collection crashing to destruction. Make sure any shelves and/or cabinets that hold your pottery are securely bolted to a wall and anchored into studs, not just drywall.

Probably more damage is done to pottery by wagging dog tails or cat curiosity than any one 6.5 Richter earthquake. An excellent preventative is to secure your pottery to a display area with the use of a hot glue gun. (Inexpensive hot glue guns are sold at hardware stores everywhere.) Hot glue will work on wood, glass, laminates, plastics, etc., but always test an area first to make sure that the hot glue will not damage the surface. Hot glue should not be used on painted surfaces or on valuable furniture with original old finishes.

Quickly apply a bead of glue around the bottom ridge of the pottery and immediately press the pottery down onto the display surface. Because the glue cools in a matter of seconds, have the display location cleaned and prepared before you begin, and figure out beforehand which side of the piece will be displayed outward.

When you need to remove the piece, tap the pottery gently with the palm of your hand to break the seal. The ring of glue will easily peel off the pottery.

Hairline Cracks, Damage, and Repairs

Hairline cracks can fill with dirt and become more obvious than they need be. Again, apply hydrogen peroxide mixed with a few drops of ammonia to a cotton ball and tape over the hairline. Seal the pottery in a plastic bag. Check and change the solution every day.

When the dirt has been removed, you may use a two-part epoxy to fill the hairline (and hope to halt its progress), carefully sponging off the excess before it dries.

By and large, repairs are best left to experts. A repair

SHAPE NUMBER REFERENCE CHART

SHAPE NUMBER	INITIAL CREATION DATE	REISSUE NUMBER	DATE REISSUED	SHAPE NUMBER	INITIAL CREATION DATE	REISSUE NUMBER	DATE REISSUED
19	1963					H510–H511	1952
43–44	1961			514–539	1936		
46–48	1961			541–564	1936		
50	1933			566–576	1936		
A51–A54	1926–29			579–601	1936		
104–108	1926–29	104–105/108	1961	605	1936	608/610/612	1964
		110/112	1961	610–677	1937	634–651	1959
114–115	1926–29					652–676	1960
119–129	1926–29			678–716	1938	678–682	1960
131–133	1926–29					684–687	1960
135/137/139	1926–29					689–697	1960
143–179	1926–29			717	1936		
181–184	1926–29			718	1938		
186–192	1926–29			720–722	1938		
194–220	1926–29			724–730	1938		
223–256	1926–29			731	1936	730—734	1960
257–266	1926–29			732–734	1938	735	1961
267–268	1933			736–737	1938	737	1960
270–333	1933					738–756	1961
335–339	1933			739–741	1938		
341–358	1933			744–778	1938	758–765	1961
360–428	1933	400–402	1951			766–778	1962
		403–408	1952	780–849	1938	780–799	1962
		410–419	1952			805–807	1962
		421–423	1953			808/810/812	1960
		425–430	1953			813–817	1962
429–433	1936	431–432	1954			818–832	1963
435–455	1936	433–442	1955			837–848	1963
		443–448	1956			849–852	1964
459–463	1936			850	1939		
474/478/480	1936			852	1938		
482–497	1936			854–865	1938	857–862	1964
499–510	1936	H503–H505	1952			857–862	1964
		H507–H508	1952	870	1938		

Shape Number Reference Chart (cont.)

SHAPE NUMBER	INITIAL CREATION DATE	REISSUE NUMBER	DATE REISSUED	SHAPE NUMBER	INITIAL CREATION DATE	REISSUE NUMBER	DATE REISSUED
867–869	1940			B1433–B1437	1953		
871–892	1939	871–881	1964	M1438–M1468	1954		
		882/884	1964	M1470–M1479	1954		
		889–890	1964	M1480–M1489	1955		
		893	1964	M1491–M1500	1955		
894–967	1939	896–907	1964	M1501–M1507	1956		
		908/910/912	1960	M1509–M1520	1956		
		909/911/913	1965	M1525–M1540	1956		
		916–932	1965	M1541–M1574	1957		
		934–948	1966	M1575	1958		
969–974	1939			1576–1615	1958		
977–1007	1940			1616–1633	1959		
1010–1023	1940			B2000–B2015	1950	M2000–M2007	1958
1025–1060	1940			B2016–B2019	1951		
1061–1082	1941			B2100–B2110	1950		
1084–1131	1941			B2111–B2112	1951		
1132–1178	1942			B2113	1952		
1179–1190	1943			B2200–B2206	1951		
1194–1214	1943			2300–2314	1953		
1215–1243	1946			B2315–B2317	1953		
1245–1246	1946			M2318–M2319	1953		
1248–1257	1946			B2500–B2509	1951		
1259–1276	1946			3000–3018	1959		
1277–1296	1947			3019–3020	1960		
1299–1304	1947			M4000–M4013	1955		
1306–1336	1947			M5000–M5014	1957		
1337–1350	1948			5015–5023	1957		
1351–1388	1949			5031	1957		
B1389	1950			5032–5033	1958		
B1390–B1411	1951			6001–6008	1949		
B1412	1952						
B1414–B1419	1952						
B1420–B1422	1953						
B1425–B1431	1953						

YEAR OF PRODUCTION REFERENCE CHART

YEAR OF PRODUCTION	SHAPE NUMBER	LINE
1926–1929	A51–A54	various glazed and *Brushed Ware*
	105–270*	various glazed and *Brushed Ware*
1933	50 Water Jug	RumRill
	52–54	RumRill
	271–428*‡	various pieces of Red Wing's #166–#267 remarked RumRill
1934–36	429–601/605/717/731*‡	RumRill
1937	610–677*‡	RumRill
1938 (Jan)	678–740*	Red Wing selling the "RumRill" shapes
1938 (July)	745–870*	Belle Kogan 100 and others
1939	871–953*	various animal novelties
	954–966	*Terra-Craft Pottery* by Belle Kogan
	967–974*	various animal novelties
1940	975–1032*	*Magnolia Group* by Belle Kogan
	1033–1060	
1941	1061–1121*	
	1121–1125	hand painted figurines designed by Charles Murphy
	1129–1131	*Sgraffito*
1942	1132–1178	
1943	1179–1214*	
1944–45	No known new pieces	
1946	1215–1234	new pieces of the *Magnolia Group*
	1235–1276*	
1947	1277–1324*	
	1327–1332	"African" handled pieces *Brown Engobe* glaze
	1171, 1278–1336	crackle glazes
1948	1336–1350	new figurines
1949	1351–1388	
	6001–6008	"6000" series
1950	B2000–B2015	*Tropicana* by Belle Kogan
	B2100–B2110	*Textura* by Belle Kogan
	& B1389	
1951	**400–402**	
	B1390–B1411	
	B2016–2019	

Year of Production Reference Chart

YEAR OF PRODUCTION	SHAPE NUMBER	LINE
	B2111–B2112	
	B2200–B2206	*Matched or Classical*
	B2500–2509	*DeLuxe*
1952	**403–408/410/419**	
	B2113	
	H503–H511*	*Hand Painted* /dinnerware patterns
	B1412/B1414–B1419	
1953	**421/422/425–430**	
	B1420–B1437*	
	2300–2319	*Over–lay* glazes
1954	**431–432**	
	M1438–M1479*	
	2300–2319	*Oxford Line* (black/white stipple)
		Fleck glazes offered on everything except 2300's
1955	**433–442**	
	M1480–M1500*	
	M4000–M4013	*Sgraffito* by Charles Murphy
1956	**443–448**	
	1501–1540*	
1957	1541–1574	
	5000–5023 & 5031	*Garden Club Pottery*
1958	1575–1615	
	M**2000**–M**2007**	*Hobnail* ashtrays by Charles Murphy
	5032 & 5033	
1959	1616–1633	
	M3000–M3018	*Decorator Line* by Charles Murphy
	634–651	
1960	**652–660**	
	661–667	*Doric Ensemble*
	668–670	
	671–678/680–685*/3006	*Chromoline Handpainted*
	730–734	*Birch Bark Line*
	679/686–697*/737/	
	808/810/812/908/910/912	

YEAR OF PRODUCTION REFERENCE CHART

YEAR OF PRODUCTION	SHAPE NUMBER	LINE
	M3019–M3020/H**1600**/H**1610**	
1961	46–48	baby figurines & bowl
	104/105/108/110/112	*Floraline*
	738–746	ashtrays
	747–765*	
1962	**508/510/512/766–784***	
	785–799	*Prismatique Line* by Belle Kogan
	800–804	Relishes—Chip 'N Dips
	805–807/813–817	
1963	19	ashtray (lowest shape number)
	818–820	
	821–824	cherub's
	825–832	various ashtray's
	837–848	*Belle Line* by Belle Kogan
1964	757	Madonna figurine
	849–850/851/852	
	857–862/871–873	
	874–881	additional *Belle Line*
	882/884/889–890/893	
	896–908	
1965	909	
	911–913/918	*Bronze Line* (4 new shapes/plus 12 existing shapes)
	916–917	
	919–931	various figural planters
	932	planter in *Crystalline Glaze*
1966	**934–936**	
	937–944	*Monarch*
	945–948	additional *Bronze Line*

Bold indicates shape numbers that have been used on different earlier shapes

*Some numbers not used

‡Many of these also marked only with shape number

NOTES/BIBLIOGRAPHY

NOTES

Chapter 1

1. Following are the standards chosen for the listing of pottery, glazes and the identifying shape numbers:
a) The shape number and actual measurement will be listed. The height is always listed unless noted with a "D". The "D" represents the widest measurement (width, diameter or length). When two numbers are listed, the height will be first.
b) We will denote the company mark only if it is unusual for the era.
c) Pieces within the photo are always described from left to right unless otherwise noted.
d) Official glaze names are spelled as listed in company literature and are italicized.
e) Official lines of Art Pottery and patterns of dinnerware are italicized.
f) Although the catalogs varied over the years as to how they designated the lining glaze, the book will consistently always use an "em" dash between the outside and the inside glaze (sometimes the "em" dash was used as part of the official name—between the glaze name and its description, for example).
g) Although the vast majority of pieces marked with the "M" prefix had a dash between the M and the shape number (see page 49), for clarity sake it is not used.
h) In a few rare cases the catalogs list a letter after the shape number such as "S" (for small). They will be listed in the caption although they almost never appear on the pottery itself.

2. Due to a lack of surviving early catalogs, best judgement was used in matching glaze names to glaze colors. An example is this early piece whose glaze was deduced as *Gypsy Orange*, that glaze being the only "orange" listed in any existing catalogs.

Chapter 2

1. Tefft, Gary and Bonnie. *Red Wing Potters and Their Wares.* Menomonee Falls, Wisconsin: Locust Enterprises, 1987, p. 2.

2. Pahnke, Ray. "The Largest Pottery," *Red Wing Collectors Society Newsletter* (August 1980): p. 10.

3. Schwartau, John. "The Red Wing Clay History: How it All Began," *Red Wing Collectors Society Convention Supplement* (1993).

4. Schmeckebier, Laurence E. *Art in Red Wing.* Minneapolis: University of Minnesota, 1946, p. 71.

5. Red Wing Union Stoneware company records privately owned.

Chapter 3

1. *Red Wing Argus,* October 18, 1887.

2. Reported by Helen Bell, a life-long Red Wing resident, and the town's "unofficial historian." The rumor was that Mrs. Cleveland threw the vase off the train at Prairie Island (around the bend and out of site of Red Wing). Officially, Mrs. Cleveland did write to express her thanks.

3. Red Wing produced duplicates of the Cleveland Vase. According to a November 2, 1901, *Minneapolis Journal* article a Cleveland Vase was awarded as a prize: *"One of the prettiest pieces is a vase made by the Red Wing Stoneware Company, a copy of the one presented to Mr. Cleveland's wife, when she visited the potteries several years ago."*

4. Robinson-Ransbottom and Red Wing also were distributed together out of Red Wing's Twin Cities Branch in the 1960s.

Chapter 4

1. $300,000 was the figure quoted in an October 1929 *Crockery and Glass Journal* article. The December 31, 1926, Red Wing Union Stoneware Company annual statement listed the value of the tunnel kiln at $77,229.

2. The *Brushed Ware* style of artware had been made for many years previously, and this seems to be what is referred to in this article.

3. *Crockery and Glass Journal* (January, 1934): p. 24.

Chapter 5

1. *The Gift and Art Shop* (March, 1932): p. 113.

2. Fig. 5–4, *Crockery and Glass Journal* (August, 1937): p. 40; Fig 5–5, *Crockery and Glass Journal* (February, 1937): p. 22.

3. Author's phone interview with Harry Rumrill, salesman for Rumrill Pottery Company (no relation to George). George Rumrill had called him one day while in Chicago as Harry was the only Rumrill in the phone book. They had a few drinks together, and Harry was soon a salesman for George.

4. *Wall Street Journal*, October 1, 1951, p. 1.

5. This is the first documented usage of the new name, Red Wing Potteries, which became official three years later when the original thirty-year 1906 charter for the company expired.

6. *Crockery and Glass Journal* (August, 1934).

7. Actually luncheon ware; dinnerware was the more formal china, but for the sake of convenience we will follow today's practice of calling it all "dinnerware." In the Trade Names and Marks - Names of Shapes section of the December, 1935, *Crockery and Glass Journal Annual Directory,* the trade name *Gypsy Trail* first shows up listed to RumRill Pottery.

8. Transfers of Patents, U.S. Patent Office, June 8, 1936.

9. Zaeske, Mike. " George & RumRill: The Man, the Myth and the Pottery," *Journal of the American Art Pottery Association* Volume VIII No 4 (July-August, 1993), citing *Polk's Directory, Little Rock, Arkansas.*

10. Articles of Incorporation on file at Arkansas Secretary of States Office, Little Rock, Arkansas.

11. Various sources researched by Jim Pfeifer, Little Rock, Arkansas, some of which were displayed at a show he curated at The Old State House Museum, Little Rock, Arkansas.

12. Author's interview with Louise Bauer.

13. Mangus, Jim and Bev. *Shawnee Pottery.* Puducah, Kentucky: Collector Books, 1994, p. 10.

14. From research and interviews done by Jim Pfeifer, Little Rock, Arkansas.

15. From research and interviews done by Leo Frese and published in the auction catalog of the sale of his collection in Red Wing, April 1, 1995.

16. *The Morrow County (Mt. Gilead, Ohio) Sentinel*, December 1, 1938, p. 1.

17. *China, Glass and Lamps* (July, 1940): p.10.

18. Advertisement, *Crockery and Glass Journal* (July, 1941): p. 12.

19. Author's phone interview with Harry Rumrill.

20. Author's interview with Harold E. West.

21. *The Morrow County Sentinel,* October 16, 1941.

22. *The Morrow County Sentinel,* December 4, 1941.

23. *The Morrow County (Cardington, Ohio) Independent,* December 4, 1941.

24. *Crockery and Glass Journal* (January, 1943): p. 95.

25. Author's phone conversation with Georgine R. Mickler and as first published in an article by Jim Pfeifer titled "RumRill Pottery," *American Clay Exchange* (January 15, 1982): p. 11–13.

26. Also, Red Wing Potteries, Inc. 1940 Annual Statement shows a write-off for "Overdrafts salesman com." of $8,293—presumably George Rumrill's.

27. *Crockery and Glass Journal* (January, 1943): p. 95.

Chapter 6

1. *Crockery and Glass Journal* (May, 1939): p. 26.

2. *China, Glass and Lamps* (July, 1939): p. 12.

3. *Crockery and Glass Journal* (July, 1939): p. 17.

Chapter 7

1. *Crockery and Glass Journal* (March, 1943): p. 35.

2. Dietz, Ulysses G. *Newark Museum Collection of American Art Pottery.* Newark, New Jersey: The Newark Museum; Salt Lake City: Gibbs M. Smith, Inc., Peregrine Smith Books, 1984.

3. Glaze is *Luster Rose—Grey Lined* as per the 1942 *Red Wing Art Pottery* catalog. Note—this was the only year Gray was spelled with an "e."

4. Nelson, Marion John. *Art Pottery of the Midwest.* Minneapolis: University Art Museum, University of Minnesota, 1988, p. 85.

Chapter 8

1. Robert Boyce, president of Harker Pottery Co., Chester, West Virginia, quoted in the *Wall Street Journal*, October 1, 1951, p. 1.

2. *Daily Republican Eagle (Red Wing, Minnesota)*, May 24, 1957.

3. Gillmer, Richard S., Ph.D. *Death of a Business.* Minneapolis: Ross & Haines, Inc., 1968, p. 22.

4. *Home Furnishings Daily* (January 13, 1958).

Chapter 9

1. Gillmer, p. 11.

Chapter 10

1. *Home Furnishings Daily* (January 26, 1942): p. 42.

2. Schmeckebier, p. 74.

3. *Eva Zeisel: Designer For Industry* exhibition catalogue (published in conjunction with the exhibition organized by the Musée des Arts décoratifs de Montréal) 1984, p. 36–40.

4. Bougie, Stanley J., and Newkirk, David A. *Red Wing Dinnerware.* 1980, p. 67.

Chapter 12

1. Jim Ormerod—Franklin Park, IL, as shown in: DePasquale, Dan & Gail, and Petterson, Larry. *Red Wing Collectibles.* Paducah, Kentucky: Collector Books, 1985, p. 142.

2. Tom Trulen lecture at the Red Wing Collectors Society 1993 Convention.

Chapter 14

1. *St Paul Pioneer Press*, April 13, 1947.

2. *Minneapolis Tribune*, December 15, 1946.

Chapter 15

1. Tefft, Gary and Bonnie, p. 2.

2. *Belle Kogan Design, 1930-1972—Catalogue of the Retrospective Exhibition at the Center for Technological Education.*

3. Oral History Interviews Transcripts, OH 130, Minnesota Historical Society, as originally done for Goodhue County Historical Society, Red Wing, Minnesota.

4. ibid.

5. ibid.

6. Author's interview.

7. Oral History Interviews Transcripts, OH 130, Minnesota Historical Society, as originally done for Goodhue County Historical Society, Red Wing, Minnesota.

8. ibid.

9. *Eva Zeisel: Designer For Industry* exhibition catalogue (published in conjunction with the exhibition organized by the Musée des Arts décoratifs de Montréal) 1984, p.13.

10. Linde, Ron. "Interview with Charles E. Murphy, Designer of Red Wing Pottery for 19 Years," *Red Wing Collectors Society Inc. Newsletter* (June/July, 1992): p. 7.

11. Schouweiler, Sara. *Red Wing Potteries, Inc. 75th Anniversary Exhibit catalog.*

12. An interview with Harry Barghusen, July 28, 1978, Goodhue County Historical Society, Red Wing, Minnesota.

13. 1939 Statement of Red Wing Potteries, Inc., at the Minnesota Historical Society.

14. Oral History Interviews Transcripts, OH 130, Minnesota Historical Society.

15. Hanson, Vera Darr. *Red Wing Collectors Society Inc. Newsletter* (February/March, 1995): p. 12.

Chapter 17

1. Viel, Lyndon C. *The Clay Giants Book 3*. Lombard, Illinois: Wallace-Homestead Book Company, 1987, p. 188.

BIBLIOGRAPHY

Bougie, Stanley J., and Newkirk, David A. *Red Wing Dinnerware*. 1980.

Creative Clays: American Art Pottery From The New Orleans Museum Of Art. Organized by the New Orleans Museum of Art, 1992.

DePasquale, Dan & Gail, and Petterson, Larry. *Red Wing Collectibles*. Paducah, Kentucky: Collector Books, 1985.

DePasquale, Dan & Gail, and Petterson, Larry, *Red Wing Stoneware*. Paducah, Kentucky: Collector Books, 1983.

Dietz, Ulysses G. *Newark Museum Collection of American Art Pottery*. Newark, New Jersey: The Newark Museum; Salt Lake City: Gibbs M. Smith, Inc., Peregrine Smith Books, 1984.

Duke, Harvey. *Official Identification And Price Guide To Pottery And Porcelain, (Eighth Edition)*. New York: House of Collectibles, 1995.

Gillmer, Richard S., Ph.D. *Death of a Business*. Minneapolis: Ross & Haines, Inc., 1968.

Hoopes, Ron. *The Collectors Guide and History of Gonder Pottery*. Gas City, Indiana: L-W Book Sales, 1992.

Mangus, Jim and Bev. *Shawnee Pottery*. Puducah, Kentucky: Collector Books, 1994.

Nelson, Marion John. *Art Pottery of the Midwest*. Minneapolis: University Art Museum, University of Minnesota, 1988.

Schmeckebier, Laurence E. *Art in Red Wing*. Minneapolis: University of Minnesota, 1946.

Simon, Dolores. *Red Wing Pottery with Rumrill*. Paducah, Kentucky: Collector Books, 1980.

Supnick, Mark and Ellen, *The Wonderful World of Cookie Jars*. Marion, Indiana: L-W Book Sales, 1995.

Tefft, Gary and Bonnie. *Red Wing Potters and Their Wares*. Menomonee Falls, Wisconsin: Locust Enterprises, 1987.

Viel, Lyndon C. *The Clay Giants*. Lombard, Illinois: Wallace-Homestead Book Company, 1977.

Viel, Lyndon C. *The Clay Giants II*. Lombard, Illinois: Wallace-Homestead Book Company, 1980.

Viel, Lyndon C. *The Clay Giants Book 3*. Lombard, Illinois: Wallace-Homestead Book Company, 1987.

Zeisel, Eva: Designer For Industry exhibition catalogue (published in conjunction with the exhibition organized by the Musée des Arts décoratifs de Montréal) 1984.